Edward Stratemeyer and the Stratemeyer Syndicate

Twayne United States Authors Series

Ruth MacDonald, Editor

TUSAS 627

EDWARD STRATEMEYER, ABOUT 1925

Courtesy of Simon & Schuster/Pocket Books

Edward Stratemeyer and the Stratemeyer Syndicate

Deidre Johnson

West Chester University

Twayne Publishers • New York
Maxwell Macmillan Canada • Toronto
Maxwell Macmillan International • New York Oxford Singapore Sydney

Twayne's United States Authors Series No. 627
Edward Stratemeyer and the Stratemeyer Syndicate
Deidre Johnson

Twayne Publishers   Maxwell Macmillan Canada, Inc.
Macmillan Publishing Company   1200 Eglinton Avenue East
866 Third Avenue   Suite 200
New York, New York 10022   Don Mills, Ontario M3C 3N1

Library of Congress Cataloging-in-Publication Data

Johnson, Deidre
    Edward Stratemeyer and the Stratemeyer Syndicate / by Deidre Johnson.
        p. cm — (Twayne's United States authors series ; TUSAS 627)
    Includes bibliographical references and index.
    ISBN 0-8057-4006-6 (hc)
    1. Stratemeyer, Edward, 1862–1930—Criticism and interpretation.
2. Literature publishing—United States—History—20th century.
3. Children's stories, American—History and criticism.
4. Children's literature—Publishing—United States. 5. Stratemeyer
Syndicate—History. I. Title. II. Series.
PS3537.T817Z72 1993
813'.52—dc20   92–45602
                                                                    CIP
                                                                    AC

The paper used in this publication meets the minimum requirements of American
National Standard for Information Sciences—Permanence of Paper for Printed Library
Materials. ANSI Z3948-1984.∞ ™

10 9 8 7 6 5 4 3 2 1 (hc)

Printed in the United States of America

To Dr. John T. Dizer,
Stratemeyer researcher extraordinaire

Contents

Preface

A month ago, I shocked a woman by saying there was no such person as Carolyn Keene. Staring at me in disbelief, she protested that Carolyn Keene *had* to exist—she'd written the Nancy Drew books, hadn't she? Such is the fate of Edward Stratemeyer, a man overshadowed by his own creations. Ironically for a writer whose series have sold over 200,000,000 copies, his name sparks little recognition, a fate not shared by the characters and pseudonyms he created. Carolyn Keene is not real—nor is Franklin W. Dixon, or Laura Lee Hope, or Victor Appleton, or many other names associated with popular series. Some of the best-known, most-loved "authors" and series of this century sprang from the mind of one man, Edward Stratemeyer, a veritable fiction factory.

In his 47-year career, Stratemeyer used 83 pen names. He authored approximately 275 stories and outlined roughly 690 others, hiring writers to complete the latter. After his death, his daughters assumed control of his empire, the Stratemeyer Syndicate, publishing over 480 more books. When they died, the publisher Simon & Schuster purchased the Syndicate, issuing over 290 more titles. The fiction factory Stratemeyer built grinds on. He began in obscurity and went on to become a major force in twentieth-century series; although his name has returned to obscurity, his creations have not. The older ones live on in readers' memories; updated versions delight a new generation today.

The difficulty in discussing Stratemeyer's writing lies in the numbers: studies of his work concentrate on a handful of popular series and gloss over or omit the rest. Yet to overlook Stratemeyer's early works or his less successful ones is to ignore the foundation and scope of his writing career. Stratemeyer's success came through his willingness to experiment with and adapt material, continually tinkering with popular formulas. He shaped his books to the times, trying series after series in almost every possible area—careers, travel, school, home life, mysteries. Above all, he showed ingenious young protagonists triumphing, whatever the odds.

This study surveys much of the fiction by Edward Stratemeyer and the Stratemeyer Syndicate, looking at the early works that launched Stratemeyer's career, the rapid development of stories and series in different genres, and the prevalent traits and themes in the works. Because the protagonist's eventual triumph plays a crucial part in the stories, the study pays particular attention to the concept of success in the different genres.

A study of this sort, unfortunately, cannot be comprehensive. The reader familiar with Stratemeyer and the Syndicate's books will find several of the technology-based series omitted, owing to the nature of the treatment. Some series dealing with transportation or technology are covered with career stories; the remaining number was too small to merit its own chapter. Most adult works and some series within the genres covered have also been omitted, owing to either unavailability of the work or space limitations. Nonetheless, the discussion encompasses a number of the major stories and series as well as less popular or less successful works.

Several previous studies have discussed the validity of examining children's literature from a literary and cultural perspective. In *Mother Was a Lady: Self and Society in Selected American Children's Periodicals* R. Gordon Kelly addresses the role of children's literature in transmitting cultural values. Kelly explains that in order for a society's values to continue they must be conveyed to succeeding generations. Children's books provide one means of passing on value systems and beliefs, for they depict problems along with acceptable responses and solutions. They reveal the views of the world adults wish to show children, the goals adults feel are significant, and the "permissible behavior" allowed for achieving them.[1]

Others have given reasons for studying not just children's literature but also children's popular fiction. Chief among these are the popularity of the works, which have touched millions of children's lives with their messages, and the scant attention paid them in histories of children's literature or conventional studies.

Finally, John Cawelti's discussion of formula fiction in *Adventure, Mystery, and Romance: Formula Stories as Art and Popular Culture* suggests additional reasons for examining series books. Although Cawelti deals with adult fiction, his description of formula fiction and the reasons for its success also applies to series fiction for younger readers. Formulaic fiction's familiar story pattern provides its readers with a "basic emotional security" while simultaneously allowing a "temporary escape from the frustrations of life." While mimetic literature portrays "the world as we know it," formula fiction offers "an ideal world, without the disorder, the ambiguity and the limitations of the world or our existence."[2] The protagonist, an idealized figure, does not promote self-exploration, but "takes us out of ourself . . . by confirming an idealized self-image"(18).

To provide successful escape, such fiction offers "intense and immediate kinds of excitement . . . stress[ing] action and plot" (14) over complex characterizations. This, essentially, summarizes the appeal of series books.

Cawelti also notes formula fiction's cultural ties. Formulaic literature combines "specific cultural conventions with a more universal story form or archetype"(6). It reflects "conventional views of life and society"(19), a "network of assumptions"(32) shared by reader and writer. Moreover, since writers gradually alter elements of the formula in response to changing attitudes, formula fiction can "ease the transition between old and new ways of expressing things and thus contribute to cultural continuity"(35–36).

Series books offer a rich field for study. Like other formula fiction, they combine wish fulfillment and escape with cultural awareness. They contain moral and social teachings, some overt, some subtle. Their use of idealized protagonists clearly delineates prescribed and proscribed behaviors. In their emphasis on success, they show the social and cultural values presented to readers. This can range from encouraging competition between business rivals to proving oneself among one's peers. The temporal changes within genres can reflect cultural shifts, as with attitudes toward technology. Studying Stratemeyer and the Syndicate series provides descriptive information about the work of an author who exerted a powerful influence on popular children's fiction and about some of the methods that contributed to his success.

Acknowledgments

Many people contributed time, patience, suggestions, and information to this project.

All Stratemeyer researchers owe an immeasurable debt to Dr. John T. Dizer, whose writings on Stratemeyer provide a firm foundation for others' investigations. Those working with dime novels owe a similar debt to Edward T. LeBlanc and J. Randolph Cox, whose bibliographic studies provide necessary factual data and whose willingness to share information has helped many a researcher through difficult times. Dr. Dizer and J. Randolph Cox also read many of the chapters, offered valuable suggestions, and generously loaned copies of scarce material. Their kindness to researchers—especially this one—is exceeded only by their knowledge of the field.

This project began life as a dissertation, and much of the material in chapters 1 through 5 and chapter 9 appeared there. My adviser, Chester Anderson, and my two readers, Karen Nelson Hoyle and Dianne Monson, made thoughtful comments that helped shape that material. Ruth MacDonald, editor of this series, waded through a massive manuscript and gave wise and gentle suggestions for revisions.

Several people offered time and encouragement at times when completing this manuscript seemed an unreachable goal. I would especially like to thank Anita Schlieder, Pat Pflieger, and Joe Bodziock for their support.

Others, learning of the research, sent photocopies of articles or citations to investigate; indeed, so many contributed material it is impossible to name them all. Dave Farah, however, deserves special mention for sending scores of photocopies of articles about Nancy Drew and Harriet Adams. Ernie Kelly graciously gave permission to reprint excerpts from his article "Inside the Stratemeyer Syndicate."

A research project of this type would have been impossible without the resources of the University of Minnesota Libraries, including the staff at Interlibrary Loan, who filled numerous requests for elusive articles and books. Most crucial, however, were the dime novels, story papers, and series books in the Hess Collection, part of the Children's Literature Research Collections at the University of Minnesota. I am grateful to the curator, Karen Nelson Hoyle, and her staff for their patience and assistance. Another debt is owed to the curator and staff of Special Collections, University of Oregon, for photocopying correspondence and scarce materials in the Edward Stratemeyer–Harriet Stratemeyer Adams Collections there.

Chronology

1862   Edward Stratemeyer born 4 October.

1883   *Our American Boys*, Stratemeyer's first abortive attempt at a story paper using his own fiction, is published.

1889   Makes first sale ("Victor Horton's Idea") to a story paper.

1890   Makes first dime novel sale ("Match").

1891   Marries Magdalene Van Camp.

1892   Harriet Stratemeyer born 11 December.

1894   *Richard Dare's Venture* and *Last Voyage of the Spitfire* published in book form (first clothbound books).

1895   Edna Camilla Stratemeyer born in May [date not known].

1896   Stratemeyer's story paper *Bright Days* begins publication in April.

1898   *Under Dewey at Manila*, first major hardcover success, is published.

1899   Rover Boys series, prototype for many boys' series, begins.

1904   Bobbsey Twins, first tots' series, begins.

1905   Stratemeyer Syndicate founded [approximately].

1908   Dorothy Dale, first girls' series, begins.

1910   Tom Swift series begins.

1927   Hardy Boys series begins.

1930   Nancy Drew series begins. Edward Stratemeyer dies 10 May. Harriet Stratemeyer Adams and Edna Stratemeyer assume responsibility for Syndicate.

1942   Edna Stratemeyer Squier becomes inactive partner.

1948   Andrew Svenson hired as ghostwriter and editor.

1961   Andrew Svenson becomes Syndicate partner.

1974   Edna Stratemeyer Squier dies [date not known].

1975   Andrew Svenson dies 21 August.

1979   Stratemeyer Syndicate switches publishers, from Grosset & Dunlap to Simon & Schuster. Nancy Drew and Hardy Boys are first published in paperback. Lawsuit is brought over publishers' rights to series.

1982   Harriet Stratemeyer Adams dies 27 March.

1984   Stratemeyer Syndicate sold to Simon & Schuster.

1

Edward Stratemeyer and the Stratemeyer Syndicate

The greatest mystery Edward Stratemeyer and the Stratemeyer Syndicate ever created was the one surrounding their own history and success. During his lifetime Stratemeyer gave few interviews and told the same anecdotes over and over; after his death his family reserved information for a biography that never materialized. The best glimpses into his character and the operations of the Syndicate come from reminiscences by former employees, but these reveal only a small part of the picture. To this day much remains hidden. It seems particularly ironic that books by Stratemeyer fill shelf after shelf, while information about him can be covered in a few pages. That he was successful as a writer and businessman is evidenced by the many books to his credit and the mushrooming of the Syndicate series. Why he selected such a career, how and why he chose to develop the Syndicate, and what his other activities and interests were remain a mystery.

Edward Stratemeyer

Childhood Only sketchy information is available about Stratemeyer's childhood. Like his series heroes, he grew up in the northeastern United States. His father, Henry Julius Stratemeyer, emigrated from Germany in either 1837 or 1845 and joined the California gold rush with the first expedition of the Forty-Niners. His father's experiences must have impressed Edward, for he later used goldfields as the setting for several books, even noting in the preface to a volume in the Bound to Succeed series, *Oliver Bright's Search* (1899): "the scenes in the mining district of California . . . were drawn very largely from the narratives of a close and dear relative who spent much time out there, going as an Argonaut of '49 and to whom the vicinity of Sutter's Mill and the Mokelumme River became as an open book, not only then but later on. To write down these descriptions was, therefore, not only a work of interest, but of love."[1]

The death of a brother prompted Henry Stratemeyer to return, in 1851, to Elizabeth, New Jersey, where he became a tobacconist. He helped—and eventually married—his brother's widow, Anna Seigal Stratemeyer, already the mother of three. The couple had three more children, a daughter and two sons. The youngest child, Edward, was born on 4 October 1862.

Stratemeyer grew up within the middle class, with opportunities to develop his interest in literature. One of the few tales about his boyhood is that he had a printing press and amused his playmates by writing and printing stories. Stratemeyer's own reminiscences omit this story, but he does mention his library of children's books, especially Horatio Algers and Oliver Optics, and his wish to write books like those.[2] His education placed some emphasis on writing; after high school he was privately tutored in rhetoric, literature, and composition. Despite this literary training, he worked as a clerk in his brother Maurice's tobacco shop.

First Efforts   During this period Stratemeyer experimented unsuccessfully with several types of writing. In January 1883 the first and only known issue of *Our American Boys* appeared, with Stratemeyer listed as publisher. This eight-page story paper (an inexpensive magazine for children) contained short fiction, jokes, and fillers, at least some of which are his work.

Stratemeyer also tried another type of writing, in conjunction with one of his half-brothers. In March 1887 Edward Stratemeyer and Louis Charles Stratemeyer deposited a book with the Library of Congress for copyright registration, "The Complete Libretto of Love's Maze, Comic Opera in Two Acts," written by Edward and composed by Louis. No performance records for "Love's Maze"—a convoluted romance, intended to be comic—have been found, although it may have been produced locally. Undaunted, the two apparently resolved to try again, for the February 1888 Copyright Office records show that they deposited another title, "The Complete Libretto of The Perfume Prince, Comic Novelty in Three Acts."[3]

Early Boys' Fiction   Finally, in 1888, Stratemeyer drafted "Victor Horton's Idea," a boys' story. He frequently told interviewers about this first writing sale, a tale that delighted biographers and has often been reprinted, lately with some skepticism. To quote from one of the earlier versions:

> His initial long story—18,000 words—was written on store wrapping paper and later copied on white paper. The author, who was then twenty-

five, was not satisfied with it, so he laid it aside. After a year . . . he revised his manuscript carefully and sent it to *Golden Days*. The check for $75 he received Stratemeyer bore proudly to his father . . . who had [previously] told him he was wasting his time writing the tale and might better be engaged in a more useful activity. . . .

"[They] paid you that for writing a story?" his father repeated. "Well, you'd better write a lot more for them." ("Newarker")

"Victor Horton's Idea" marked the start of Stratemeyer's success in the juvenile market. *Golden Days* purchased a second story in 1890, the same year Street & Smith, one of the leading publishers of popular literature, published his first dime novel. Over the next few years Stratemeyer developed his formula fiction, turning out dime novels and boys' serials quickly and steadily. By 1893 he had published 49 dime novels alone, including humor books, westerns, and mysteries.

Along with Stratemeyer's growing success came changes in his personal life. About 1890 he moved to Newark, where he owned and ran a newspaper, magazine, and stationery store for approximately six years. On 25 March 1891 he married Magdalene B. Van Camp of Newark, in that city. Their first child, Harriet, was born on 11 December 1892; their second, Edna Camilla, was born in May 1895.[4]

In 1893 Stratemeyer enhanced his knowledge of boys' fiction by taking the job of editor for *Good News*, a boys' story paper. This position proved an ideal training ground, for *Good News* was owned by Street & Smith. Stratemeyer also used the opportunity to run many of his own stories in *Good News*. His serials ranged from science fiction to outdoor tales to mysteries, although the majority were success stories loosely patterned on Alger's "rags to riches" formula. The heroes in Stratemeyer's success stories often aspire to own small businesses, as did Stratemeyer himself and his father; one even ends up owning a stationery store.

Stratemeyer's time at Street & Smith may have suggested the basis for the Stratemeyer Syndicate, since Street & Smith used several of the techniques Stratemeyer later employed in his own organization. Most writers worked under house pseudonyms assigned by Street & Smith and wrote about characters controlled by Street & Smith. Consequently, even if a writer left for other employment, readers remained unaware of the departure and continued to read tales about their favorite character with the pseudonym still attached. Sometimes authors contracted to write stories after receiving only the title. They were expected to use series characters created by other writers, thus blending their own ideas with other people's. Dime novels also adhered to a strict format. Writers had little leeway in the length of the story: they wrote to fit the format, not the reverse. The standard practice for payment was a flat fee, which conveyed all publishing rights to the publisher; whether it printed the story once or several times, the writer could expect neither royalties nor any share in the profits—and Stratemeyer lived to see some of the stories he wrote for Street & Smith reprinted up to four times.

In 1894 Stratemeyer expanded the market for his fiction by revising some of his story-paper serials for publication as books, a practice he continued through 1907. Such reissues were common practice, despite the story papers' frequent claims that their serials would not appear in book form. This experience, too, must have impressed upon him the lesson that it was better to be publisher than author, for when he bought back the rights to some of his serials, he ended up paying the publisher twice what he had received for writing them.

During this period Stratemeyer also experimented with other genres. As early as February 1896 he had a romance published under the name Edna Winfield in Street & Smith's family story paper, the *New York Weekly*. He may have sold more romances under that pseudonym to another family story paper, the *Chicago Ledger*. Six other Edna Winfield titles, again Stratemeyer's work, were published in paperback in 1899.

Stratemeyer left Street & Smith about 1895 to become associate editor of Frank J. Earll's boys' story paper, *Young People of America*. This probably led to one of his few unsuccessful ventures, for he launched his own short-lived story paper, *Bright Days*, in April 1896. It lasted only until February 1897. Although Stratemeyer attempted to imitate popular story papers, he seems to have lacked both the willingness and the funds to hire many writers. As a result, much of the writing had a certain uniformity, rather than the variety expected of such a publication. Even though the serials and fillers carry an assortment of names, most seem to be his efforts. Stratemeyer may also have been under pressure to keep up the publication schedule, for the *Bright Days* serials are structurally among his weakest works, starting well but degenerating into hastily reached conclusions.

After the demise of *Bright Days*, Stratemeyer offered less material to story papers. In 1898 he began selling directly to book publishers and had two works of historical fiction issued that year. One of them, *Under Dewey at Manila* (1898), established Stratemeyer with Lee & Shepard, one of the foremost publishers of juveniles. Although his foray into historical fiction lasted for only a few years, it was long enough to transform his name and one of his pseudonyms, Captain Ralph Bonehill, into highly marketable commodities.

The close of the century saw Stratemeyer in an enviable position for a juvenile writer. He had one historical fiction series in progress and had initiated four more. He was also adding volumes to his career series. Under the pseudonym Arthur M. Winfield, he had just started a popular school series, the Rover Boys. With the Rovers, Stratemeyer introduced the formula that would work so well for many of his future series: a group of personable, young, upper middle class protagonists travels to different locations, finding adventures and sometimes a light mystery. When the first edition of *Who's Who in America* appeared in 1899, it listed Stratemeyer's name and credited him with 30 published books. If anything, his only possible problem was having more ideas than time to develop them in writing.

As he grew more successful, Stratemeyer was able to devote more time to his craft. At first he worked at home in his third-floor studio and wrote stories longhand, until he mastered the typewriter. He would spend the mornings writing, usually two chapters, and then "stroll out around Roseville, study ideas, and return to his machine."[5] In a rare interview from around 1904, Stratemeyer described his method: "When starting to write a story . . . I generally make a careful outline and cast of characters. After this I compose directly on the typewriter, working four to six hours a day. Sometimes I make half a dozen changes, and then make more when the proof sheets come along. In addition, I usually mark all the subjects for illustration, as a guide to the artist." He also noted that he "rarely work[ed] during the hot weather" and was at the time "looking forward to a vacation in the mountains and at the seashore, with a camera and a fishing rod."[6]

In the same interview, Stratemeyer discussed his work. By then he had abandoned dime novels and was writing primarily clothbound fiction along with an occasional magazine serial. Although serious controversy about the quality of his books was yet to arise, his comments, even then, defend their style and content:

I have no toleration for that which is namby-pamby or wishy-washy in juvenile literature. This is a strenuous age. . . . [The boys and girls] of today are clever and up-to-date and appreciate that which is true to life quite as much as their elders. They love incident and adventure. . . . The best an author can do is to give them a fair proportion of legitimate excitement, and with this a judicious dose of pleasantly prepared infor-

mation. Every story ought to be of a high moral tone, but the moral
ought to be felt rather than mentioned. ("Newark Author," 75–76)

Even at this stage of his career Stratemeyer was moving toward the
development of the Syndicate; he faced the problem of a growing number of ideas and an insufficient amount of time. He commented that he
had "the plots and outlines of a score of books in [his] desk . . . and
[kept] adding to them constantly." He continued, "When a new idea
comes to me I make a note of it, and if I can gather in any information
on the subject I do so" ("Newark Author," 76).

The Stratemeyer Syndicate

Sometime between 1904 and 1908, probably about 1905, Stratemeyer
embarked on a new venture, the Stratemeyer Syndicate. It was a production factory for series books. Stratemeyer recruited writers and
assigned them to work on volumes in various series for which he owned
the rights. His full role and the actual workings of the Syndicate during
its early years have never been detailed, just as many of the writers who
contributed to Syndicate books have never been identified. In later years
Stratemeyer (and subsequently his daughters) drafted two- to three-page
outlines for each book, sketching the plot, subplot, characters, and major
incidents. Writers-for-hire would take these outlines and write full-
length manuscripts, then return them to the Syndicate for editing.
Writers received a flat sum for each book—with no royalties—and
signed a contract agreeing not to use the pseudonyms for their own
material or even to acknowledge their connection to them. The reward
for satisfactory work was the opportunity to write more books for the
Syndicate.

About 1910 Stratemeyer took offices at 17 Madison Avenue; sometime after 1916 he moved to the Ashland Building at 315 Fourth
Avenue.[7] There Stratemeyer edited incoming manuscripts and continued
his writing. By then he had progressed from typing to dictating chapters
to his secretary; one article noted that the newer method "irked him at
first but he persisted and eventually was able to dictate three chapters a
day easily" ("Services").

Establishing the Syndicate allowed Stratemeyer to increase book production dramatically. Prior to 1906 he had established 19 multivolume
series, approximately one-third of which incorporated reprinted material. From 1906 through 1930 (the year he died) Stratemeyer created 82

more series, primarily composed of new stories. Although some series were short-lived and not all received new volumes annually, the Syndicate kept between 19 and 32 series in progress each year from 1910 through 1930 and averaged 31 new titles a year.

Several marketing tactics were used to promote sales. Generally, the Syndicate launched a series by issuing the first three titles (called "breeders") simultaneously, so that readers were greeted with a ready-made series. Each book worked an enticing summary of the characters' previous adventures into the first or second chapter; the dust jacket and endmatter carried advertisements for other titles and series. About 1906 Stratemeyer further increased sales by negotiating an agreement with one of his publishers whereby his series books were priced at 50 cents. This made the books more affordable and helped usher in the era of the "fifty-centers."

Syndicate Series   Ultimately, of course, the success of the series rested on the books themselves, and Stratemeyer took care that no possible reader would be overlooked. Variety and versatility were the keynotes of the Syndicate. Within a decade of its creation, Stratemeyer was issuing series on topics that appealed to almost every imaginable interest. From about 1906 through 1912 the Syndicate concentrated on boys' series, using a variety of school, outdoor, and technology-based stories, although a few still followed the pattern of Stratemeyer's career stories. This period saw publications like the series on the three Motor Boys, who travel about the continent using the most modern conveyances, from motorcars to motorboats and airplanes; the Great Marvel science fiction series, which takes the reader from the polar caps to the outer planets; and a series on Jack Ranger, a lively schoolboy who hunts, travels west, and even sails the ocean. After 1910 the Syndicate began to develop sports series, like Baseball Joe.

The Syndicate's girls' series began in 1908 and flourished after 1913; soon these works constituted 30 percent of the Syndicate's production. Girls could enjoy the adventures of Ruth Fielding, a schoolgirl who becomes a scriptwriter and movie producer; the Outdoor Girls, a group of "bright, fun-loving girls" who go "camping and tramping for fun and health"; and the Girls of Central High, a high school sports series. Letters to the Syndicate from 1928 to 1929 show female readers eagerly inquiring after the fates of different characters and forming clubs to imitate them.[8]

Series aimed at young children were developed last. Although the Bobbsey Twins date from 1904, similar series did not emerge until the mid-1910s, when characters like Bunny Brown and His Sister Sue and the Six Little Bunkers appeared. Other tots' titles featured anthropomorphized animals and toys in series such as the Kneetime Animal Stories and Make-Believe Stories.

As the Syndicate grew, the number of books written under Stratemeyer's name and the two pseudonyms he claimed declined. In 1899 the names Edward Stratemeyer, Captain Ralph Bonehill, and Arthur M. Winfield accounted for nine books. During the next decade Stratemeyer averaged five books per year. By 1913 the name Captain Ralph Bonehill was no longer used on new stories, and the only volumes that can be definitely attributed to Stratemeyer are the annual additions to the Dave Porter and Rover Boys series. The former series lasted until 1919, and the latter until 1925.

Unlike his outgoing, assertive characters, poised and admirable in all situations, Stratemeyer has been characterized as a nervous man who did not display emotion readily and avoided speaking to groups. Moral and slightly old-fashioned, Stratemeyer eschewed tobacco and alcohol and faithfully observed the Sabbath, traits echoed by his series characters.[9] His elder daughter, Harriet Stratemeyer Adams, described him as "very strict," the same phrase she used about her paternal grandmother (DeWitt).

He was also interested in current affairs. Edna Stratemeyer recalled that "he paid close attention to the contents of magazines, journals, and newspapers . . . [looking for] information and inspiration [for his books and] strove to maintain his reputation for timeliness" (Soderbergh 1973, 239). One of his prefaces noted he was "the proud possessor of a touring car, and . . . enjoyed numerous trips around his home and beyond."[10] In the summer of 1909 he "covered about seven thousand miles of our great western country," a trip reflected in series titles set in the West.[11]

Among his friends he counted Howard Garis, who lived nearby. Some sources say he enjoyed bowling and watching baseball games, and he admitted to being "a good deal of a baseball 'rooter.'"[12]

Syndicate Ghostwriters   Stratemeyer had a talent for selecting skilled writers for the Syndicate. Some of its first known employees came from dime novel or journalistic backgrounds. Howard and Lilian Garis, both from the *Newark Evening News*, were two such writers—probably the first the Syndicate employed. Howard Garis's own records credit him with 20 volumes of the Motor Boys series, an accomplishment that would have him working for Stratemeyer as early as 1906. He also penned some titles in the Great Marvel and Baseball Joe series, wrote 35

Tom Swift books, and contributed to some of the children's series, including several Six Little Bunkers titles, 6 Bunny Browns, and 15 Bobbsey Twins.[13] Lilian Garis, his wife, worked on the early Bobbsey Twins, Dorothy Dale, the Outdoor Girls, and the Motor Girls series.[14] Both also wrote extensively under either their own names or other non-Syndicate pseudonyms: Howard Garis's much-loved Uncle Wiggily characters (not a Syndicate property) appeared in 15,000 stories during the years 1909 through 1954. How much direction—either written or verbal—Stratemeyer gave such experienced writers about plots and secondary characters remains debatable. Stratemeyer's elder daughter, Harriet Adams, once recalled her father and Howard Garis prancing around the Stratemeyer home acting out ideas for stories, suggesting a fair amount of collaboration between the friends.

Other experienced writers also leased their pens to the Syndicate. About 1911 the former dime novelist St. George Rathborne contributed camping and outdoor stories for the Outdoor Chums and the Boys of Columbia High series.[15] Like many other Syndicate writers, he also published children's books under his own name.

Another adept writer, W. Bert Foster, joined the Syndicate's staff of writers about 1913. Foster started the Ruth Fielding and Corner House Girls series, working on approximately the first 12 and 10 titles, respectively, and handled most or all of the Carolyn and Oriole books. Under the Syndicate pseudonyms James A. Cooper and Chester K. Steele, he also wrote stories for adults. Several originally appeared in Street & Smith's pulp magazines, along with many of Foster's non-Syndicate stories. Foster's association with the Syndicate lasted until about 1927 or 1928.[16]

By the mid-1920s Stratemeyer's empire had extended to the point where he began advertising for writers in trade papers. One respondent, a journalist named Leslie McFarlane, later provided a detailed account of the recruitment process. While working on a Springfield, Massachusetts, newspaper in 1926, McFarlane answered Stratemeyer's advertisement in *Editor and Publisher*. He received a letter from Stratemeyer explaining "that the Stratemeyer Syndicate prepared book manuscripts for publishers, with special emphasis on series designed for juvenile readers." Stratemeyer's role was primarily "planning new series and plotting new books, which he hired others to write."[17] Stratemeyer sent books from two current Syndicate series and asked McFarlane to read them and pick one. After that, as McFarlane explained, "he would then send me an outline of the opening chapters of the series volume presently in prepara-

tion, which I would be asked to expand into about 2,000 words of pub-
lishable fiction. . . . If the two chapters pleased Mr. Stratemeyer, he
would commission me to complete the book, twenty chapters in all, for a
guaranteed sum of $100, flat rate, no royalty, with the prospect of fur-
ther lucrative employment to follow" (10–11).

McFarlane made his selection, wrote the trial chapters, and sent
them in. His material was accepted, and McFarlane proceeded to finish
the book, a Dave Fearless title. Stratemeyer sent a $100 check, "anoth-
er three-page outline of the next book in the saga . . . [and an inquiry
about whether] I would take on an assignment every month and make
myself available for work in other series" (39). McFarlane agreed and
worked on the final Dave Fearless titles, most of the first 26 Hardy
Boys books, the first 4 Dana Girls stories, an X Bar X Boys title, and
other unidentified series, continuing his association with the Syndicate
until 1946.

Soon after employing McFarlane, Stratemeyer added another important author to the Syndicate roster. After a year on an Iowa newspaper,
Mildred Wirt Benson (then Mildred Wirt) journeyed to New York in
1926 looking for a job writing or editing. She interviewed with the
Stratemeyer Syndicate and left samples of her work. Although she did
not find employment in the city, she received a letter from Stratemeyer
after her return to Iowa. He offered her free-lance work on the Ruth
Fielding series, which needed a writer after W. Bert Foster's departure.
Wirt Benson accepted and began a 24-year association with the
Syndicate.[18] Among the titles to her credit are most of the first 25 volumes of the Nancy Drew series, many early volumes in the Dana Girls
and Kay Tracey series, and 5 titles in the Honey Bunch series. In addition to her Syndicate work, she created other series and nonseries titles
under her own name and assorted pseudonyms.[19]

Yet another writer may have joined the Syndicate about this time.
Frank Dorrance Hopley, who "worked as a secretary in New York City
for some thirty years . . . claimed to have authored a number of volumes
in the Bob Chase and Jerry Ford series," as well as some X Bar X titles.[20]
Hopley's connection with the Jerry Ford series seems questionable since
he died in 1930, a year before the series started; his association with the
other two remains a possibility. He also wrote magazine and newspaper
stories and published a book under his own name.

By then, the Syndicate was approaching its peak production. Thirty-
one series were in progress in 1926, and an indeterminate number of
unidentified ghostwriters were busily turning out titles. In 1929, even

with the Depression looming, the Stratemeyer Syndicate still managed to publish 36 books.

The following year Stratemeyer's health began deteriorating rapidly. In February thrombosis of the leg restricted his movements for a time. Even after it had cleared up, he needed assistance commuting to and from his office. He had his first heart attack in the spring but returned to work until a second heart attack struck him on 2 May. While he was recovering from that, lobar pneumonia set in and was complicated by a third heart attack. During his illness he dreamed he was part of one of his own baseball series. He died on Saturday, 10 May 1930, and was interred at Evergreen Cemetery on 13 May ("Services"; Soderbergh 1973, 247). Appropriately, the monument was carved to resemble a bookshelf holding series books. His marker bore the epitaph, "The final chapter closes, leaving in young hearts the memory of fine ideals."[21]

Stratemeyer's will left $1,000 to his brother Maurice, $1,000 to his niece, $20,000 to each of his daughters, and the remainder— including "royalties due and becoming due, copyrights, bookrights, printing plates"—to his wife. Howard Garis was one of the witnesses. Although the actual will makes no mention of the ghostwriters, both McFarlane and Wirt Benson recalled receiving bequests: apparently Stratemeyer had arranged that "each of his writers [be sent] a sum equal to one fifth of their earnings from the Syndicate" (McFarlane, 191).

After Stratemeyer's death, his family and publishers faced a crisis. For all its use of ghostwriters, the Syndicate had still been controlled by one man, and except for a few manuscripts waiting for editing, its machinery had ground to a halt. Stratemeyer's widow, now full owner of the Syndicate, was a semi-invalid, and his younger daughter still lived at home with her. However, Harriet Adams, Stratemeyer's elder daughter, was another matter entirely. If any of the family had inherited Stratemeyer's ambition and business acumen, it was indeed she.

Harriet Stratemeyer Adams

Adams's Background   As a young woman, Harriet Stratemeyer Adams had attended Wellesley, majoring in English, music, and religion, with an interest in archaeology, and had even played piano with the college symphony orchestra. She joined the newly formed Press Board while a freshman and had served as a college correspondent for the *Boston Globe* by the time she graduated in 1914. According to one account, two churches and a newspaper offered her jobs when she finished college.[22]

Appalled at the thought of one of his daughters working, Stratemeyer made a counteroffer: she could edit manuscripts for the Syndicate, providing she did the work in the Stratemeyer home. The female characters in the Syndicate series may have enjoyed a certain degree of independence, but Stratemeyer apparently did not extend this freedom to members of his family.

Harriet Stratemeyer's employment ended in 1915 when she married Russell Vroom Adams, an investment banker, because Stratemeyer felt that as a married woman she should devote herself to her husband and home. Or, as she put it, "my father had the idea that a woman's place was in the home. . . . I didn't agree with my father's view and I asked him several times if I could work for him, bringing home manuscripts and proofs, but he said no. I think he would be amazed that I carried on his work" ("Author").[23] Adams was not—and never became—an ardent feminist; she respected her father's wishes. Rather than seeking other employment, she directed her energies to church and community activities, writing miscellaneous items for Sunday Schools and women's clubs.

By 1930 Adams had been away from the Syndicate for almost 15 years. She had four children to look after: Russell, Jr., Patricia, Camilla, and four-year-old Edward. Nonetheless, after discussing the situation with her husband, she decided to assume management of the Syndicate in conjunction with her sister. The two daughters stepped in to continue the Syndicate's publishing ventures, forming a fifty-fifty partnership on 20 August 1931.

Adams and the Syndicate   Almost immediately, the sisters moved the Syndicate office from New York to the fifth floor of the Hale Building in East Orange, New Jersey, a 15-minute drive from Adams's home. Adams's first duties involved editing five manuscripts Stratemeyer had left. She gradually began writing stories, beginning with titles in the Bobbsey Twins series.[24]

At this stage in her career Adams tried to avoid publicizing her role in the Syndicate. An entry in a book prepared for the twenty-fifth reunion of her class at Wellesley practically buries the reference to her job amid her other activities: "Besides the serious jobs of marriage and the rearing of two boys (one at Princeton, one thirteen) and two girls (about ready for Wellesley) and being co-partner in a juvenile literary syndicate, I have done a good bit of club work, including organizing the New Jersey Wellesley Club, and dabbled in various kinds of writing, poetical, religious, and editorial. My hobbies are dancing and the collection of antique books for children."[25]

Edna Stratemeyer also assisted with Syndicate management, though she seems to have played a less active role than Adams. An article written in 1934 (after its author failed to receive an interview from the sisters) described the two thusly: "Miss Edna, who stays at home managing affairs, waggles her bobbed grey head emphatically and says that their business is their business. Mrs. Adams, who takes care of personal contacts with New York publishers, smiles graciously and says the same."[26]

The sisters soon faced more challenges. The Garises, still key writers for some of the more successful series, left the Syndicate about 1932, as did Wirt Benson. The reason for the Garises' departure is not known, although it seems possible they left for the same reason Wirt Benson did: the Syndicate's decision that the Depression made it necessary to reduce the payment for manuscripts. In Wirt Benson's case, at least, the suggested cut was quite severe: from $125 to $75 per book.[27]

To compensate for this loss, the sisters enlisted Walter Karig to write several volumes in the Nancy Drew, Doris Force, X Bar X Boys, and Perry Pierce series.[28] A seasoned journalist, Karig also worked for the *Newark Evening News* for 21 years and later became book editor of the *Washington Post*. In addition to his Syndicate books, he penned many fiction and nonfiction titles under his own name and pseudonyms. His association with the Syndicate lasted from about 1932 to 1936. Around the time he left, Wirt Benson resumed work on the girls' series.

Mrs. Stratemeyer died in 1935. After making assorted small bequests to friends and relatives, she willed the remainder of her estate to her daughters, naming Edna Stratemeyer, Harriet Adams, and Russell Adams as executors. Under the daughters' management, the number of Syndicate series decreased from 27 in 1930 to 7 in 1942. Rather than experimenting with new series, the Syndicate increasingly relied on a few durable characters.

In 1942 Edna Stratemeyer became an inactive partner. She married Charles Wesley Squier and moved to Florida for health reasons.[29] Adams continued to manage the Syndicate, aided by her office staff.

After the war, Adams began rebuilding the Syndicate's portion of the market. She hired the former journalist and journalism teacher Andrew Svenson as a writer and editor in 1948. Svenson's arrival infused the Syndicate with new energy: it soon reissued two series in new formats, and he initiated and wrote one of the more popular postwar series, the Happy Hollisters. In 1959 the Syndicate also started revising many of the older volumes in its three most successful series (Nancy Drew, the Hardy Boys, and the Bobbsey Twins) to keep them contemporary. This project spanned almost 20 years and meant updating or rewriting close to 100 titles. The Syndicate officially recognized Svenson's valuable assistance on 1 January 1961 when it made him a Syndicate partner.

During this burst of renewed activity the Syndicate enlarged its stable of writers. In 1954 Jim Lawrence joined the staff, taking over the newest project, the Tom Swift, Jr., series, with volume 5. His previous experience included scripting radio series such as *Sky King* and *Green Hornet*; he later created such non-Syndicate properties as the *Friday Foster* comic strip and the Binky Brothers juvenile series. In the 1960s he developed the Chris Cool series for the Syndicate and wrote the first few volumes, but he left in 1967 after some differences with Svenson. Even after severing his official connection, he continued free-lancing for the Syndicate, ghostwriting some of the Hardy Boys, Bobbsey Twins, and Nancy Drew titles.[30] The Syndicate acquired another experienced craftsman in the 1960s when it hired the western author S. Omar Barker for the Bret King series.[31] Other writers also came and went, some staying with one series for several years, others taking on volumes in assorted series as needed.

Syndicate Methods

The Syndicate still retained Edward Stratemeyer's methods for testing writers, but with some differences. Ernie Kelly, a researcher who interviewed many Syndicate employees from this period, summarized the process by which an aspirant was incorporated into the Syndicate staff: "Writers and editors often started out on a contract basis before becoming full time employees. New writers had to submit sample chapters written from copious outlines. [Next] they were involved in editing. Then they were either given older books to rewrite or work preparing new titles for series [for younger readers] like the Bobbsey twins and Honey Bunch. . . . Over time they might be able to establish themselves as reliable enough to begin producing their own outlines and stories."[32] Harriet Adams and Andrew Svenson supervised operations: Harriet for girls' series and the Bobbsey Twins; Andrew Svenson for the boys' series, the Tollivers, and the Happy Hollisters (E. Kelly, 2:8).

Adams's and Svenson's Syndicate duties included "setting up the outlines, doing background checks and visiting the sites [for the books' settings], selecting the writer and scheduling the deadlines and then doing the first editing" (E. Kelly, 2:8). Although the amount of writing each did is debatable, both described their writing habits in various interviews. Adams's comments are perhaps the most telling, for they show the increasing loss of individual responsibility for a title. One interviewer described her methods: "She begins one of her books with a precis—a brief description of plots and subplots. She then jots down an incident-by-incident outline of the book on a yellow pad [linking plot and subplot together]. And when she is ready to begin the actual writing, she turns to her dictaphone machine."[33] After secretaries transcribed the tapes, she and the staff edited the manuscripts. Writing a book typically took two months, although she admitted it was possible to do one in two weeks.[34]

Eleven years later another interviewer described the procedure as "a system that is part division of labor, part subcontracting, and part writers' collective." He then elaborated on the process: "First comes a brief summary of the story, then a detailed chapter-by-chapter outline written by a member of the syndicate's writing team of Harriet Adams, Lieselotte Wuenn, Nancy Axelrad, and Lorraine S. Rickle. The outline is passed around for editorial comment before it is taken over by a team member who specializes in a particular series. She either writes the book or farms it out to a free-lance writer. The manuscript is scrutinized, revised, and checked for accuracy before going to the publisher."[35] Ernie Kelly, too, noted the overabundance of helping hands, commenting that sometimes as many as five editors worked on a title, "render[ing] the final product almost unrecognizable" (1:5).

Neither Adams nor Svenson seemed disturbed by the formulaic approach to the books—indeed, as early as the 1950s they took to referring to "the Stratemeyer formula," as if it were a magic potion for success. Definitions of the formula varied, depending on the time and speaker. In 1954 Svenson stressed the rapid action in the books: "A low death rate but plenty of plot. Verbs of action, and polka-dotted with exclamation points and provocative questions. . . . The main character introduced on page one and a slam-bang mystery or peril set up. . . . The end of every chapter is a cliff hanger."[36]

Adams took a different approach, pointing out the books' conservative moral code. In this, she was aided by the press, who delighted in running headlines like, "100 Books and Not a Hippie in Them," or, "Squeaky-Clean and Still 18; Nancy Drew, Girl Detective, Marks Half a Century." Interviewers consistently cataloged some of the prohibited material: "No use of guns by the hero. No smooching" ("Tom, Jr.," 26); "[no] big-city suffering, no sex, and no violence" (DeWitt); and, of course, "no profanity"("Adams," 15). Adams also mentioned the books' accuracy and informational value, stating that "a battery of specialists goes over everything to eradicate the slightest error" ("Tom, Jr.," 26). In later years the Syndicate summarized the Stratemeyer formula as "Good mystery and lots of action, with some educational material."[37]

Adams and Svenson also cited the educational nature of the books to explain their extensive travels. One article included the following partial list of Svenson's research sites: "He wrote his most recent book after a trip to Greece, and found inspiration for his book now in progress while in Hong Kong. . . . The action in [another book] takes place in Iceland. While there interviewing the chief of the Icelandic Navy . . . Andy was invited on a cruise to the Arctic Circle. The result—*The Arctic Patrol*, another success in the Hardy Boys series."[38]

Changes in the Syndicate

After the riots in East Orange in the late 1960s, Adams moved the offices to Maplewood. The Syndicate was now in its final phase as a family-owned business. Harriet Adams's husband had died in April 1965; her sister, Edna Squier, died in 1974. A more serious loss to the Syndicate came with Andrew Svenson's death in August 1975.

After Svenson's death, Adams offered several of the office staff the opportunity to become junior partners. Four of them did: Nancy S. Axelrad, a writer and editor; Lieselotte Wuenn, an editor and former secretary to Svenson; Lorraine Rickle, Adams's personal secretary; and Gordon Eyler, an accountant (E. Kelly, 2:11). The Syndicate again cut back to its three central series, the Hardy Boys, Nancy Drew, and the Bobbsey Twins; the sales of the first two were bolstered by the brief success of a prime-time television series, "The Nancy Drew/Hardy Boys Mystery Hour" (1977–79).

In 1979 the Stratemeyer Syndicate also decided on another major change. It acquired a different publisher, Simon & Schuster, which issued paperback editions of new titles in the Nancy Drew, Hardy Boys, and Bobbsey Twins series. Grosset & Dunlap, which had handled these series practically since their inception, was understandably distressed by the thought of losing them. It filed suit against the Stratemeyer Syndicate and Simon & Schuster, claiming "breach of contract, copyright infringement, and unfair competition" and asking "punitive damages of $300 million, unspecified compensatory damages and a variety of declarations of . . . contractual rights."[39] In the midst of this, Gordon Eyler resigned from the Syndicate, leaving the partnership between Harriet Adams and the three junior partners. After the 1980 trial, the Syndicate won the right to choose its own publisher; it decided to continue with Simon & Schuster. The court granted Grosset & Dunlap the right to continue issuing all previously published titles, but in hardcover editions only.

Two years later, on 27 March 1982, Harriet Adams suffered a fatal heart attack while watching *The Wizard of Oz*. Although one of her grandsons had worked briefly on the Hardy Boys series, none of the family was closely involved with the Syndicate or able to step in as Adams and her sister had done over half a century before. The three remaining active partners managed the Syndicate for two more years.[40] After the publisher expressed interest in purchasing the Syndicate and ownership of the series, those involved eventually decided—not without some reluctance—to sell (E. Kelly, 1:12). In 1984 Simon & Schuster became owner of the Stratemeyer Syndicate.

With the Syndicate sale to Simon & Schuster, Stratemeyer's fiction factory and its creations had come full circle. In the 1890s Stratemeyer had strengthened his craft by writing about series characters owned by the publishers Street & Smith. He built a one-man empire, which was managed successfully for more than half a century by his offspring. Now, with the original participants gone, a publishing company again controlled the rights to his fictional creations.

2

Dime Novels

In the early 1890s dime novels provided an inviting market for beginning writers like Stratemeyer. Their publishers required an enormous amount of formula fiction: by then the dime novel had evolved to a 16- or 32-page adventure story for adolescents, issued weekly or semimonthly. Most dime novel series centered on a particular genre—such as westerns, war stories, and mysteries—or on the adventures of a series character. They catered to a faithful audience that expected regular doses of similar fare. Stock characters, situations, and plots were played and replayed with minor variations, an almost unavoidable consequence of the pressure on writers to keep pace with production by turning out 25,000 to 50,000 words of frenetically paced story on a weekly, biweekly, or monthly schedule.

Stratemeyer proved to be a capable dime novelist. From May 1892 to November 1893 he wrote 42 dime novels; an additional 17, which may have been written in this period, were published over the next five years.[1] Writing dime novels provided Stratemeyer with a valuable introduction to formula fiction, from both a business and a writer's perspective. Much of what he learned from his publishers resurfaced when he founded the Stratemeyer Syndicate. On a more immediate level, his dime novels show that he quickly mastered the rudiments of formula fiction, and that he adapted content and style to suit the market. In sharp contrast to the Syndicate's series, the dime novels are set in a rougher, less sanitized world and, accordingly, offer different, less moral protagonists. Marginally, it could be said that Stratemeyer's dime novel characters gradually become less like adult dime novel heroes and more like those in boys' fiction, but overall his stories show little change. His dime novels indicate his reliance on formulas and stock characters, his readiness to capitalize on current events and popular fads, and his willingness to use more adult, less savory characters and situations in his stories, in keeping with dime novel traditions.

Comic Dime Novels

Before he began writing regularly for the market, Stratemeyer published two comic dime novels in Street & Smith's Nugget Library under the pseudonym Ned St. Meyer. Issued in 1890, "Match; or, The Golden Wedding at Turkey Hollow" and "Match as Fakir; or, The Pumpkinville County Fair" both follow the adventures of a boy named Match, a prankster ever in search of mischief. These stories invert the traditional hero tale: rather than fighting scoundrels and righting wrongs, the protagonist is himself the swindler. The dramatic tension stems from seeing how far he can go before his schemes backfire. In the first story, Match, a city lad, meets up with an old farmer who has come to the metropolis to make preparations for his golden wedding anniversary. Delighted by such an easy mark, Match feigns friendship and takes his newfound acquaintance for a tour of the city, alarming him with wild and fictitious tales of modern life and maneuvering him into buying dinner, theater tickets, and lodgings for them both. Emboldened by his success, Match returns to the country with the farmer and turns the anniversary party into a shambles, ruining the food for the banquet and reawakening old feuds among the guests. When he is finally discovered as a fraud, Match lights out, unrepentant, in search of new territory to conquer.

This is hardly a heroic tale. Match narrates his story, but even so, it is difficult to empathize with him. He is, at best, a selfish and destructive lad, delighting in disruption and waste, with nary a thought for his victims. Ironically, Match does have some of the qualities that will show up in other Stratemeyer heroes—spunkiness, quick wits, courage (for it takes some courage to go through with a prank of that magnitude), and an impish sense of humor—but he uses them for nonproductive ends, something most later Stratemeyer heroes scorn.

Stratemeyer's three other comic dime novels were written for the Nugget Library and the New York Five Cent Library in 1892 and 1893, under the pseudonym Peter Pad, a house name used by several writers. Two follow the misadventures of a German emigrant; the third tells of the intrigues of a black manservant. "Hans Liederkranz; or, A German Emigrant's Trials and Tribulations" inverts another popular formula, the city success story, wherein a bright lad comes to the city and gains fame and fortune—poor Hans acquires neither. The story becomes a humorous cautionary tale. The newly emigrated Hans takes the reader on a tour of New York's seamier side, stumbling into a disappointing dime museum (the attractions are all on the poster outside), a seedy tailor shop (where he is almost forced to buy a suit he does not need), a dishonest auction gallery, and a flea-ridden hotel. Hans gets and quickly loses several unpromising jobs before finally finding his brother and security. Hans's later adventures continue to parody the success tale. By the last story he has achieved fame, but not in New York: he becomes the mayor of Hoboken through brawling and ballot-box stuffing, a post he eventually resigns.

Like other comic dime novels, Stratemeyer's tales use a cruel humor reliant on slapstick and exaggerated situations. Published only a few years after George Peck's *Peck's Bad Boy and His Pa* (1883), they operate on similar lines, satirizing human weaknesses and institutions.[2] Disagreements are resolved by farcical violence. Characters are punched and pounded; clothing and crockery are splattered or shattered. Dishonesty, greed, and cronyism prevail, with every man out for himself. In the midst of their comedy, the dime novels sketch a world filled with con men and corruption—the same world that would appear in the mystery and adventure dime novels but that is here seen without an avenging hero.

For Match, Hans, and others like them, the city is not Horatio Alger's golden land of opportunity, filled with philanthropic businessmen, but a place of deprivation and deception, made livelier by the opportunity for playing pranks and plotting revenge. Benevolence is in short supply, as is a desire to rise through honest effort. The Alger combination of industry and thrift is not a part of the protagonists' makeup. Instead, the characters' main concerns are making money, not necessarily through honest means, and having a good time. While Alger heroes renounce such frivolous and costly pastimes as attending theaters and gambling, the dime novel characters embrace them.

The comic dime novels show their characters in the most unflattering light, highlighting their greed, ignorance, and other weaknesses. Like Richard Outcault's "Yellow Kid" and similar comic strips, the comic dime novels incorporate a diverse group of characters—including a flow of immigrants, blacks, and rustics into the city—using them as the basis for conflict and humor. Unfortunately, the characters, especially peripheral ones, often become caricatures or crude stereotypes. The eight men on the corrupt town council in "Mayor Liederkranz of Hoboken" typify this mixture and treatment: "Fritz Stimmermann, a [German] saloon keeper like Hans; Andy O'Grady, an Irish contractor; Moses Rosenbaum, an eagle-nosed Jew; Lincoln Stump, a remnant of the

Fifteenth Amendment; Clarence De Roy, a dude from Dudedom; Golf Traderisky, a Swede; Josiah Homestead, from the annexed district; and Giorgio Shina, an Italian, who . . . had been a bootblack."[3] All eight speak in dialect or heavily accented English and have one or two unflattering traits; even the protagonists do not escape this kind of characterization. Such diversity was reserved for the comic tale, for Stratemeyer's later works never again show such a varied group working together. Other elements took longer to fade: most of the stereotypes persist in his other works.

Adventure Dime Novels: Mysteries, Westerns, and Sports Stories

In May 1892 Stratemeyer began writing mysteries for Street & Smith's Nick Carter Library. This marked the true beginning of his dime novel period. For the next year and a half, rarely did more than a month elapse without a Stratemeyer story in one of the dime novel series.

His detective fiction for Street & Smith was essentially ghostwriting: using pseudonyms shared by other writers, he turned out stories about already established characters created by other authors. His most notable contributions were 22 Nick Carter stories. These involved well-known characters and preconceived notions about the nature of the story, leaving only limited room for experimentation or originality. Readers expected that the setting would be contemporary and usually urban; that Nick, as an outsider, would be summoned to solve a baffling crime; that he, like almost every other dime novel detective, would don a variety of disguises in pursuit of the criminals; and, of course, that he would eventually capture the wrongdoers and bring them to justice, thus demonstrating his skill.[4]

Under the pseudonym Ed. Strayer, Stratemeyer also sold mysteries to a rival publisher, Norman L. Munro, for his Old Cap Collier Library of detective fiction. Munro left Stratemeyer free to develop his own characters, yet the first one he created, Dash Dare, bears a striking resemblance to Nick Carter. Dash appeared in five stories from 1892 to 1895. From 1893 to 1898 Munro published six other Stratemeyer mysteries in the Old Cap Collier Library. Each features a different detective, usually with an unusual trait or trademark heralded in the story's title ("Vasco, the Magician Detective," "Placer Dan, the Yukon Detective").[5]

After his first Nick Carters, Stratemeyer branched out to write adventure dime novels for Street & Smith. He penned eight westerns for the

Log Cabin Library. Most are set in Colorado and depict miners living near rough gambling towns, harassed by claim jumpers, barroom brawlers, and highwaymen. Four stories feature a character Stratemeyer created, Cool Dan, a road agent turned mine owner. The Log Cabin Library stories were the only 32-page dime novels Stratemeyer tried for Street & Smith and are his weakest work in the genre; they degenerate into a series of often pointless chases, unintentionally underscoring the open spaces of the West.

The remainder of Stratemeyer's work went to Street & Smith's New York Five Cent Library. This series contained a variety of tales, predominantly urban adventures—mysteries and sports stories—featuring a rotating cast of characters. Stratemeyer contributed three sets of series heroes. Dead Shot Dave, a gentleman gambler, appears in eight stories published under the pseudonym Jim Bowie. Gentleman Jack, a boxer (so named to capitalize on the popularity of Gentleman Jim Corbett), stars in seven tales written under the pseudonym Jim Daly, the name of one of Corbett's trainers. Jack and Jerry, "the bicycle wonders," pedal their way through four stories published under the name Zimmy. Stratemeyer's works comprise over one-third of the series during its early run; indeed, Dead Shot Dave's was one of the portraits decorating the series masthead. Loosely defined, these are sports stories: a scheduled competition is ostensibly the goal, though the plots are complicated by rivalries, dishonest opponents, and other obstacles, so the emphasis is also on whether the hero will survive these difficulties and reach the competition.

Characters   Stratemeyer's adventure dime novels differ greatly from his other works, not so much in style as in tone. Designed to titillate and thrill young readers rather than to edify or enlighten them, the dime novels create a pseudo-adult world, a blend of boyish concerns and attributes overlaid with adult settings and pastimes. The moral values espoused in Stratemeyer's hardcover fiction are noticeably absent, and the heroes serve as far less appropriate role models. Although the seeds of some of Stratemeyer's later characters are there, the dime novel characters also engage in actions practically every self-respecting series book hero would shun. It is as if Stratemeyer felt he addressed a different audience, with different goals: the dime novels would not be purchased by adults for children but rather consumed as forbidden fruit by the children themselves. Consequently, he provides glimpses of a lurid world, where characters indulge in actions and activities forbidden to children.

Stratemeyer patterned several of his protagonists on existing dime novel characters. As has been mentioned, Dash Dare is almost a duplicate of Nick Carter. Cool Dan is patterned after the famous Deadwood Dick. Stratemeyer's pugilist, Gentleman Jack, debuted in the New York Five Cent Library 13 weeks after Billy Madden (A. B. Tozer) began writing stories about a fictitious boxer named John L., Jr., an obvious parallel with John L. Sullivan. In addition to being based on real boxers, both Gentleman Jack and John L., Jr., live in New York and travel throughout the country as pugilists and actors, and both include a trainer, a fellow boxer, and one or more newsboys in their entourage, with the newsboys providing comic relief and an occasional rescue.

Standard Traits   Like other dime novel heroes, the protagonists of Stratemeyer's stories have many of the requisite heroic characteristics. They are courageous, generous, and physically fit, as well as resourceful, quick-witted, and prone to act while others stand agape. The heroes do not develop these traits in the course of the series but possess them from the start, just as most begin the series with their reputations already established. Despite the heroes' noble natures, however, their habits often leave much to be desired. In some ways they seem far more representative of the Gilded Age than of Alger heroes; if they are not sybarites, they are certainly not ascetics.

The standard Stratemeyer hero is an adult, although he is rarely described beyond the term "young man," leaving his age and appearance conveniently flexible. His background is somewhat obscure: if his family is mentioned, its members are either far away or deceased, leaving him reliant on his own resources. This appearance of adulthood is also bolstered by the characters' independence. Despite their assorted and unorthodox occupations, all of the heroes possess ample funds. Like grown-ups—or like the appearance of grown-ups to a child—they have enough money to spend it freely, buying drinks, lodgings, meals, or other items without ever worrying about budgets.

Their lives, too, show a freedom that must have delighted young readers who were forever caught between parental strictures and the discipline of school. Only one of the characters, Cool Dan, appears even to have a home to return to, although Dash Dare does have an office. The others spend their time traveling about the United States, stopping at hotels or the homes of acquaintances, unencumbered by restrictions, chores, or household rules.

The work ethic is notably absent from many tales: Jack and Jerry tour various towns perpetually in search of bicycle races to enter; Dead Shot

Dave is a "professional gambler" and shows no inclination to change. (Ironically, although Dave does not work his girlfriend, Jessie Dowling, does. Night after night she performs with a comic opera while he lounges backstage, yet neither considers this an odd arrangement.) Cool Dan's life is almost a reverse success story: he began as a hardworking horse trader, then moved west and took up highway robbery, before marrying a wealthy woman. Only Gentleman Jack, whose history parallels Stratemeyer's later career stories, works his way to success through determination and effort—and that occurs in the first story in the series.

The characters' handling of finances is enough to make a thrifty hero shudder. They spend money lavishly, buying dinners for their friends and, when in bars, drinks for the entire place. None too surprisingly, Dead Shot Dave is the most profligate. As he follows the opera company from city to city, his money provides the good things in life. He and Jessie stay at fine hotels and enjoy excursions to local sights. On one occasion, he hires a paddleboat and takes the opera company on a day's outing.

Vices   The heroes' habits—or vices—are those of adults. They patronize bars, dance halls, and gambling houses (but never brothels), enjoying the entertainment and joining in games of chance. The number and type of establishment pictured vary with the series. Cool Dan lives outside Creede, Colorado, "a gambler's paradise," where the local saloons serve as a combination bar, gambling house, and dance hall.[6] Dead Shot Dave frequents places like "the Golden Pick, the liveliest gambling saloon in Spokane," and also visits private clubs, racetracks, dogfights, and even dice games in back alleys.[7]

All drink freely and usually prefer hard liquor or champagne, the latter underscoring their affluence. The heroes regularly encourage other characters to imbibe; drinking is presented as a natural, pleasant pastime. Although the heroes are never seen drunk, some of their cronies are. Dave's friend Soapy Jack is often inebriated—at one point he is unable even to make his way back to his hotel—yet his condition earns not one word of censure from Dave or the author.

Other questionable behaviors are also evident. Cigars are one of Dash Dare's trademarks, and the other characters smoke them, too. Most heroes also use slang, a habit criticized in Stratemeyer's hardcover fiction. Jack and Jerry's dialogue is peppered with comments like, "Push your pedals, old man, and I'm with you," or, "You're a corker."[8]

The characters choose friends who would be considered highly unsuitable in other circumstances. Both Dan and Dave have heavy drinkers and gamblers as close friends. One of Jack's other companions, Stumpy the newsboy, is a contentious, rough lad, given to fighting with other newsboys and insulting anyone he dislikes. Jack's contribution to Stumpy's upbringing is to teach him some boxing tips so he can do better when he gets into fights!

These traits, incidentally, were not essential to a dime novel hero. Characters like Frank Merriwell stood firmly against alcohol, tobacco, and gambling. Even within the New York Five Cent Library, John L., Jr., never touched liquor, in sharp contrast to the real John L. Sullivan, who was noted for his barroom challenges. Stratemeyer's character Gentleman Jack frequently imbibed, though the real Gentleman Jim Corbett gave up alcohol early in his career.

Additional Traits   While the heroes' vices display their worldliness, other aspects of their characters appeal to a reader's desire to be admired and in control of situations. The heroes' most outstanding characteristic is their cool: they stay self-possessed and confident, a fact commented on repeatedly. Stratemeyer's heroes are "as cool as a cake of ice" (Gentleman Jack as a relatively unknown boxer before the match with the champion of the world),[9] as cool as a mountain snowbank (Cool Dan robbing a stagecoach) ("CD," 10), or just plain cool. Other characters confronting the hero become angry, edgy, or fearful, creating an additional contrast to the hero's calm.

Similarly, the hero has a strong sense of his own worth and is ready to stand up for his rights or his good name, both of which are often challenged by overbearing adults. When a man takes Gentleman Jack's seat on a crowded train, Gentleman Jack lifts him out of it bodily, telling the man, "I mean to have my rights, and don't you forget it. . . . [I] won't be squashed by anybody" ("GJ," 6). Although the heroes are usually good-natured, they show little tolerance for those who question their integrity. Many stories have at least one scene where another character accuses the hero of cheating or lying. The response is immediate: the hero insists that the speaker take back the remark and backs up his demand by pulling a gun or otherwise threatening the speaker, refusing to let the matter drop until the insult has been withdrawn. As Dead Shot Dave puts it, "I never allow any man to ride it over me" ("DSD," 3). The hero's willingness to stand up for himself, even to return rudeness for rudeness, never earns criticism from the crowd—and there is often a crowd observing. Instead, they applaud his spirit, a situation that must have appealed to readers not yet accorded the respect or privileges of adults.

Even more amazingly, the hero is not alone in his good opinion of himself. He has a presence that a later age would have labeled charismatic. He makes friends easily; people like and admire him, listen respectfully to him, and express concern for his welfare. Friends and strangers marvel audibly over his deeds. Only scoundrels fail to respond to his fine qualities. In the first Gentleman Jack story, every page has someone praising Jack: approximately 15 percent of the text is devoted to friends or strangers offering Jack encouragement, criticizing his opponent, thanking him for favors or rescues, or praising his actions, abilities, or physique. How could a reader fail to admire the hero with such a chorus of approval flowing from each page?

At the same time, however, the characters are not real adults but man-boys—or adolescents in men's clothing. They may indulge in pastimes that make them look grown-up, but they take an adolescent's view of the world. Most show an almost total lack of concern for the future; the next contest or the current problem is all-absorbing. They remain unencumbered by adult responsibilities. Even Dan, who has a wife and child and manages a mine, never worries about household or business affairs and is not even seen at work. For Jack and Jerry, life is like one long summer vacation: the weather is always warm as they bicycle from town to town, enjoying good times on the road with no thought of winter.

Humor   Finally, most characters in adventure dime novels show a generous dose of the schoolboy prankster, delighting in a bit of fun at another's expense. The New York Five Cent Library characters, especially Jack and Jerry, engage in the most high jinks. Their pranks range from light jokes to surprising cruelty, and from spontaneous actions to carefully planned creations, although the more extreme jokes are usually designed to humble or humiliate a rude or pompous character. In "Jack and Jerry's Tight Squeeze" the two shame an arrogant young man by luring him up a tree, then stirring up a hornet's nest. He is stung repeatedly and ruins his clothes when he seeks refuge in a shallow stream, while Jack and Jerry join with other members of his party in laughing uproariously at his predicament. Dousing people with water is a favorite trick. After helping to fight a fire, Jack and Jerry decide to have some "fun" with the country people who have been laboring to put out the blaze. They grab the fire hose, feign confusion, and give most of the crowd a thorough drenching.[10]

Such humor appeals to an adolescent reader's love of slapstick as well as to hostile feelings about structured society or authority. Freud observes that jokes can provide a means of humbling the powerful. Similarly, a study of children's humor notes that children "feel often oppressed by adult superiority and coerced by adult moral rules"; consequently, they use humor to turn "the envied bigness and powers of adults into something ridiculous, [and] expose adult pretensions."[11] The dime novels use pranks in a similar fashion.

The humor takes two forms: exaggeration and physical humiliation. In "Jack and Jerry's Tight Squeeze" the young man the duo embarrass is a caricature of high society. The portrayal highlights the more arbitrary aspects of society: elegant clothes, proper (or, in this case, affected) speech, artificial mannerisms. The joke then shatters all of this, ruining the clothes, reducing speech to primitive yells, turning careful movements into a mad scramble for the safety of the stream. Even in the escapade with the fire hose, the townspeople represent an established community and a way of life in which Jack and Jerry—and most dime novel heroes—have no part. Such mockery reinforces the dime novel hero's place outside of society.

Formulaic Plots   Just as Stratemeyer's protagonists conform to a similar pattern, so, too, do his dime novel plots follow fairly consistent lines. The stories fall into two groups: the New York Five Cent Library, a 16-page "nickel weekly," and the Old Cap Collier Library, which ran from 32 to 48 pages.

Most New York Five Cent Library tales are 14 to 15 pages long and use competition as a plot-unifying device. The Gentleman Jack and the Jack and Jerry stories build to a contest at the conclusion; the Dead Shot Daves contain a number of games throughout the story. Although the incidents and their order of occurrence vary, a typical New York Five Cent Library plot can be summarized as follows: The hero is presented with a challenge, such as an upcoming fight or race, and accepts. Soon after, he wins a quarrel with a dishonest antagonist connected with the upcoming contest, making an enemy. While pursuing his daily affairs, he sees someone being swindled or mistreated and intervenes, thus earning the friendship of the intended victim and the animosity of yet another miscreant. This new opponent soon meets and teams up with the first one. In a subsequent encounter (usually a sneak attack), the villains rob or injure the hero and escape. More clashes follow, usually one or two between the existing antagonists and the hero and his friends, and another with a walk-on character who, quickly shamed or bested, slinks off and disappears from the story. (This allows the hero a clear triumph while maintaining the ongoing conflict.) The villains unite to dispose of the hero, sometimes capturing him, sometimes trying an indirect attack, such as setting fire to his lodgings. After a fierce battle, the hero emerges victorious, and his opponents are either captured or killed. He recovers just in time to win the competition. His friends celebrate his triumph and the story ends, after readers are assured that the hero will return soon in new adventures.

The New York Five Cent Library plots emphasize competition and fair play: the hero's honesty is continually pitted against his opponents' treachery. To some measure, this approach is occasioned by the nature of the protagonist. Since the story begins with the hero's virtues and numerous victories already established, it has little room for details about character building or Algeresque struggles to succeed. Still, the readers expected action and adventure aplenty, so the problem facing the novelist was how to provide exciting conflict in a story. The solution, for Stratemeyer, was to set up a series of challenges to the hero's superiority: boxing matches, gambling matches, bicycle races. But once again the nature of the hero—and of the dime novel—interferes with plans for any type of traditional sports story. Given the hero's incredible ability, his win against any normal opponent seems assured and thus anticlimactic—unless the odds against him are increased by outside circumstances, such as cheating. Thus what begins as a simple challenge soon snowballs into a mass of complicated schemes and underhanded deals.

Despite the similarity of plots and characters, Stratemeyer gave each of the three New York Five Cent Library series its own flavor by shaping situations to incorporate each character's particular abilities. Hence, Dead Shot Dave stories contain numerous situations in which Dave uses his keen eyes and knowledge of gambling to catch dishonest players. Gentleman Jack resolves most problems with his fists, knocking down quarrelsome thugs, locked doors, and even a runaway horse. With Jack and Jerry, Stratemeyer used even more ingenuity to work the bicycles into plot lines, sending the duo racing along to spread alarms and pursue runaway horses or, alternatively, creating situations in which the bicycles could be used in lieu of grappling hooks or ladders.

Stratemeyer's Old Cap Collier Library stories, which usually run from 29 to 44 pages, employ a more complex narrative style and a different type of plot. They sometimes open before the crime has occurred, in which case the first chapter follows the actions of secondary characters before and during the crime. Even after introducing the detective, the story alternates between the two perspectives for several chapters. Occasionally, the story shifts back and forth in time, chronicling the detective's investigation, then moving back to describe the coroner's inquest or the actions of other characters before finally tracing the detective's final steps to unravel the crime. Large stretches of the novel are one-sentence paragraphs relying heavily on dialogue, a convenient method for filling pages rapidly.

Again, although some plots vary, many follow a standard formula. A murder is committed, and one of a pair of young lovers stands suspected of the crime. Through incompetence or deliberate deceit, officials introduce enough evidence at the coroner's inquest to charge that person with murder. The detective becomes interested in the case and decides the accused is innocent. His investigation reveals that what looked like a simple domestic homicide, motivated by thwarted love or greed, is actually a more complex affair concealing a ring of professional criminals. He locates the gang's hideout and either eavesdrops on or infiltrates the gang by using his skill at disguises—but he is captured. In the nick of time, reinforcements arrive or he overcomes the gang. The criminals end up in jail or dead, the lovers are happily reunited, and the detective departs with his fee and the satisfaction of a job well done.

"Dash Dare on His Mettle; or, Clearing up a Double Tragedy" (1892) is unusual in that it parallels an actual event: the crime Dash solves is a thinly disguised copy of the Lizzie Borden case. The basics of the murder are almost identical with the original case: father and stepmother killed with an axe, daughter suspected. When Dash investigates at the request of the girl's fiancé, he discovers a major counterfeiting ring. One member has been fabricating clues to implicate the girl and to conceal the real killer's identity. Dash learns that a neighbor engineered the murders after the stepmother discovered he was a counterfeiter and threatened to tell her husband, a far cry from the actual incident.

Crime and Violence   Crime and violence, or threats of violence, are quite common in the stories. In the New York Five Cent Library, the combination of the shorter length and the need for rapid action results in a crime or confrontation on almost every page. "Dead Shot Dave in Chicago; or, High Times among the White City Sharps" (1893) begins on page 2 and ends on page 15. In that short space, all of the following occur: one illegal dogfight, in which the dog also attacks an onlooker and is killed; two illegal gambling clubs, both with rigged games; four confidence games; three attempted thefts; two robberies, both involving injuries to innocent people; two kidnappings; one attempt at torture, resulting in the torturer accidentally burning to death; eight fistfights; two attempted stabbings; two stabbings; two attempted shootings; five shootings (three fatal). Almost anyone can become a victim: the criminals and their confederates, the hero and his associates, innocent bystanders, and friendly or unwary citizens who fall prey to confidence men's schemes or pickpockets' talents.

In the Log Cabin Library and Old Cap Collier Library stories, the violence is often more brutal or more graphic, and the crimes against innocent persons quite severe, again perhaps an indication that these stories were intended for older readers. The Old Cap Collier tales frequently begin with a murder; the victim is someone who has run afoul of criminals, rather than someone guilty of wrongdoing. Additionally, the accused and his or her friends, also innocent, suffer from the misery caused by false accusations and imprisonment. In the first Dash Dare story grief is a constant undertone: the victim's daughter spends most scenes sobbing, swooning, or looking strained as she tries to bear up under the double anguish of her father's death and the incarceration of the man she loves; the accused's mother is so shattered by his arrest that she falls ill and is placed under a doctor's care.

The violence in these adventure dime novels exceeds that in series books. The number of innocent victims leaves the impression that crime and its consequences are widespread and likely to affect innocent bystanders. Even the hero is less liable to try to defuse the situation than he is to respond in kind. All of the protagonists carry guns and use them, sometimes killing their opponents. Even when the criminals do not die by the hero's hand, many of them perish in other ways—through flaws in their own schemes or in accidents or natural disasters. In these instances the situations are designed so that the hero cannot effect a rescue and sometimes, recognizing the futility of the effort, does not even try.

Other factors contribute to the dime novels' picture of an uncivilized and uncertain society. One is a lack of faith in the police or the judicial system. Time and again, when a character is caught committing a crime, the victim frees him by deciding it is too much bother to file a complaint with the police. The criminal, untouched by this gesture, waits for a more opportune moment and commits another crime. Alternatively, on the few occasions when the criminal is turned over to the law he usually escapes within a few paragraphs or pages, demonstrating the unreliability of the police.

A second factor is the sheer extensiveness of evil: it occurs in every profession, in every place the protagonist visits, and in almost all walks of life. Petty crimes occur continually as he walks along the street or stops in a bar, and beneath it all an underworld of professional criminals unites to plot more serious affairs. While the dime novel plots are wildly improbable, they gain a touch of verisimilitude through their links to actual events and places. The Jack and Jerry stories capitalize on the bicycle craze of the 1890s, suggesting even that new sport was rife with dishonest players. The Columbian Exposition figures in most stories about Chicago; on visiting the city Gentleman Jack observes, "The World's Fair is what brings all the scum of the country here"—hardly a comforting thought to would-be tourists![12]

One offshoot of this continuous evil is that it presents an unusual picture of the world—a forerunner of the bleak landscape of the hard-boiled detective story, with Pollyanna-like characters spread throughout the tale. On all sides are vicious persons harboring disproportionate feelings of hatred and vengeance toward the hero, confidence men eagerly looking for their next victim, selfish or ruthless thugs setting up gambling dens or brutalizing women. Yet in their midst, confidently trying to right every wrong he encounters, stands the hero, an optimistic soul who is rarely, if ever, emotionally troubled by the continuing stream of misery and villainy he sees.

The dime novels present their own mixture of heroism and vice, violence and victory. Their adult protagonists, who remain outside of conventional society, possess some noble traits, but many questionable ones, too. The settings depict more vice and brutality than do series books, although the plots retain the emphasis on the hero's success. For Stratemeyer, the dime novels served as a training ground, a means of making additional money, and a first arena for working with formulas and series characters. They formed a brief period in his career, one he rarely mentioned. It was with his other works, published in story papers, that he moved away from slightly disreputable heroes and began the career success stories that gave him a foothold in clothbound fiction.

3

Career Stories

Career stories and series were a longtime staple for Stratemeyer and the Stratemeyer Syndicate. Beginning with Stratemeyer's first published story in 1883 and running through the Wynn and Lonny series in 1975, their history is, perhaps appropriately, a history of the growth and success of the Syndicate. Like the hero of one of his own tales, Stratemeyer began his rise to riches with these stories, and their format reveals the changes between nineteenth-century literature and the writings of the newer age. Just as the external form of the stories evolved from the now obsolete story papers to the multivolume, recurring-progatonist series books, so, too, did the contents change to reflect newer attitudes and ideas. These stories show Stratemeyer's ability to adapt his material to the times while retaining patterns and concepts based on his earlier writings. The result, "up to date books" for "up to date boys and girls," kept the Syndicate firmly entrenched in popular fiction well into the twentieth century.

In the Stratemeyer career story the central character takes a job either to support himself or to contribute substantially to his family's income. Although circumstances vary, the plot usually includes unraveling a mystery and concludes with the hero's success in his career or in solving the mystery, or both. Stratemeyer developed the patterns he used in his earlier stories fairly quickly, drawing on models like Alger's success tales. But as the new century unfolded, the single-story character who reaches respectability and security yielded before the trend toward recurring heroes who face constant competition as they rise to fame. Although Stratemeyer preserved some of the formulaic elements of plot and characterization, many of the stories' internal elements changed over time. The technological advances of the twentieth century—and more important, the prevailing faith and delight in such advances—colored the stories, which substituted scientific and mechanical information for moral instruction.

Background and Influences

Horatio Alger Stories chronicling the success of young working boys emerged sporadically in the 1830s and appeared more frequently as the century progressed. In 1867 Horatio Alger, Jr., published his *Ragged Dick*, which traces an orphan's progress from newsboy to businessman. Its popularity prompted Alger to write other, similar books. One of his young readers was none other than Edward Stratemeyer, who hoped someday to write books like Alger's—and did.

Scholars have analyzed the formula and values in Alger's fiction. In the typical "rags to riches" story,

> a teen-aged boy whose experience of the sinister adult world is slight yet whose virtue entitles him to the reader's respect, is cast unexpectedly into that sinister world and forced to struggle for a livelihood. At some point . . . the hero enters the City, both a fabled land of opportunity and a potentially corrupting environment, where he . . . struggle[s] to maintain his social respectability, to clear his or another's name of false accusations, [and] to gain a measure of economic independence. . . . At length, the hero earns the admiration of an adult patron who rewards him with elevated social status, usually a job or reunion with his patrician family.[1]

In the course of his rise the Alger hero is usually contrasted with another boy, "a parochial snob who neither travels nor struggles, whose behavior is supremely selfish, who aspires to wealth, and who invariably ends the novel a rung lower on the social ladder than the one attained by the hero" (Scharnhorst, 68). Most of these elements—except, ironically, the trip to the city (one of Alger's strong points)—also appear in Stratemeyer's stories. The Alger hero's success, however, does not depend solely on his character; what is described as "earn[ing] the admiration of an adult patron" is rarely a matter of hard work but of incredible luck. Ragged Dick, for example, is conveniently nearby when a banker's son falls off a ferry. After Dick leaps into the water and rescues the boy, the banker offers him a job, providing the path to his success. Or, as Russel Nye summarizes the Alger formula, "success [is] made out of labor plus the breaks of ability plus the opportunity to capitalize on it," a philosophy Stratemeyer's heroes took to heart.[2]

Story Papers Stratemeyer's stories shared similarities of plot and character with those created by Alger and others. He also imitated their publishing patterns, selling his stories first to periodicals and later reprinting them in hardcover as part of a series. At that time the juvenile periodical market was divided into two camps: quality magazines (such as *Youth's Companion* and *St. Nicholas*) and the less literary story papers. The former, often published by some of the better publishing houses, carried prose and poetry by writers dear to historians of children's literature. They "attempted to entertain children with realistic events from the everyday lives of ordinary families," shunning tales with violent adventures and implausibly successful heroes (R. Kelly, 38). Whether Stratemeyer ever submitted any of his early material to these literary magazines is not known; what is known is that he did not succeed in breaching their pages with any of his early stories.

Instead, Stratemeyer, like many another writer, turned to the story papers. These publications provided a ready market for would-be authors. They were often issued by dime novel publishers, and like the dime novels they were priced inexpensively, published weekly or monthly, and used an enormous amount of fiction. Each issue offered a mixture of material: installments of three to eight serials, often in different genres, plus shorter fiction, informational tidbits, jokes, puzzle columns, and letters.

The tone of the papers varied considerably: some strove for a more respectable approach; others stressed "blood and thunder" stories with heightened violence. Accordingly, Stratemeyer tailored his material to the market. Two of the papers that carried some of Stratemeyer's earliest fiction, *Golden Days* and *Golden Argosy*, can be considered transitional papers. They "bridge[d] the gap between the 'respectable' juveniles and the blood-and-thunder bang-bang-bang type of cheap weekly for boys."[3] *Golden Days* was probably the more sedate and reputable of the two, and Stratemeyer's stories for *Golden Days* differ from his later writings: they come closer to the "reform" stories found in the more literary magazines.

After several of his stories appeared in *Golden Days*, Stratemeyer also sold material to *Golden Argosy*, a periodical founded to publish "inspirational stories" (Mott, *History*, 4:418). Although what generally resulted was more adventure filled than inspirational, the stories still carried moral overtones, with an emphasis on career. Horatio Alger was one of its staunch supporters.[4] Stratemeyer's *Golden Argosy* serials from 1891 and 1892 alternate between stories about boys who pursue traditional careers and tales about young boys who demonstrate their ability to manage business affairs in their parents' absence.

Several other story papers for which Stratemeyer wrote were less restrained. In 1893 his fiction began appearing in Street & Smith's *Good*

News. Although *Good News* published stories with moral heroes, its contents emphasized exciting adventures and came far closer to the "blood and thunder" school than to respectability; its authors included those who, like Stratemeyer, had gained experience writing the action-filled dime novels. During 1893 and 1894 Stratemeyer also edited *Good News* and published most of his writing in its pages. He penned many of his more unusual pieces for *Good News*, including his early science fiction and adventure tales, and even his career stories showed more variety in their choice of occupation. Tales about "Camera Bob," "Joe the Surveyor," and others highlighted an assortment of careers, many of which involved unsupervised work outdoors that allowed the protagonists a great deal of mobility.

That these career stories were keyed to the interests of readers of *Good News* becomes evident from a reading of several of the regular columns in the story paper. Boys wrote from all across the country to ask for advice about jobs. Correspondents ranged in age from 13 to 21, with the majority aged 16. They wanted information on wages and qualifications for various occupations and assessments of the practicality of entering others. A sampling of letters from early 1894 shows the boys who wrote in expressed interest in a variety of careers. The three that received the most queries were musician, writer, and civil engineer or surveyor—all occupations used in Stratemeyer's stories. Roughly one-third of the letters came from boys who were already employed and who were usually considering changing jobs. Here, reality diverged from fiction: five worked in offices or "business houses"; others were tailors, factory workers, or in similar occupations that seemed to preclude the type of open-air work that many of Stratemeyer's heroes favored.

For these readers, stories like Stratemeyer's provided both escapist reading and a measure of wish fulfillment. His characters were about the same age as many of the letter writers. Like them, the heroes begin the story in unpleasant, unrewarding jobs but then progress to the type of occupations readers asked about. While the stories offer little practical information about the working world, they depict boys employed in challenging occupations and hold out hopes for adventure and success. No matter how unpromising the original situation, the hero's innate ability, luck, and determination eventually secure him a good job and a comfortable nest egg, while he encounters enough thrilling adventures to satisfy the most restless reader.

The last few story papers that printed Stratemeyer's material were *Young Sports of America*, *Bright Days*, and *Golden Hours*. Stratemeyer's stories for these papers placed the protagonists in less traditional careers and also continued his experimentation with other types of tales. *Young Sports of America* (later retitled *Young People of America*) emphasized sports and athletic stories; *Bright Days* appears to have been modeled after *Golden Days* (but with less emphasis on the inspirational). Stratemeyer edited *Young Sports of America* and both published and edited *Bright Days*. This gave him greater freedom to use his own material and possibly to reprint it: several of his *Young Sports of America* serials resurfaced in *Bright Days*.[5] *Golden Hours* was issued by a dime novel publisher and favored sensational fiction.

Story-Paper Fiction

Like Alger, Stratemeyer can be said to have told the same tale many times over. A boy deprived of his rightful inheritance faces numerous trials as he attempts to regain it. In the process, he confronts and overcomes opposition by several key figures, usually an adult in a position of authority, a boy approximately his own age, one or more thugs, and the legal system. This is the Stratemeyer career tale reduced to its simplest form. (For clarity's sake, in my discussion of Stratemeyer's story-paper writing I use "career stories" and "career tales" to refer to publications in the story papers and "career series" to refer to Stratemeyer's and the Syndicate's hardcover career fiction.) Stratemeyer's early stories, some of which are described in detail below, show the rapid development of this formula.

For at least the first few years, as Stratemeyer changed publishers, he altered certain elements in the stories. Although not all of his works conform neatly to a pattern, in general the plots follow a chronological development and fall into three stages. His first stories, from *Our American Boys* and *Golden Days*, show various combinations of the formula's elements, which coalesce in his fourth tale, "Alvin Chase's Search." Except for the first story, these tales lack employment for the hero, an element remedied in most of the fiction from the second stage, the *Argosy* tales. The *Argosy* stories usually feature a boy trying to support himself or help his family, but they vary the hero's origins or situations, often involving him in temporary or menial labor from which he is released by acquiring his inheritance. They also move further away from the protected hero, one sheltered by a father or benevolent guardian. Finally, the *Good News* stories shift the focus to the working hero and intensify the dangers.[6]

"Harry's Trial": The Basic Formula Stratemeyer's first career tale was "Harry's Trial," published in January 1883 under the name of Ed Ward. It appeared in the premiere issue of *Our American Boys*, Stratemeyer's initial attempt at publishing his own story paper. A two-page story, "Harry's Trial" is a stripped-down, bare-bones version of a career tale. There are no extraneous characters, no subplots, no scenes designed to provide background or acquaint readers with the characters. Harry Melville, a "boy of fifteen, with a frank pleasant face," works as an errand boy in a grocery store to help support his widowed mother.[7] Although Harry works industriously, one of his coworkers, Mr. Olward, resents him, for "he had wanted his son, Tom, to have the place Harry now occupied" ("HT," 5).

One evening Olward unexpectedly walks Harry home and asks him to change a ten-dollar bill, which Harry does. The following day, at work, Olward sends Harry out to change another ten-dollar bill, which turns out to be counterfeit. Olward accuses Harry of substituting a fake bill for the genuine one; though Harry denies the charge, he knows he will be unable to prove his innocence. When Olward informs their employer of the alleged theft, the employer pulls the bill in question from his pocket. He explains that he had stopped at Harry's the night before and had changed the bill for Harry then. Disgusted by Olward's plot, the employer fires him and promotes Harry to clerk, so all ends happily. The basics of the later stories are all there: the honest young boy, a half-orphan, who is falsely accused and unable to prove his innocence; the dishonest and mean-spirited older man (and his dissolute son, mentioned only in passing in "Harry's Trial"); the friendly benefactor, who here and in some later stories serves double duty as employer; the unveiling of deceit and the punishment of the deceiver; and the final success of the hero—in this case, rather limited.

After "Harry's Trial," almost seven years passed before Stratemeyer published another story. "Victor Horton's Idea," serialized in *Golden Days* in November 1889, was a longer and more polished affair, patterned after the reform story. Victor, a troublesome boy, is falsely suspected of starting a fire and runs away from home. After learning that life in New York is not as wonderful as the dime novels picture it, he is found by his father, who explains that his name has been cleared. Victor returns home, wiser and repentant. The protagonist's decision to flee from trouble (and usually from possible arrest) rather than to face up to false charges proved a favorite plot device of Stratemeyer's, becoming almost a standard convention.

"Captain Bob's Secret": Developing the Formula in Longer Fiction   Stratemeyer's next sale to *Golden Days* introduced more of the standard elements. In "Captain Bob's Secret" (1890) the hero serves as the narrator and is actually a lost heir, believed dead, who has been deliberately concealed from his family. The lost heir—a forerunner of another favorite theme of Stratemeyer's, the missing parent—continued to appear intermittently throughout the career stories. This approach allowed the hero to claim a place in society and an inheritance by right of birth, showing he was not a social climber but someone who belonged in better circumstances.

Other elements from the story also became regular components in Stratemeyer's tales. In "Captain Bob's Secret" Shep, the protagonist, works briefly for a businessman and his daughter and also befriends an amnesiac. All three instinctively like and admire Shep—and turn out to be none other than his uncle, cousin, and older brother, bringing about a wonderful reunion. Later stories, too, would include sympathetic characters who turn out to be relatives or friends of the hero's family—and would explain that the hero's true joy was in acquiring not a fortune but a family. "Captain Bob's Secret" also instituted the idea that unscrupulous persons could use information about the hero's past for gain.

"Alvin Chase's Search": The Penultimate Formula   Finally, Stratemeyer's third story for *Golden Days*, "Alvin Chase's Search" (1890), introduced most of the remaining elements of the career story—almost everything, in fact, except employment for the hero. The recently orphaned Alvin Chase lives with his miserly stepfather and spoiled stepbrother. Although Alvin's mother had told him he would be cared for after her death, her will leaves him only a living interest in the family home, where he is mistreated by his stepfather, Dr. Bardell, and bullied by his stepbrother, Tom. Alvin endures numerous trials; then, aided by a young man, he goes to New York, where he learns that his stepfather has swindled him. Faced with overwhelming evidence, Dr. Bardell confesses and reforms, some of the coconspirators are jailed, and Tom flees to the West and eventually disappears. This is the essence of Stratemeyer's version of the career story: swindled out of an inheritance, the protagonist faces assorted dangers as he gradually uncovers the truth.

Unlike Stratemeyer's earlier pieces, "Alvin Chase's Search" places more emphasis on the protagonist's own efforts to regain his inheritance and less on the reformation of either the central or secondary characters, marking the transition to the different philosophy of the career tales. It is Stratemeyer's first use of the "rites of passage" story, moving the sheltered Alvin from his secure home into a corrupt and scheming adult world, in effect testing and preparing him for some of the pitfalls of the business world. Although Alvin deals with an assortment of natural dangers and disasters, they are secondary to the real conflicts in the story—those with human antagonists.

Other Story-Paper Fiction   Stratemeyer's first full-length career story was "Richard Dare's Venture," serialized in *Golden Argosy* in 1891. This was one of the few stories that touched on an area close to Stratemeyer's own experience: the hero eventually joins with another young man in running a stationery store, the same occupation Stratemeyer held when he began writing. Like "Alvin Chase's Search," most of Stratemeyer's *Argosy* stories deal with young boys proving their ability to face the treachery of the adult world. Their titles reflect this emphasis on self-reliance: "Luke Foster's Grit," "Fighting for His Own."

While adhering to the basic "search and discovery" pattern and most of the same types of conflicts found in "Alvin Chase's Search," several of the *Argosy* stories introduce another Stratemeyer trait: the weak, missing, or ailing father. Typical of these is the 1892 serial "True to Himself; or, Roger Strong's Struggle for Place." The book opens with Roger Strong's father in jail for embezzlement and follows Roger's struggle against the prejudice of some of the townspeople and his own difficulties when he is falsely accused of theft. Stories like this replace the unjust guardian with a dishonest rich man who possesses similar characteristics but has no claim to the boy. In "True to Himself" Roger's two nemeses are Mr. Woodward, a wealthy, mean-spirited man, and his son, Duncan, a "wayward" boy "who had many of the traits of the bully about him"—virtual duplicates of the stepfather and stepbrother in "Alvin Chase's Search."[8] Predictably, Roger Strong not only clears his own and his father's name but discovers that the real embezzler is none other than Mr. Woodward.

These stories, like most of Stratemeyer's career tales, differ from works such as Alger's *Ragged Dick* in several respects. Although Stratemeyer, like Alger, faithfully includes mention of salary and the cost of meals and lodging, the Alger emphasis on thrift is missing. The Alger hero's two favorite books are his Bible and his bankbook, and the reader is continually given a running tally of his account in the latter. Stratemeyer's characters have the appearance, but not the substance, of these thrifty souls: they do not make nightly reviews of the bank balance, and quite often they have moneyed friends who dole out funds to pay for lodgings, transportation, or even private detectives as needed.

Moreover, although the hero profits from a combination of providence and pluck what he usually ends up with is his own money, which was taken from him. Unlike Alger heroes, who receive midlevel positions in respectable firms, the Stratemeyer hero is equally apt to receive an inheritance and to go off to college to study law or medicine in the final pages of the book.

After his first sales to *Argosy*, Stratemeyer did not return to the career story until late in 1893. Then, for the next year and a half, almost every issue of *Good News* carried an installment of a Stratemeyer story. Although most of his heroes were so much alike as to be almost interchangeable, Stratemeyer continued to use the single-story hero who achieves success and a comfortable position at the end of the tale. His stories from this period are among his most action filled. Harrowing adventures, vengeful foes, and mysteries provide the hero with continual excitement, even overshadowing his drive for success. Some dangers occur on the job, foreshadowing the types of plot found in the career series.

The *Good News* career stories also differ from Stratemeyer's earlier tales in that some contain a light—usually very light—romance. Generally, the hero meets his girl after he rescues her, a pattern continued in several of the series books. Although the text makes occasional references to the girl being special, it includes few, if any, sentimental scenes between the two. Readers are left to conclude that she shares his feelings by references to her pleasure in seeing him and by the mention of their marriage in the summary at the end of the story, again underscoring the hero's growth to maturity.

The Story Papers: Themes and Traits

The central theme in Stratemeyer's stories is the hero's growth to manhood, which is accomplished not so much by character development as by weathering conflicts with different types of adversaries. This usually involves four basic types of antagonists: the guardian or adult authority figure, the adolescent peer, the adult criminals or "hired help" (usually in league with the adult authority figure), and the judicial system. The hero's earliest confrontations are with a peer or authority figure, underscoring the rites of passage aspect of his struggles. Here, the protagonist demonstrates his ability to hold his own against other adolescents and his readiness to move from a childhood dependence on adults to a more equal footing with them. Both sets of confrontations operate partly as a symbolic conflict over the protagonist's rights and independence, and partly as a morality play illustrating the effects of appropriate and inappropriate behavior.

The Guardian   In the simplest sense, the protagonist's struggle with and final victory over his guardian or authority figure can be seen as the child breaking free from his parents, overthrowing his subordinate role to become an adult. Stratemeyer, however, sidesteps the issue of filial disrespect or disobedience by replacing the natural parents with a substitute figure, one who is clearly misusing his authority. The stories quickly establish that the protagonist is powerless, unappreciated, and usually mistreated. "Alvin Chase's Search" begins when Alvin's stepfather, Dr. Bardell, grabs Alvin by the collar "so tightly that [the boy] was in great danger of choking" and accuses him of hitting his stepbrother.[9] When Alvin wrenches free, protesting this treatment, his stepfather is outraged by his actions and ingratitude—further evidence of the stepfather's skewed sense of justice.

Alvin also points out the unfair treatment he receives at home. He tells Dr. Bardell, "I get just about enough to hold body and soul together . . . [and] I do all the work around the house, while your son Tom plays the gentleman." Alvin's stepfather "loftily" replies, "My son has certain rights in this house which you do not" ("ACS," 721–22). However, the house and money that allow Dr. Bardell and Tom this gentlemanly life belonged to Alvin's late mother; neither Alvin nor the reader can believe she expected her son to be reduced to resident servant.

Soon after the hero's lowly position has been established, he makes a crucial decision to stand up for himself and his rights. This is the beginning of his transition into adulthood, marking his recognition that the position of a child (that is, one who has no rights, only a duty to obey his parents) is no longer appropriate. He now wants the responsibility and respect accorded an adult. At one point Alvin Chase tells Dr. Bardell, "I've always done my duty and I don't propose to be treated like a dog," in effect, renouncing the servile role of a child in favor of adulthood ("ACS," 721). (Other stories note the significance of the hero's momentous decision to assert himself even more emphatically. The hero of "Paul Raymond's Rovings" [1895] states: "I came to a decision *which was destined to change the course of my whole life*. I would stand up for my rights, be the consequences what they may."[10])

The protagonist's first attempt to assert himself often occurs within the confines of his own home when he questions the guardian about his finances, endeavoring to move from the limited knowledge of a child and penetrate the business affairs of an adult. The attempt is flatly rebuffed. Although the guardian usually reveals some measure of guilt by blanching or appearing startled, he recovers and reasserts his rights to the boy's funds. Alvin Chase's stepfather not only denies any wrongdoing but takes a whip to Alvin—the punishment for a disobedient child. Essentially, the boy cannot have it both ways: he is attempting to remain in the home as a child yet also to act as an adult.

Soon after this, in a second confrontation, the guardian calls for the police and the boy runs away. This development moves the boy out of the house, giving him his first opportunity to face life on his own, yet it ends in his arrest. While survival in the outside world is essential for the transition to adulthood, running away from one's problems is not a proper solution; the hero, freed from prison by a benevolent adult, must find another way.

Here, despite their insistence on the hero's virtue and honesty, the stories display an odd sense of morality, for cunning succeeds where honesty and forthrightness fail. In his first confrontation with the guardian (questioning him about finances) the boy uses the direct approach and learns that directness or the guilelessness of a child is not an effective method for dealing with adult affairs. When he resumes his investigation, he tries more devious methods: eavesdropping, rifling through desks, and reading personal mail. After hiding and listening to a conversation between his stepfather and a lawyer, Alvin searches Dr. Bardell's desk, justifying his action to the reader by explaining: "That conversation I had just heard proved to me . . . that my stepfather was not treating me justly; that he was withholding property that legally belonged to me. This being so, it was certainly right for me to investigate matters, and to that end I approached his desk" ("ACS," 762). Finding an incriminating letter with the address of a New York conspirator, Alvin takes it without hesitation and uses it to establish his stepfather's guilt. This type of information leads the hero into numerous confrontations in the outside world, usually with the hired help— avaricious and violent adults who people the world outside of the home, the kind of people from whom the boy has been sheltered by his previous position as a child. Having proved his ability under those circumstances, the boy returns home with evidence of the guardian's deception. At the end of "Alvin Chase's Search" Alvin regains the title to his mother's estate and assumes his position as keeper of the finances and owner of the house, in effect displacing his stepfather and completing his transition to adulthood.

The protagonist's clash with his guardian also illustrates one of the apparently contradictory themes in Stratemeyer's novels: financial gain. The goal of Stratemeyer's heroes is money—making it or regaining it— yet most of their problems arise from the antagonists' desire to do essentially the same thing. The distinction, blurred in many of Stratemeyer's tales, stems from Alger's economic values, which in turn are derived from the concept of the Christian gentleman or of stewardship: it is not wealth but the use of wealth that marks one as bad or good.

In "Alvin Chase's Search" Alvin's stepfather and stepbrother exemplify wealth gone wrong: the stepfather has used dishonest means to acquire money and, having it, hoards it for his own use. Like almost every other Stratemeyer guardian, he is reluctant to spend money even for the needy in his own home—Alvin. By extension, one assumes, he is equally unwilling to spend it helping others. His reformation underscores this, for after returning Alvin's estate, he "devoted [himself] to repairing the wrongs he had done and to founding the Cedar Cove Hospital"—a life of service ("ACS," 63). Alvin's stepbrother follows an equally unacceptable path. He is not miserly, but wasteful, squandering money on cards and drink and mistreating his own and others' belongings. Alvin, however, possesses the correct philosophy. He is willing to work, and he is generous, demonstrating his openheartedness by helping others, even risking his life to do so on occasion. In the course of the story, Alvin thus learns three lessons about money: one from his mother, demonstrating the consequences of misplaced trust and failure to attend carefully to one's own financial affairs; and one each from his stepfather and stepbrother about the misuse of wealth. Having mastered these lessons, Alvin is ready to handle his fortune responsibly.

The Peer The hero's second adversary in the story is his peer, usually a relative, coworker, or local lad. The protagonist's problems can be summarized simply: the peer tries to bully the hero, and the hero resists. In "Alvin Chase's Search" Alvin's stepbrother Tom treats Alvin with contempt, insulting him, appropriating items belonging to him, and interfering with his activities. Alvin responds by standing up for himself, verbally and physically. When his stepbrother orders him out of a boat because he wants to use it, Alvin refuses to obey; when Tom takes Alvin's boots and throws one at him, then prepares to throw the other, Alvin "wrenche[s] it from his grasp and hit[s] him over the head with it" ("ACS," 722). Alvin does not initiate the quarrels, nor does he retaliate by taking Tom's belongings; he does, however, refuse to be cowed by Tom's behavior.

Although the peer is usually involved in all manner of mischief, he does not try to entice the hero to join him in his dissolute habits; given the protagonist's character, he would not be tempted. These clashes are not lessons in how to resist temptation but an object lesson in how to deal with intimidation by or corruption in one's peers: hold fast to your rights, and fight for them if necessary. This sentiment reflected the cry of the times. One of Stratemeyer's contempories, Theodore Roosevelt, noted in his autobiography that some of the best lessons he learned from his boyhood reading were teachings about "the individual virtues . . . self-reliance, energy, courage, the power of insisting on [one's] own rights."[11] This is precisely what the protagonist does, and significantly, he is able to hold his own against his peer unaided, even to defeat him.

The confrontations with the peer also carry their own lesson. Like the two-dimensional characters in a morality play, the two boys, personifying virtue and vice, run through their prescribed roles following a foreordained course. The peer is every parent's nightmare: he lies, steals, drinks, and gambles; he is also rude, irresponsible, and dishonest, lacking a single saving grace. Alvin Chase's stepbrother Tom begins the story in a pampered, respectable position but moves steadily toward a ruinous end. He disobeys his father, accrues gambling debts and steals to pay for them, hires a man to kill Alvin, and finally runs off to the West, where he falls in with a bad crowd and is sentenced to prison, "the last [Alvin] heard of him" ("ACS," 63). In contrast, as Alvin weathers the trials he faces and searches for the truth about his family's finances, he moves closer to wealth and respectability. The message is clear: good and right eventually triumph, and corruption leads to ruin.

The Hired Help and Other Criminal Adversaries   The protagonist's confrontation with the hired help also pits the innocent boy against corruption, but these adversaries are adults, not equals. Unlike the guardian or authority figure, they are not parental figures or white-collar criminals involved in embezzling or paper theft, but thugs, sometimes with jail records for violent crimes. They lack the traits of gentlemen: they are poorly or loudly dressed; their speech is ungrammatical or slangy; they have no established homes or roots in the community but instead skulk in and out of the area, stopping at roadhouses or other hangouts; and they are capable of cold-blooded violence. While the authority figure occasionally threatens or assaults the protagonist, these acts usually spring from a moment of rage rather than from premeditation; the white-collar criminal is unable to manage a dispassionate killing. In contrast, the hired help readily resort to violence. Theirs is the physical work—breaking and entering, robbery, attempted murder.

The hero's clashes with these men often place his life in jeopardy, increasingly so in later stories. These conflicts reinforce the idea that the hero's growth occurs not just through personal development but through surviving external challenges. He must prove himself by exhibiting agility, strength, courage, and endurance.

It could be suggested that these conflicts add a mythical element to the hero's quest. Just as mythical heroes often venture into the underworld in their journey for enlightenment, so, too, do these Stratemeyer protagonists face the criminal underworld, or the underbelly of society. (Indeed, many of the criminals actually inhabit an underworld of sorts: their hideouts are in dark cellars or other places below ground.) The hero's battles with the hired help draw him into conflicts with superior forces, for the opponents are bigger and stronger than he is, and often armed besides. He also faces elemental forces in these battles: captured by the villains, the hero is usually imperiled by fire, water, or nature, left to burn or drown, or tied up and abandoned in a forest or a cave. Like a mythical hero, he must survive these ordeals in order to continue his quest. And just as the mythical hero has a helper to guide him, the hero has an older friend who offers suggestions and occasionally provides timely rescues.[12] Although unlike the mythical hero Stratemeyer's protagonists do not emerge bringing a boon to mankind (unless one considers the arrest of the hired help to be beneficial to society), they do learn about the darker side of life and prove their ability to survive and conquer it.

The Judicial System   The protagonist's conflict with the judicial system also forms part of his initiation into the adult world. Like most of his other problems, the hero's troubles with the law spring from conflicts with his guardian or another adult authority figure, who fills out a complaint to have the boy arrested. Usually this involves two separate clashes, one with the police, the physical arm of the law, and the second with the court, the bureaucratic aspect. Both illustrate the hero's changing status during the story. In almost all of Stratemeyer's writings prior to the mid-1920s the police are more of an inconvenience than a menace, a bumbling, rather incompetent crew. In the success stories they provide material for a few chase scenes, eventually capturing the hero more by luck than skill.

They do, however, reinforce the general division between adults and children, for their response in most situations is to side with the adult rather than the young protagonist. In "Alvin Chase's Search" although the local constable has presumably known Alvin for most of the boy's life, he readily accepts Dr. Bardell's assessment of Alvin's character and is ready to condemn Alvin. However, as the story progresses and the hero gains more knowledge of the world, his relationship with the police gradually changes. By the final chapters of the tales the police are willing to cooperate with him—again, an indication that the protagonist is being accepted in the world of adults.

The hero's conflict with the court, usually a more serious affair, also illustrates his growth. It is, of course, the fear of an unjust trial rather than guilt that motivates the boy's original flight. Alvin Chase believes that Dr. Bardell will "shape his story to suit himself," and that Tom and a servant will corroborate the falsehoods. Although he remarks, "Had I known as much as I do now I would certainly not have taken the course I did," the courtroom scene justifies his original fears rather than the placatory statement ("ACS," 745). Standing alone, Alvin faces the constable, Dr. Bardell, and Bardell's dishonest lawyer, Doddington; all these adults paint him as a "disobedient, good-for-nothing boy" (789). There is no evidence to incriminate Alvin, yet Doddington asks that he be held to face a grand jury; unless the virtually penniless boy can come up with $300 bail, he will remain in jail for a month. Although the judge remains impartial—indeed, almost sympathetic to Alvin—he is still compelled to order that Alvin be held pending trial.

For Alvin, neither force nor wits can be used successfully against the court. Nor do Alvin's character and appearance (the type of elements that often help the protagonist) gain him freedom. In this and other trials, the judge is often favorably impressed by the lad's appearance and demeanor and tries to be helpful, but he is still unable to circumvent the law. Alone, Alvin is lost. Then the young man he befriended arrives and speaks confidently and knowingly to the judge. Although he is a stranger in town, he understands what is required, and "in five minutes," virtually no time at all, Alvin is "free to go" ("ACS," 790). Like Dr. Bardell and the lawyer, Alvin's older friend understands the legal system and can maneuver within it easily even though he is not a lawyer. Time and again, this type of scene appears in later stories: the hero is unable to prove his innocence and, although he is not convicted of a crime, still loses his freedom until an older person posts bail or otherwise aids him. In the first confrontation with the legal system, the hero fails. No matter how good his intentions or how strong his determination, he still lacks the experience and funds the situation requires.

Unlike many of the later stories, "Alvin Chase's Search" has a second courtroom scene, illustrating Alvin's growth to maturity. This time, though his stepfather is again present, spluttering with rage, a wiser

Alvin presents his case, standing "addressing [the judge] very much as a lawyer would have done" ("ACS," 821). The furious stepfather actually tries to attack Alvin in the courtroom, but the judge intervenes, reiterating that force has no place in the courtroom. The judge orders Dr. Bardell to remain silent and encourages Alvin to tell his story, according him the respect given an adult; he then agrees to investigate the matter. Although the stories rarely describe the final courtroom scenes in which the criminals are sentenced, they mention that the hired help (and sometimes the guardian and peer) are sent to prison or otherwise punished and that the hero regains the funds stolen from him. By the end of the tale the legal system that once supported the guardian has reversed itself, thus demonstrating that the protagonist is now able to maneuver within the intricacies of this institution and have his claim validated.

Characteristics for Success   In addition to the rites of passage theme, several other ideas about success surface periodically in the stories. Most presage concepts in the series fiction. The hero's success springs from several characteristics, among them charity, self-culture, and innate abilities. In this, it could be said that Stratemeyer espoused a form of social Darwinism: an endorsement of competition coupled with the belief that the deserving would secure success—the survival of the spiritually and innately fit.

All of Stratemeyer's protagonists are Good Samaritans always ready to help those in danger or in need. Their selfless impulses are generously repaid when they receive crucial assistance from those they have befriended. In *Joe the Surveyor* (1903) young Joe Hurley comes to the aid of a man being attacked by two thugs. The victim, a surveyor, hires Joe as his assistant, thus starting him in his career. Although the hero does not necessarily create the circumstances that give him his "lucky break," it is still his response that determines his fate. This is especially evident in stories where the hero aids not a great man but a less influential one. On several occasions, heroes deal gently with tramps or the poor, even risking their lives to save them; in turn, those characters later provide crucial information, helping the boy to receive his inheritance.

Two other factors in the hero's rise are his willingness to learn coupled with his innate ability or natural aptitude for a particular profession. Almost all of Stratemeyer's heroes endorse self-improvement, a philosophy promulgated by many of the popular success philosophers of the time. Unlike some of Alger's street urchins, Stratemeyer's heroes are already literate, so their course of study is usually concentrated in their intended profession. While all of the protagonists are hard workers and remarkably rapid learners, many also possess a natural talent for their work; that gift is commented on by either the author or other characters. Even in professions requiring technical expertise, the hero displays a natural talent. Joe the surveyor, for example, "took to the profession as a duck takes to water," learning more in a few days than his predecessor had in a month.[13] Although his aptitude makes the hero's meteoric rise more credible, it also suggests that success is more than a matter of hard work and training—put another way, some workers achieve success because they are more able than others.

Stratemeyer's Career Series

While Stratemeyer was publishing his later stories in *Good News*, he was also preparing his early *Argosy* stories for publication in clothbound editions as the Bound to Succeed series (3 volumes, 1894–99) and the Ship and Shore series (3 volumes, 1894–1900). Both series were a group of unrelated books united only by the series title and general theme of success, sharing neither common characters nor occupations. Stratemeyer's next two career series, Bound to Win (12 volumes, 1897) and Working Upward (6 volumes, ca. 1898–1903), also used material from the story papers, again gathering diverse stories under a general series title.

Another of Stratemeyer's pre-Syndicate series can be considered only marginally a career series, even though it features working heroes. Old Glory (discussed in more detail in chapter 4) is a historical fiction series about three brothers who run away from a harsh guardian and become self-sufficient by enlisting at the outset of the Spanish-American War. After that, Stratemeyer did little with traditional career series except continue existing ones, mostly reprinting story-paper materials. He returned to the classic success story for the Rise in Life books (11 volumes, 1900–1912). The initial volumes are completions of stories begun or plotted by the late Horatio Alger, Jr.; the series was published under Alger's name.

Syndicate Career Series

With the formation of the Stratemeyer Syndicate around 1905, Stratemeyer was able to increase his book production and experiment with different types of series. It was an ideal time for new career series, for twentieth-century readers faced exhilarating opportunities owing to an exploding technology. Although the first few Syndicate series still depicted traditional occupations, after 1910 a new breed of working boy emerged, one active in contemporary careers, and thus one more suited to contemporary readers. Two areas in particular appealed to Stratemeyer, moviemaking and aviation, and he offered them packaged in several different forms. He also kept up a practice begun with the Old Glory series: instead of wrapping up the heroes' success in one book, he continued their adventures in succeeding volumes. This practice proved an ideal way to build audiences and reflected the tone of the times: new inventions were continually being improved in the quest for new records and successes.

After about 1910, the Syndicate also began a line of girls' career series. Although girls' stories never contained the same emphasis on technology or quite as many hair-raising adventures as did the boys' series, they were responsible for several trends, including the renaissance of story-paper formulas in slightly modified form.

With Stratemeyer at its head, the Syndicate launched roughly 20 career series from 1906 through 1930. After he died, the Syndicate allowed many to lapse. It briefly and unsuccessfully tried to resurrect them, with more glamorous heroes, almost 30 years later. Its golden age for career series was the 1910s and 1920s, when it produced a host of new series reflecting the changing times and the excitement over new technology.

Early Series Although the Syndicate's first few series maintain the conservative strain, a holdover from the story-paper era, and use traditional careers that could have been lifted straight from Stratemeyer's writings, they abandon the complications involving the hero's lost inheritance and place a stronger emphasis on his business trials and successes. The Boys of Business (4 volumes, 1906–8; retitled the Boys of Pluck, 5 volumes, ca. 1906–11) are a group of boys who pursue careers as storekeepers, printers and newspaper publishers, land agents, and the like. The series uses a novel approach to link titles while retaining the single-story hero: although each story has its own protagonist, the characters from other books reappear as friends and mentors of the struggling hero. Thus, in *Two Boy Publishers; or, From Typecase to Editor's Chair* (1906), when Darry and Bob consider opening a printing business, their friend Bart Stirling, hero of the previous book, is there to encourage them and place orders to help them get started. In turn, Darry and Bob befriend a stranger in town, Frank Newton, who shows up as the central character in the next book. Advertisements for the series also emphasized the books' functional value, noting that *The Young Express Agent* (1906) "gives a good idea of the express business in general," and that "all youths who wish to go into business will want to own [*A Business Boy's Pluck*]."[14]

The Webster series (25 volumes, 1909–15) was a final attempt to utilize the old patterns by publishing unrelated stories under a general series title. The name of the series derived from the pseudonym used on the books, Frank V. Webster. Several titles, such as *The Newsboy Partners; or, Who Was Dick Box?* (1909), use occupations straight out of the story-paper era; others, like *Airship Andy; or, The Luck of a Brave Boy* (1911), suggest the influence of the new century. Even the series advertisements note the blend of old and new, stating that the stories are written in a style like that of Horatio Alger, Jr., but are "thoroughly up-to-date."

The last of the early series, and a transitional one, Ralph of the Railroad (10 volumes, 1906–28), combines a staid, steady job with one involving transportation and technology, the latter being key areas for Stratemeyer's subsequent career series. According to the publisher's ads, the books "revealed the whole workings of a great American railroad system." Ralph's fortuitous appearance at the railroad during a crisis and his bravery while resolving same wins him a job in the roundhouse. A typical Stratemeyer hero, his diligence, courage, and luck result in a promotion in the final pages; the series follows his rise from engine cleaner to train dispatcher. Ralph gradually ages during the series run. Ralph also marks the Syndicate's first use of a sole protagonist as the continuing central character in a career series, and the books' success probably contributed to Stratemeyer's decision to try others with this format.

New Technology The Tom Swift series (40 volumes, 1910–41) marked the shift from the old technology to the new, as well as the continuing use of the recurring hero working his way up to prominence. Tom, the son of the inventor Barton Swift, is an inventor and mechanical genius in his own right. Actively interested in the century's new technology, he continually tinkers with inventions. In early titles, he makes his motorcycle and motorboat faster and more efficient; later, he develops airplanes, television, and weaponry (Dizer 1982, 49). Early advertisements stressed the series' connection with the most recent developments in technology, commenting, "Every youngster is filled with the marvels of invention displayed in motorcars, motor boats, submarine boats and airships." Later advertisements claimed that one goal was "to interest the boy of the present in the hope that he may be a factor in aiding the marvelous development that is coming in the future."

Tom Swift can be only marginally labeled a career series, for it contains several types of books. Some reflect the newer trends in the career story, emphasizing contests and business competition as Tom struggles to prove the superiority of his inventions or to overcome rivals trying to steal his patents. Others are adventure stories in which Tom travels to faraway parts of the globe, and later stories are science fiction—for instance, Tom uses a giant telescope to discover life on Mars (Dizer 1982, 47–59). Tom begins with a number of advantages, such as the use of his father's laboratory and expertise, and he is self-employed. Although the costliness of his experiments occasionally causes financial problems, these are more evident in conversations than in action: he spends money on equipment and lives in a comfortable house (complete with servants) with ready access to his motorcycle, motorboat, and airplane. In this respect, he is similar to the newer breed of career heroes, who, while not wealthy, usually move from poverty to an adequate income in the first book.

After 1910, one of the growing trends in the country was the motion picture phenomenon, and Stratemeyer, like countless others, was fascinated with the silver screen. Most Syndicate series published in the early 1910s include at least one encounter with moving picture crews: two of the Rover Boys manage bit parts in a picture filmed near their home; Dave Dashaway assists a moving picture company before he becomes an aviator; even Tom Swift manufactures a new type of camera. Film crews were almost everywhere in the world of Syndicate series books, and soon Stratemeyer created four series dealing specifically with different aspects of the field. The Moving Picture Boys (15 volumes, 1913–22) travel around the world filming movies, as do the Motion Picture Comrades (5 volumes, 1917); the Motion Picture Chums (7 volumes, 1913–16) manage a succession of movie houses; and the Moving Picture Girls (7 volumes, 1914–16), two sisters, act in photoplays. All of these offer a behind-the-scenes look at the profession, telling readers of the hard work and challenges involved in bringing stories to film.

The same year the Motion Picture Chums and Moving Picture Boys premiered the Syndicate launched a series in another new field, one destined to overshadow even the movies in popularity. Dave Dashaway (5 volumes, 1913–15) follows the adventures of a young boy who runs away from his cruel guardian and finds work with a famous aviator. Dave, whose passion is flying, becomes a licensed pilot himself and competes for aerial records, ending the series by winning a race around the world. Shortly after the series concluded, World War I began, providing the Syndicate with material for another aviation series—the Air Service Boys (6 volumes, 1918–20), two Americans with the Lafayette Escadrille in France.

After World War I, aviation books languished for a time. When Charles Lindbergh gained worldwide attention in 1927 with his nonstop flight to Paris, however, the Syndicate rushed an appropriate response into print. *Over the Ocean to Paris* (1927) heralded the start of the Ted Scott Flying Series (20 volumes, 1927–43). Unlike Dave or later series pilots, Ted is no mere aviator but a national hero. Quickly moving from mechanic to pilot, he learns to fly and makes the title trip all in the first volume of the series. Subsequent volumes continue his stellar career. Everything he does earns national attention and adoration. He visits with the President, breaks aerial record after aerial record, flies supplies to Mississippi for the Red Cross and airmail over the Rocky Mountains, and tries his skill at almost all aspects of aviation. The Syndicate's other aviation series, Slim Tyler (6 volumes, 1930–32) and Randy Starr (Sky Flyers) (4 volumes, 1931–ca. 1933), never achieved the same longevity.

Girls' Series   Like the Moving Picture Girls and Ruth Fielding, the Syndicate's three other career series for girls use more domesticated heroines, usually in far less glamorous occupations. Two of the series, Amy Bell Marlowe's Books for Girls (7 volumes, 1914–16) and the Barton Books for Girls (15 volumes, 1926–31), resemble the early boys' series in that each groups diverse stories without continuing characters under a general series title. Ads suggested that they strove for a blend of old and new: both were billed as reminiscent of Louisa May Alcott, "but thoroughly up-to-date." Not all the books concern employment; the general theme is proving oneself or establishing (rather limited) independence.

Finally, one of the Syndicate's best and most realistic career series for girls is the Blythe Girls (12 volumes, 1925–32). After the deaths of their parents, the three Blythe sisters, Helen, Margy, and Rose, move to New York in search of employment. Helen, the artistic and domestic sister, finds a job coloring prints for an art store and does some painting on the side; Margy, ambitious and self-possessed, becomes a social secretary for an eccentric older woman; pragmatic Rose takes a position as a clerk in the millinery department of a major department store. In the course of the series, they meet a number of other young people, almost all of whom are defined by their occupations: Joe, a furniture mover; Hugh, a young lawyer; Dale, a newspaper reporter; Annabelle, Rose's coworker in the millinery department. The stories concern the day-to-day prob-

lems of survival in the city and in the working world. There are no meteoric rises here. After 12 books, the sisters still hold essentially the same
positions: Helen is being paid more for her artwork, and Rose has just
been promoted to manager of the junior dress department, but none
have become wealthy, famous, or powerful. Rose's goal is to become a
buyer for a store; Helen's, to be able to work full-time as an artist;
Margy is the only one content with her job.

Surprisingly for an organization that had introduced working girls in
series as early as 1913—not to mention an organization headed by a
woman—the Syndicate let its girls' career series fade in the 1930s (along
with most of its boys' series) and never revived them. Even though the
1940s saw other writers begin successful girls' career series, the
Syndicate opted to remain with amateur sleuths like Nancy Drew and
the Dana Girls. When it did finally start experimenting with new series
in the 1950s and 1960s, the only girls' series created was about another
amateur detective.

Later Series Three of the Syndicate's later boys' series, Tom Swift,
Jr. (33 volumes, 1954–71), Tom Swift (III) (12 volumes, 1981–84), and
Christopher Cool/TEEN Agent (6 volumes, 1967–69), are marginally
career series. Far more than years separate them from "Harry's Trial." In
all three the heroes are already employed when the series opens. The two
Toms (the son and grandson of the original Tom Swift) are inventors,
with high-level positions in the vast Swift Enterprises; Chris Cool is a spy
for the teen division of the CIA. (The series premiered during the height
of the television spy craze and owes a great deal to "The Man from
U.N.C.L.E.")

Lavish is almost too mild a term for the boys' life-styles. At the start
of the Tom Swift, Jr. series Tom is developing a space lab, busily building, redesigning, and rebuilding with never a thought for the cost of the
materials. He has his own car and plane (and is soon at work on a rocket
ship), is consulted by members of international scientific organizations,
and jets off across the globe at a moment's notice. His son, also named
Tom Swift, spends much of his series in outer space, traveling in ships
he and his father designed, helping establish scientific bases on
Ganymede and, in the later books, participating in intergalactic travel
and preventing interplanetary war. Chris Cool attends an Ivy League college and drives a Jaguar. In the first book he is sent on a special assignment to Paris and St. Croix and provided with an Alfa-Romeo for his
jaunts across France; after successfully completing his mission, he
receives a week's vacation in Paris at Uncle Sam's expense. Glamour is

the keynote here: the books seem designed to cater to a middle-class audience's dreams of excess.

Only the Wynn and Lonny series (6 volumes, 1975–78) presents a comfortable familiarity to a reader accustomed to story-paper heroes. Having worked part-time to save money to enroll in a racing-driver's course, Wynn and Lonny journey to California only to find they are victims of a mail-order swindle. Nearly broke, they rescue the son of a racing car manufacturer and are given jobs as "gofers" at the manufacturer's workshop, where they work part-time and learn more about the profession. Even though their living habits can hardly be called frugal—they rent furnished rooms, enroll in a racing course, and even rent a car to use for the classes—there are overtones of old Stratemeyer heroes here, for the two are industrious, enterprising, and charitable, even helping another driver to reform. Touchingly, Wynn and Lonny, almost the last of the Syndicate career series, returned to the themes of the early ones.

Syndicate Series: Themes and Traits

The theme that runs through the Syndicate series is the new versus the old, or, more accurately, the triumph of the new, which improves all it touches. A belief in progress, especially as evidenced by technology, permeates the books, as, indeed, it permeated the decades that produced them. If ground frontiers were steadily closing, scientific frontiers were opening up, rearranging and revolutionizing the future in the most glorious ways imaginable. Change itself serves as a theme in some of the stories, especially the early ones, as new ways or ideas struggle to defeat the old. In other books the changing world is almost a fait accompli, and one of the underlying themes, if it could be called that, is to acquaint the reader with the marvels of the new world.

The attitudes undergo a slight shift over time. Books from series started prior to 1910 suggest the redemptive influence of modern ideas and technology on communities or secondary characters. Young boys with fresh ideas prevail over older men, and new businesses revitalize towns and the people therein. Such series portray a more insular world, with the protagonists tied to one community and content to remain there. By the later series, modern technology allows Americans to gain recognition around the world, to challenge and conquer nature, and, of course, to make their fortunes. The books depict the dramas and dangers intrinsic to a particular field, the professional rivalries and financial concerns, and the greater glory for the individual and the nation.

Competition virtually replaces the rites of passage theme. While this change of theme can serve as a vehicle for demonstrating the superiority of the new ways, in the series started after 1910 it also marks a shift in the nature of the hero. He no longer moves toward regaining his inheritance and settling comfortably into a "happily ever after" life but remains in stasis, continually reasserting his superiority with each new challenge. This change in the hero is, perhaps, one of the effects of the new technology, for as it improved men were able to set and demolish records with amazing rapidity. Consequently, the series emphasize the hero's battles with natural obstacles or human opponents.

Early Series and Progressivism The Boys of Business series typifies the earlier pattern, tracing the effects of new ways on the hero's career and on the community. In *A Business Boy; or, Winning Success* (1908), the protagonist, Nelson Cady, dreams of someday "own[ing] and run[ning] a busy, up-to-date store."[15] During a visit to a local shop Nelson discovers the manager is stealing from his employer by passing merchandise to his cronies for resale elsewhere. He alerts the owner and is given temporary management of the shop, which he promptly begins renovating, using "hard work and new ideas" (*BB*, 48). His "new programme" is twofold (46). First, he cleans and inventories the store, thus symbolically sweeping out the old and creating a new order; he even gives the place a facelift by gilding the letters on the sign and varnishing the showcases. Finally, he introduces new marketing strategies in the form of advertising, souvenirs for customers, and a big renovation sale. Nelson's new ways are contagious: he "infuse[s] his clerks with the ambition and energy he himself experienced" (77) and eventually works a complete transformation on one of his employees, who changes "from a dull, listless boy . . . into an ambitious energetic business fellow" (109). Nelson's innovative sales techniques produce impressive results: the town "had rarely been so stirred up," and "by the end of the week . . . [the store] had won back many old customers and had made friends of many new patrons" (94–95).

It does not stop there. Nelson refuses to join another shopkeeper in raising prices when the circus comes to town, and he rejects an offer to buy factory seconds at low prices even when informed that his rival regularly purchases them. His honesty and fresh approach result in increased trade. This goads a rival shopkeeper to criminal activities, which end in an insurance fraud that drives the man from town. Impressed by his son's success, Nelson's father buys him a half interest in the store, and the original owner has a new sign made showing the partnership. Thus, almost everyone benefits from Nelson's new ideas: the now ambitious clerks are paid higher wages because business has improved; several of the townspeople (as well as a stranded circus troupe) receive temporary employment and thus additional income; the customers have a "brisk, neat and attractive" shop to patronize, one that sells good merchandise at reasonable prices (*BB*, 93); the town is rid of a disreputable businessman and several criminals; and Nelson is able to realize his dream.

Whether by accident or design, *A Business Boy* portrays a microcosm of Progressive reforms, even though politics is not mentioned. Three of the wrongdoers who fall before the new order are the insurance man, busy with his illegal schemes; the former store manager, who is stealing from the owner to do favors for his associates; and the rival storekeeper, who tries to create his own version of a trust during the circus. All three have visible parallels in targets of Progressive reform: the insurance companies, whose dealings were brought to light by reformers and modified by legislation; machine politicians and party bosses, who used their office to sell legal protections to cronies, shortchanging the people, their employers; and corporate trusts, which tried to corner the market and raise prices. And just as Progressivism is said to have had an agrarian bias, some of the first beneficiaries of Nelson's new programs are the farmers. In addition to blocking the price-raising scheme (which would have especially hurt the farmers coming to town), Nelson later gives the farmers special discount coupons in exchange for permission to post advertisements on their property. The farmers show their support for the store, which gives them favorable treatment. Like the Progressive politicians, Nelson believes that, given a choice, people will flock to a new store, a new way.

Modern Ways in Other Early Series   The appeal of new technology surfaces in some early series in connection with the conflict between young boys and older men and between new and old ways of doing business. *The Young Firemen of Lakeville*, part of the Webster series, provides one example. The story takes place in Lakeville, "a very nice place, but [one where] the principal citizens lacked a progressive spirit."[16] The town's old-fashioned ways are typified by the volunteer fire department, a bucket brigade ("All they've had in Lakeville since the time it was founded by Christopher Columbus," says one character sarcastically) run by the men of the town (*YFL*, 5). The boys, full of new ideas, want to see the department updated and organize their own volunteer fire department, arranging to purchase a hand-operated fire truck from a nearby village.

Rivalry between the two brigades grows, with the men opposing the boys on two fronts, age and technology. The town seems perpetually ablaze as the boys keep demonstrating the effectiveness of their machinery, continually outperforming the men and their antiquated methods. In gratitude, local businessmen whose buildings the boys have saved purchase more modern equipment, and the townspeople begin to acknowledge the advantages of the newer ways. By the end of the book the boys are in charge of the fire department, and both town and fire department have blossomed: Lakeville is "now quite a city," boasting not one but "two steam fire engines" (*YFL*, 203).

Differences between Earlier and Later Series The Webster series was one of the last to focus on protagonists with strong ties to a community and on the local effects of their business. Series published after 1910 generally rely on changes in setting rather than in protagonists or professions for variety. Characters rarely settle in a town for more than one book and have few friends in the community other than business associates.

With a few exceptions, the new series adhere to their own pattern. The first book uses a premise lifted almost intact from the story papers: either mistreated by a miserly guardian or employed in a menial job, the hero runs away from his surroundings, meets up with someone connected with a new field, and finds employment. By the end of the book he is well established in the profession. Subsequent stories chronicle the hero's work experiences and successes in other locales and often continue the threads of the story line suggested in the first book. The protagonists of the Moving Picture Boys series, two orphans working on failing farms, spot a motion picture company filming a show and are offered jobs as assistants to a cameraman. Their employer teaches them the basics of the business and, by the end of the book, they are firmly established as cameramen and preparing to go west as independent filmmakers. In subsequent volumes they travel around the United States and even to Europe and Africa, making films and winning prizes.

As the Syndicate developed its newer series, especially those about modern careers, a number of the themes and conventions from earlier books either disappeared or were relegated to the background, an indication of changing attitudes about the characters and their occupations. Rather than introducing new ideas into traditional occupations, the more recent series have characters engaged in professions that are themselves brand-new and against which, as history proved, the old ways could not compete. When the Motion Picture Chums establish their first moving picture house, there is no discussion of whether it will be overshadowed by local theater or vaudeville houses. Their existence is not even mentioned; instead, a reference is made to "whole crowds tak[ing] the trolley [to a nearby town] just to see the movies."[17] The underlying assumption is that the old cannot compare with the clearly superior new.

The conflict between older and younger men also tends to fade, partly owing to attitudes about the professions. The new fields attracted young men—aviation, for example, is called "a game for youth only"—and even the established businessmen working in related fields are often described as young.[18] Consequently, the hero's opponents are often only a few years older than he is, and rivalry occurs between men with similar backgrounds.

Finally, the impact of new ways on communities receives only passing comment rather than serving as a theme in the books. Some mention of the effects of new industry occurs in the aviation series, which note the prosperity resulting from the establishment of airfields or aircraft factories. Descriptions of Ted Scott's hometown note that the town was given "a new impetus . . . when the Devally-Hipson Aero Corporation established a mammoth airplane plant there. Hundreds of workmen and officers and executives became residents of the place. Other industries were established and the town began to boom."[19] The books concentrate, however, on Ted's flying rather than the effects on the town; the community's prosperity is an accepted by-product of progress, not the central issue.

Instead, the books acquaint readers with the delights and challenges of the new technology, partly by including informational material, which also adds a touch of realism to the stories. When aviators talk about "voplaning" to safety or "Immelman turns," it gives the impression that the characters and author are knowledgeable about the subject. Advertisements promoted this impression: those for the Air Service Boys series claimed the books were written "by one who knows all about army aviation." Some books also offer brief explanations about the new technology. The aviation series discuss the construction of planes and the basics of aviation, sometimes with surprising detail. In the first Ted Scott book, the visitor Ted is taking on a tour of the aircraft factory learns about future prospects in aviation, the advantages of air-cooled airplane engines, and the best type of silk for parachutes. The assumption is that readers are interested in technical aspects as well as in characters and adventures.

Technology and Nature   Information, however, plays only a small part; it is woven into the adventures forming the heart of the stories. The adventures show readers the challenges and advantages of the new technology. In the aviation series, one of the key conflicts is man against nature. The mere act of flying—"the conquest of the air"—is in itself a heady triumph.[20] Unlike battles with human opponents, such conquests are accompanied by a sense of power and euphoria. Pilots are "transported to [a] new world" when they fly; it is an ennobling experience (*OOP*, 45). Nowhere is this feeling expressed more rhapsodically than in the Ted Scott books. Once aloft, Ted feels "like an eagle released from its cage. . . . He was alone in illimitable space, and his spirit expanded in sympathy."[21] Like the pioneers to whom they are occasionally compared, the pilots are opening new frontiers, and as with tales of the frontiersmen their contact with unspoiled nature enriches them.

Even when the situation is not tranquil, the sense of power and euphoria remain. In aviation stories, encounters with inclement weather are almost a convention: at least once per book, pilots fly through thunderstorms or fog. (The latter was especially dangerous in the earlier books, written when pilots relied on their eyes rather than on instruments while flying.) Books devoted to long-distance flights contain an array of natural hazards. In *Sky Riders of the Atlantic* (1930) Slim and the pilot face a hurricane, a waterspout, and volcano fumes, which have a narcotic effect on the crew; if those experiences were not enough, on the return trip the plane is struck by lightning.

These situations are often treated as if pilot and plane are battling a sentient and almost supernatural foe. When the wing of Ted Scott's plane catches fire above the Pacific, he and his copilot face "the fire demon above! The water demon below! Both of them ruthless! Both reaching for their lives!" (*FSH*, 159). Such descriptions personalize and intensify both the battle and the victory, again underscoring the challenges facing the pilot and the power of technology in defeating such a formidable adversary.

In the motion picture series technology's triumph over nature occurs less frequently, although characters do brave assorted hazards to capture nature's fury on film. Additionally, the film series treat encounters with nature less as life-threatening adventures than as ways to demonstrate the characters' ingenuity and ability to turn any situation to a profit. Characters in the Moving Picture Boys and Moving Picture Girls series do not view storms as representations of the power or magnificence of nature, but as footage to incorporate into fictional dramas. When a character falls through thin ice in *The Moving Picture Girls Snowbound* (1914), the cameraman faithfully records his rescue and the director announces that since a similar scene appears in Dickens, he'll simply rewrite the story and call it "A Modern Pickwick." In one sense, perhaps nature here is even more fully conquered than in the aviation series, since it is regarded primarily as another element to be added to the script.

Technology and Distance   The conquest of distances—again, most dramatically illustrated in the aviation series—is another effect of the new ways. As early as 1913 Dave Dashaway flies around the world, with his crew chuckling over an aeronautics book from 1850, "wonder[ing] what those old fellows . . . would think of the nifty machine here, and a trip around the world in it, easy as a Pullman sleeper."[22] Aviation's ability to telescope distances also serves other purposes. In *Danger Trails of the Sky* (1931) Ted Scott flies explorers to the Himalayas; in *Following the Sun Shadow* (1932) he takes scientists to the Sahara to film a solar eclipse from the air. Long-distance flights also improve relations between distant lands. After a flight to Argentina a pilot tells Slim Tyler, "Every stunt like ours helps to strengthen friendly relations between the two Americas."[23]

In a few cases these international relations have drawbacks: new technology makes the United States more accessible to foreign criminals and more vulnerable to international crimes. Smugglers constitute a particular danger, for they "keep abreast of all modern inventions" (*LEB*, 141). Several of the aviation series have the hero temporarily deputized into the Secret Service to stop smugglers flying illegal cargo such as drugs or duty-free diamonds over the border. Additionally, America's superiority is occasionally threatened by foreigners. The Ted Scott books sound the most jingoistic note. When Ted tries for his altitude record, crowds throng to the field because "the coveted record for altitude had been held for a long time by a foreign aviator" and Americans are eager to see one of their own regain it (*FSH*, 2).

Another aspect of technology narrowing distances, that of using photographic representations to make the unfamiliar familiar, is treated so matter-of-factly that the value of it seems almost nonexistent. Although the Moving Picture Boys travel about the country and the world bringing back an assortment of footage, little is made of the value of films in introducing Americans to far-off or exotic sights. Instead, technology serves to recapture the familiar. When the Moving Picture Boys work for a newsreel company, one of the films that receives the strongest response is of an accident on the elevated. Members of the audience are all familiar with elevated trains (some even witnessed the accident) and are thrilled to watch them on film. As one pleased viewer tells a friend, "I can actually see over again in picture form what I saw only a few hours ago in reality. I wonder how they do it?"[24] Rather than introducing the extraordinary, technology here serves to present the ordinary, the familiar, in a new light.

Technological Hazards   Although the series laud the world of technology, they also indicate that much of it was still in a developmental stage, that it presents challenges for the hero in the form of mechanical hazards and dangers associated with the profession. While deciding to become a pilot, Ted Scott reflects that "scarcely a day passed without the death of one more airman being reported" (*OOP*, 48). Engines fail unexpectedly; gauges stick, giving false readings; wires cross or come loose, bringing vehicles to a standstill. So constant are the mechanical problems that even though most pilots possess a thorough knowledge of their planes, few plan jaunts without taking along their mechanics; in the Randy Starr and Dave Dashaway series the mechanics are major characters.

Accidents and mechanical failures sound a sobering note throughout the series, for although the heroes usually sustain only minor injuries, other characters do not fare as well. Randy Starr is able to lead an air circus when the original leader's plane crashes unexpectedly and the man is hospitalized. Before Ted even begins his flight to Honolulu, he learns that one of the contestants has been killed in an accident. His informant goes on to explain: "Smashed yesterday. . . . Fine fellow, too. British war ace with thirty-one enemy planes to his credit. He was circling round the field in practice about three hundred feet in the air when something went wrong with his plane. . . . Wife was there and saw it, too. Bad business!" (*FSH*, 116).

The man continues, "Well, that's that. Death has scratched him off the list. Just goes to show what a risky business we fellows are in" (*FSH*, 116). That the series books, which almost unfailingly reward good people and punish only the bad, should include incidents of "fine fellows" being killed reflects the state of aviation in its early days and the pilots' daring in remaining in the profession. For all that technology has accomplished, it has not eliminated risk. Those who choose the new profession still rely on luck as well as skill for their survival.

Human Obstacles   Finally, human agents provide another set of obstacles. Many are standard villains, only slightly modified from their story-paper days. Several series start with conflicts between the hero and a crabbed guardian or wealthy businessman who has swindled him or his parents, although these conflicts usually disappear early on. The peer reappears as a spoiled rich boy, sometimes trying to compete in business, other times merely as a local nuisance as senselessly spiteful as in the story papers. Greg and Duck Gale, brutish and dissipated sons of a wealthy hotel owner who swindled Ted's foster parents, often figure in the Ted Scott books and are perpetually jealous of Ted's success. Such characters again serve as a contrast to the hero's fine qualities. Unlike the story-paper peers, however, some of these characters are not permanently defeated but return again and again, a consequence of the series format. Similarly, story-paper thugs are paralleled by professional criminals, sometimes in the employ of rivals, other times acting on their own initiative. Their activities can either be entwined with a career-based plot or serve as the basis for the entire story.

The human antagonists who appear most often are rivals of all types, since competition occurs regularly in the series. Ironically, competition in contests or in business allows the heroes their chance at success—it is something they themselves endorse—but at the same time it is presented as riddled with corruption. Although the heroes are all for fair play, crying (if not literally, at least in spirit) "Let the best man win," their competitors are rarely honest and, of course, are never the best. Instead, they try to succeed through dishonesty, intimidation, or even out-and-out destruction. When the Motion Picture Chums purchase their first theater, their disgruntled rivals try to disrupt the show with rowdiness, noises, and catcalls; in one Ted Scott book a rival aviator plants a bomb on Ted's plane. The picture of competition that emerges—whether as part of the free enterprise system, in races, or in other contests—is one of the hero being pitted against the powerful, the devious, or the rich, who are willing to do almost anything to undermine a promising competitor. It is only the hero's determination and luck that allow him to win.

The growing emphasis on competition signals another change in the series. As a series of technological improvements made possible a continuing string of new records and achievements, contests and formal competitions became standard elements in many of the books. In some cases they provide the foundation and unifying threads for the plot: the protagonist devotes himself to preparing for, then participating in, the contest. In others they serve only as minor subplots, reinforcing awareness of the hero's superiority. In either case competition illustrates the hero's superior skill and also serves the practical purpose of providing funds for further ventures.

Stratemeyer's early story-paper fiction encompassed a variety of careers, but these remained secondary to the hero's passage to manhood.

This transition was marked by his success against different types of human opponents: his guardian, his peers, professional criminals, and representatives of the judicial system. Some elements of a boy's character contributed to his success, most notably his decision to stand up for his rights, his Good Samaritanism, and his willingness to learn. However, luck and innate ability also played a part in his triumph.

The Syndicate series shifted the emphasis from the hero's growth to new ideas and technologies. In those books the world holds all manner of futures and challenges. The "new" offers a more prosperous life for individuals and communities; it offers America more chances to demonstrate its superiority; it offers heroes the opportunity to challenge nature, visit new lands, and display their ability by winning contests. Several of the more exotic elements of the career series, however, had their roots in some of Stratemeyer's writing in other areas, as did the series' inclusion of factual information. For readers whose taste ran to a different type of information and adventure, Stratemeyer and, to a lesser extent, the Syndicate offered three other types of series: travel tales, historical fiction, and outdoor adventures.

4

Travel Stories, Historical Fiction, Outdoor Adventures

Travel tales, historical fiction, and outdoor adventures all enjoyed brief popularity as Stratemeyer or Syndicate series. Although they may seem diverse types of series, they share common subject matter, themes, and publication patterns. Stratemeyer's publications in all three areas first appeared from 1894 to 1896 and were concluded by 1911. The Syndicate offered only a few series in each genre, usually clustered during particular time periods. The historical fiction and travel tales take place in settings other than the contemporary United States. All three series feature boys "roughing it" in the outdoors, whether they are colonists or frontiersmen facing the wilderness, a group of chums on a hunting and camping trip, or world travelers threatened by exotic animals. In one form or another, all are concerned with survival outside of the confines of urban or village life, and with boys facing deadly enemies, animal or human.

Written at a time when America was in transition—ironically, a time when its frontiers were closing just as the chance for colonial empire was opening—the books reflect the paradoxical national attitudes at the turn of the century. Narrators bemoan the growing scarcity of game, then laud the growth of cities and the spread of civilization. A belief in American superiority and the need to promulgate American culture runs through the stories, as does a tacit endorsement of the strenuous life. Theodore Roosevelt's influence is evident both in the emphasis on physical and moral strength and in the characters' activities.

Stratemeyer's work in all three genres was primarily a product of the times. When he reintroduced the three types of series for the Syndicate's fiction, he altered much of the form and content. The outdoor stories became western or ranching adventures, and historical fiction practically disappeared except for a brief flurry of topical material during the First World War. Although the Syndicate series still endorsed physical ability and survival in the outdoors, many of the other messages were absent. By then Americans had been through a world war and were considerably less interested in acquiring an overseas empire and more resigned to their shrinking wilderness. Escapist fiction prevailed. The times and the literature had changed, and Stratemeyer adapted his stories accordingly.

Travel Fiction

Stratemeyer's Travel Adventures   As a genre, travel adventures were born in part of the shipwreck and the enticing but imaginary shores found in books like Johann Wyss's *Swiss Family Robinson* (1812–13) and Robert Louis Stevenson's *Treasure Island* (1883), as well as from dime novels and pulp tales; they were not constrained by the need to instruct or be accurate. Whether the flora or fauna that filled the exotic islands were figments of the authors' imaginations or actually found in geographies was irrelevant; what mattered was the excitement and danger, the exotic touch of foreign shores.

Stratemeyer's earliest travel adventures appeared in the story papers *Bright Days* and *Golden Hours*. These tended to feature ships and shipwrecks, small tropical islands or other isolated shores, and sometimes treasure. Stratemeyer also favored man-eating sharks and islands inhabited by hostile savages and predatory animals. Unlike Robinson Crusoe or the Swiss Family Robinson, Stratemeyer's stranded heroes rarely built island dwellings or other contrivances; they were too busy escaping from cannibals or other carnivores.

The early stories usually describe the adventures of children journeying to meet an adult relative. In "Island of Caves; or, The Remarkable Adventures of the Bixby Twins," serialized in *Bright Days* in 1896, Millie and Andy, the orphaned twins, undergo their "remarkable adventures" after they are shipwrecked en route to their uncle's home in Australia. Later stories often incorporate one of Stratemeyer's favorite themes, the search for the missing parent. "Lost in the Land of Ice; or, Bob Baxter at the South Pole," serialized in *Golden Hours* in 1900, involves an Arctic exploration prompted partly by the quest for knowledge and partly by Bob's hope that his father, last seen in the area, is still alive and waiting to be rescued.

One of Stratemeyer's last travel adventures for the story papers subsequently became the initial volume for a series. Dave Fearless and his father, divers who explore the world's oceans salvaging treasure, first appeared in "The Rival Ocean Divers; or, A Boy's Daring Search for Sunken Treasure" in *Golden Hours* in 1901. More fantastic than realistic, it typifies the exaggerated adventures found in the "blood and thunder" publications. The story makes no attempt to convey factual information but rather emphasizes the bizarre. Dave and his companions contend with the "Sea Devil of the Ocean's Bottom," a 20-foot fish whose eyes are "like two electric light globes" and whose head "closely resembl[es] a rubber balloon," and with a race of sea demons with a civilization on the ocean floor.[1]

The story was retitled and reprinted in book form several times, with two more volumes added to form a series. In 1926 Stratemeyer gave further evidence of his dexterity at reusing material by reissuing them to start a monthly paperback Dave Fearless series (17 volumes, 1926–27). Dave and his friend Bob Villett spend less time diving than they do dodging criminals and wild beasts. Even the titles downplay actual geographic locations, preferring the colorful phrase or generic name: *Dave Fearless on Volcano Island; or, The Magic Cave of Blue Fire* (1926); *Dave Fearless Captured by Apes; or, In Gorilla Land* (1926). At times the factual information, such as it is, is even inaccurate, and in general the tone is closer to that of the pulps than that of hardcover boys' series.

Many of the later Dave Fearless volumes were ghostwritten by Leslie McFarlane, who, pounding out as many as six chapters in one day, considered them hack work. Although Stratemeyer sent detailed outlines of the entire book, McFarlane worked through them chapter by chapter, without reading them in advance, commenting, "A chapter at a time was about all one could take" (40). No research went into the books, only peril after peril, some created by McFarlane's active imagination, most in Stratemeyer's outlines. In *Dave Fearless under the Ocean* (1926) Dave and Bob encounter, in quick succession, an angry octopus, "lethal seaweed," and man-eating sharks, as well as a storm at sea, a boat wreck, and other crises (36–37). Other titles offer similar hazards and close escapes. For McFarlane, the books represented easy money but little challenge. When the series ended, his only regret was the potential loss of a regular paycheck; he avoided that fate when he was assigned to write the Hardy Boys, a task he did with far more enthusiasm and success.

Syndicate Travel Adventure Series   The Syndicate's second travel series was Don Sturdy (15 volumes, 1925–35), which was better written, marginally more informative, and less fantastic than its predecessor. As the series ads explained, Don Sturdy and his two uncles, Amos Bruce, "a big game hunter," and Frank Sturdy, "a noted scientist," travel "far and wide—into the jungles of South America, across the Sahara, deep into the African jungle, up where the Alaskan volcanoes spout, down among the head hunters of Borneo." Like Dave Fearless, Don travels in company with his best friend and an adult relative and bypasses Europe and various centers of civilization for more isolated spots, but the similarities end there. While the Dave Fearless books race along with one- and two-sentence paragraphs and staccato sentences, the Don Sturdys, like many of the hardcover series from this period, contain smoother prose and include minor incidents that add some depth rather than merely advancing the plot. The factual information remains minimal— at best several pages per book—but it is accurate and indicates that some research was done by the author.

Most striking perhaps is the open-mindedness shown toward the inhabitants and the customs of the countries visited, though it may reflect only the ghostwriter's attitudes (not all Syndicate books exhibit such tolerance). Although Don's love for his own country is never in doubt, he remains able to appreciate the places he visits without continually comparing them unfavorably with America.

After Don Sturdy, the Syndicate tried its most unusual travel series, Bomba the Jungle Boy (20 volumes, 1926–38), a junior version of Tarzan. Raised in a South American jungle by an amnesiac naturalist, Bomba one day encounters two white hunters whose questions cause him to wonder about his family and past. Realizing he is not like the natives, Bomba sets off to learn the fate of his parents and spends ten volumes traveling through the jungle tracing clues to their whereabouts; each discovery leads to another clue to be pursued in the next volume. Like Tarzan, he has animal friends who assist him; he also has enemies among some of the tribesmen in the area, but only limited encounters with white men, most of whom he admires greatly. An underlying racism fills the books. Bomba instinctively recognizes that he is innately superior to the natives; indeed, this realization helps to spur him on in his quest. After he finds his parents and they move to New York, his father journeys to Africa and disappears, providing material for another search. At the close of the series Bomba is aboard ship, again heading for civilization while thinking nostalgically about the jungle. Not intended as educational and with none of the tidbits of factual information found in a series like Don Sturdy, the books were clearly designed to capitalize on the popularity of Edgar Rice Burroughs's Tarzan series and succeeded in doing so.

Although other Syndicate books involve travel—indeed, few series protagonists stay at home for more than one or two volumes—in keeping with their preference for America, most series have their protagonists tour the continental United States, marveling at everything from New York's hustle and bustle to southern cotton fields to western cowboys. The only other heroes who occasionally go abroad are aviators like Ted Scott; not until much later would sleuths like Nancy Drew and the Hardy Boys begin to expand their fields. Whether Stratemeyer would have introduced more travel series as technological advances made distant areas more accessible is a matter for debate, but his death and the subsequent curtailing of new series effectively ended the Syndicate's forays into the genre.

Historical Fiction

Stratemeyer began writing historical fiction in 1896, shortly before the outbreak of the Spanish-American War, and continued in the genre until 1909, returning briefly with some Syndicate titles during World War I. During the initial 13-year period Stratemeyer's historical fiction did not so much develop as explode. Under his own name and the pseudonym Captain Ralph Bonehill, he authored 32 books in 8 series and 5 non-series titles. Almost all deal with American history. The earliest period covered is the French and Indian Wars; the most recent is the then-current Russo-Japanese War.

In general, Stratemeyer's choice of historical period seems to have been determined by notable battles. A number of the books show signs of extensive research, interspersing long blocks of factual information with the story. The books are unabashedly patriotic, in keeping with the times. From the earliest stories, which show American bravery in the Spanish-American War, through the later tales, set in pioneer days, the books praise white Anglo-Saxon values and the march of progress. America's moral and economic development is tied to the hero's victory.

Theodore Roosevelt and the Spanish-American War

One influence on Stratemeyer's historical fiction, as well as on his travel and outdoor stories, may have been Theodore Roosevelt. Although Roosevelt appears in only a few of Stratemeyer's works, elements from his life and philosophy surface in many of the series from this period. For Roosevelt, time spent in the military—ideally, during war—was perhaps the ultimate making of a man, and this love of soldiering is echoed in Stratemeyer's works. While Stratemeyer never seemed to endorse war with quite the same enthusiasm, for several years during and after the Spanish-American War many of his characters served in the military, fighting in historic battles from America's past and present.

A firm believer in "physical and moral courage," Roosevelt saw the world in black-and-white terms.[2] For him, heroism was not a thing of the past but an ongoing affair. Indeed, Roosevelt's description of the ideal American boy could have been a blueprint for a Stratemeyer protagonist—"He must work hard and play hard. He must be clean-minded and clean-lived, and able to hold his own against all comers" (Roosevelt 1910, 128). Stratemeyer's protagonists did just this. They tackled their activities with enthusiasm—and scorn for those who complained—and with a belief in the rightness of what they were doing and a determination to triumph, whatever the odds. As hunters, soldiers, or explorers, in the pages of Stratemeyer's books a whole generation of mini-Roosevelts tramped off to adventure and success.

At the turn of the century America's attention was focused on the Spanish-American War. For newspapermen, writers, and adventurers, it must have seemed "a splendid little war": quickly won, and relatively bloodless for the victors. The United States emerged as the proud possessor of a stronger navy and the start of a colonial empire in the form of islands scattered across the Pacific. Some of these, like the Philippines and Hawaii, were fraught with possibilities for entrepreneurs and writers. The war provided topical, exciting material, and writers were not slow to pick up the challenge. Surveying best-selling novels of the period, Frank Luther Mott observed that historical romances "prospered by falling in with the great American expansionist ideology of the times . . . sublimat[ing] the fighting and politics in easy emotional satisfactions. They suited the mood of the times."[3]

Stratemeyer's Historical Fiction

"Estella": Historical Romance Stratemeyer's first historical fiction capitalized on this trend. Written for an adult audience, "Estella, the Little Cuban Rebel" blends romance with contemporary events and is somewhat atypical of his later works. It was serialized in Street & Smith's popular family story paper, the *New York Weekly*, in 1896, under the pseudonym Edna Winfield. En route to Cuba, the newspaperman Howard Sherwood falls in love with Estella, a Cuban girl educated in the United States who is supportive of the Cuban rebels. Estella's father, a retired general with the Spanish army, sides with the Spaniards, as does her fiancé, a lieutenant in the Spanish army. (She has been promised to him since childhood, much against her wishes.) The story follows their obstacle-strewn romance as Estella endeavors to

change her father's attitudes and Howard struggles to stay alive amid
the warring factions.

Even when writing for adults, Stratemeyer could not entirely shake
the pattern of the boys' career adventure. Rather than dealing with the
heroine's triumph over trying circumstances, as many story-paper
romances do, "Estella" focuses on Howard's trials, complete with the traditional financial problems. In addition to his other difficulties, Howard
is suspected of spying and has also been swindled out of his family fortune by some Spanish sympathizers, among them Estella's fiancé.
Though she is the title character, Estella is clearly subordinate to
Howard, just as the love interest remains secondary to the adventures.

Old Glory Series   Stratemeyer's next title, *Under Dewey at Manila;
or, The War Fortunes of a Castaway* (1898), was published after the start
of the Spanish-American War, when Admiral Dewey's victory in the
Philippines had elevated him to a national hero. As with "Estella,"
the book still draws on formulas established with the career stories. The
hero, Larry Russell, is an orphan mistreated by a cruel and miserly
guardian. Larry runs away and signs on as a sailor; halfway through the
book, he is shipwrecked and picked up by Dewey's fleet en route to
the Philippines. He arrives just in time for the historic battle with the
Spanish fleet.

At least one source suggests that *Under Dewey at Manila* was originally intended as an adventure story and was rewritten to incorporate
recent events, an assumption supported by the book's text and narrative
structure (McFarlane, 49–50). While the first half of the book contains
more adventures than information, the tone changes once Larry joins the
navy: factual material dominates. Larry receives practically an entire
course in naval procedures, as well as a review of the background of the
conflict and updates on current developments. The story again stops
once the ship reaches Manila and spends almost a chapter on a biography of Dewey. When the actual battle begins, Larry is practically invisi-
ble. An occasional paragraph shows him with his companions, but the
majority of the descriptions read as if they were compiled from newspaper accounts. Afterwards, the narrative rejoins the characters as they celebrate the victory.

Despite this uneven approach, the book proved quite popular, and
Stratemeyer added others to the Old Glory series (6 volumes,
1898–1901). A second book issued the same year, *A Young Volunteer in
Cuba* (1898), follows the experiences of Larry's brother Ben and Ben's
friend Gilbert Pennington, a southerner serving with the Rough Riders.

Again, the book is heavily laden with information, this time on commanders in the army and on Cuban leaders. It also includes descriptions of Cuban geography and culture, especially the food, which, in the Ugly American fashion prevalent in the series books, the characters do not like. The third volume, *Fighting in Cuban Waters* (1899), describes the naval adventures of yet another brother.

At the end of *Fighting in Cuban Waters* all three boys return to the United States and are reconciled with their guardian, suggesting that Stratemeyer may have intended to end the series there. However, his publisher, Lee & Shepard, had a tradition of selling juvenile series in six-volume sets, and three more books soon appeared. These introduce a new challenge for the heroes: the cashier of the local bank, in which the boys' inheritance is deposited, absconds with the funds. He flees to the Philippines, where Ben's unit is conveniently stationed. With less fighting and historical information than in the earlier volumes, the books combine a search for the cashier and his Spanish confederates with the war story. Stratemeyer used this tactic, blending business problems with battles, in a number of books; apparently military victory was not always a sufficient reward for service.

The style and structural problems of the Old Glory series are typical of Stratemeyer's historical fiction. One of the selling points of the books was their educational value. The prefaces repeatedly assure the reader (or, more likely, the adult buyer) that the information is accurate and gleaned from many sources. The information in *A Young Volunteer in Cuba* is "drawn from the very latest and best reports, including those submitted by Major Generals Shafter and Wheeler, Colonel Wood of the Rough Riders . . . supplemented by the countless personal narratives of men who went to the front, saw, suffered, fought, and conquered."[4] This can work to the detriment of the book. The narrative often teeters between history and fiction, with one or the other controlling large blocks of text. When factual information is presented, the story stops for paragraphs or pages of textbook-based facts, and when action dominates, no matter what the setting, the protagonists neither think nor act differently than their counterparts in other types of tales.

Stratemeyer's Other Historical Fiction   Stratemeyer returned to the Spanish-American War as the backdrop for the initial volumes of the Flag of Freedom series (6 volumes, 1899–1902). Like other books published soon after the war, the series capitalizes on locales that had recently been in the news. The first two titles relate the adventures of noncombatants, sons of businessmen caught up in the war while tending to their fathers' business interests in Cuba and the Philippines. By the third title, *Off for Hawaii* (1899), the war is over and the boys are off to search for treasure in the islands. The series loses its original focus after the initial three volumes, and the final books even use unrelated characters and settings.

The Soldiers of Fortune series (4 volumes, 1900–1906), a sequel to the Old Glory series, resumes with Gilbert Pennington's adventures during the Boxer Rebellion. In later volumes, characters from the Old Glory series join him to fight in the Russo-Japanese War. During 1900, the last year he would start books dealing with foreign wars, Stratemeyer also published his most unusual work, embodying the height of jingoism: a fictional war tale serialized in *Golden Hours*, then reprinted in book form in 1902.

"*Holland,* the Destroyer; or, America against the World" is set in the near future (1907), when America has grown and prospered until it "now embraces [a]ll of North America, from the Isthmus of Panama to Hudson Bay, and . . . all of the West Indies, Hawaii, the Philippines, and half a dozen other islands of the sea, as well as a corner of China and another corner of Japan."[5] The other nations of the world have become so jealous of America and so determined to quash its growth that, in self-defense, America declares war against the world. The hero, Oscar Pelham, designs a highly sophisticated submarine, the *Holland*, and takes to the seas in his creation, destroying enemy flotillas from Cuba to Alaska, rescuing the President's daughter (who bears a strong resemblance to Alice Roosevelt), and eventually bringing worldwide acknowledgment of American superiority.

Having thus subjugated the world, Stratemeyer retreated to tamer subjects from America's past for the next few series. The Mexican War (3 volumes, 1900–1902) and Colonial (6 volumes, 1901–6) series use a similar premise, that of settlers in danger of losing their homes and lives during a conflict over the land. Both series begin as pioneering adventures but become war stories when the protagonists enlist and pursue the enemy across the country.

During this time Stratemeyer also wrote his only nonfiction series, the American Boys' Biographical series (2 volumes, 1901–4), covering the lives of William McKinley and Theodore Roosevelt. Surprisingly, these are not fictionalized narratives picturing incidents of dubious authenticity from the subjects' boyhoods, but factual accounts of events from their adult lives.

Soon after, Stratemeyer began wrapping up his foray into historical fiction. He launched no new series and ended the existing ones in 1906. With the Syndicate firmly established, Stratemeyer may have felt that he no longer needed to write or plot books that required time spent researching background information. During World War I he created only one Syndicate historical fiction series, the Air Service Boys, although he did send characters from existing series off to join the military or, in the case of girls, the Red Cross.[6] The World War I stories, however, concentrate on adventures instead of information. That war was also the last to receive Syndicate recognition. Even though other writers created stories in response to World War II, the Syndicate ignored the fighting except for occasional plots involving foreign spies on American soil, uncharacteristically keeping its characters isolated from events in the outside world.

Outdoor Adventures

In some ways, placing the hunting and camping adventures into a separate section is misleading, for Stratemeyer's historical fiction and travel adventures also incorporate outdoor stories into the narratives; indeed, it is partly because of the amount of hunting and camping material in those tales that the genre is included here. In all three types of stories, protagonists view the outings with enthusiasm, hunt basically the same types of animals, exhibit the same competence, and face many of the same types of challenges. One difference occurs in the early outdoor adventures, where the hunt also becomes the stated goal of the book rather than part of a more complex plot. A second difference has to do with the books' different time periods. In historical fiction set in the colonial or Jacksonian period, the protagonists hunt as part of a regular routine to provide meat for their families. The outdoor stories set in the late-nineteenth and early twentieth centuries treat hunting and camping as a sport, an activity to occupy their leisure time. The protagonist's social situation changes accordingly: he is now part of a middle- to upper-middle-class family with sufficient funds to purchase the necessary camping supplies and ample time for such recreation.

The pure hunting and camping story faded quickly, and a second type of outdoor series emerged, westerns. These are not "cowboy and Indian" adventures but stories set in the modern-day West or Southwest, with sons of ranchers as protagonists. Characters ride, hunt, camp, and maintain their land and herds, essentially a contemporary version of Theodore Roosevelt's descriptions of ranch life. The hunt reverts to the more pragmatic role it held in the historical fiction: outings are motivated by necessity, such as losing stock to a wild animal. Hunting becomes less important within the overall tale, having been replaced by roundups, rustlers, and other aspects of range life.

Stratemeyer's Outdoor Stories: Establishing a Formula
Stratemeyer's first outdoor story, "The Tour of the Zero Club; or, Perils by Ice and Snow," ran in *Good News* from December 1894 through March 1895 and was later reprinted in book form. After an accident temporarily closes their school (a favorite Stratemeyer tactic), a group of boys elect to spend two weeks hunting and camping in the nearby woods. Before leaving, they go sledding and iceboating and manage to offend the local bully and his cronies. They also acquire another member for the expedition, a black lad, who serves as a friend, cook, and general factotum. (Early Stratemeyer heroes usually found someone to handle the menial chores on these outings.) After almost perishing during a snowstorm, the boys locate an ideal spot for camping and construct a rough, but cozy, lean-to. Once settled, they down an astounding amount of game—one afternoon's shooting yields ten rabbits—and are menaced by almost every beast indigenous to the northern woods, including wolves, a bear, and a wildcat, all of which they kill. Later, an adult who has had poor luck with his own hunting meets them and is astonished by their skill. Disaster strikes when the town bully and his friends show up and steal most of their supplies. Fortunately, the boys are able to trail the thieves, regain their possessions, and resume their outing. After several weeks, the quintet returns home triumphantly, bearing tangible evidence of its hunting prowess in the form of pelts, antlers, and meat.

"Tour of the Zero Club" includes most of the conventions found in Stratemeyer's stories. The often-episodic plots begin with the group planning a hunting and camping trip, with some references to the boys' home lives and comfortable social situation. The protagonists are four or five close friends, supposedly of slightly different personalites and temperaments, although usually indistinguishable from each other. They blend the family-based hero with the self-reliant one. The trip involves several dangers and trials: a near-fatal encounter with inclement weather; another with wild animals that either tree or otherwise trap the protagonists; the destruction and restoration of camp through human agents or forces of nature; and a confrontation with human antagonists. The rewards, however, compensate for these troubles: adults marvel at the boys' skill; game is varied and plentiful despite the boys' occasional complaints; and there is always enough left to bring home trophies and carcasses for the family.

Two of Stratemeyer's later hunting series occasionally varied elements from the formula. The second volume in the Young Hunters series (2 volumes, ca. 1900), *Young Hunters in Porto Rico; or, The Search for a Lost Treasure*, introduces a treasure hunt in Puerto Rico as a subplot. Like the Flag of Freedom series, published about the same time, it emphasizes adventures in Uncle Sam's new possessions. The last volume in the Boy Hunters series (4 volumes, 1906–10), *Out with Gun and Camera* (1910), signals a change in emphasis: ads noted that it "takes up the new fad of photographing wild animals as well as shooting them."

Syndicate Outdoor Series   The trend toward photography continued in the Outdoor Chums (8 volumes, 1911–16), a Syndicate series published under another military-sounding pseudonym, Captain Quincy Allen. Less violent and more modern than its predecessors, it was ghost-written by St. George Rathborne, the author of numerous camping and wilderness stories under his own name. Advertisements explained that the four boys "love outdoor life, and are greatly interested in hunting, fishing, and picture taking. . . . The stories give full directions for camping out, how to fish, how to hunt wild animals and prepare the skins for stuffing, how to manage a canoe, how to swim, etc." However, the books actually devote little space to practical information and rely on essentially the same plot formula as the earlier stories—a mixture of encounters with wildlife and human bullies.

Thirteen years elapsed before the Syndicate published another hunting series, although occasional outdoor stories appeared as individual volumes in other series in the interval. The Syndicate's final offering, the Bob Chase Big Game series (4 volumes, 1929–30), was fashioned after career success stories. Bob Chase works as a hunter-guide for a trio of big-game hunters and is gradually adopted into their ranks. Unlike the protagonists in other outdoor stories, Bob views the expeditions as financial ventures: he loves to hunt, but he cannot afford to unless the specimens will bring in enough money to pay for the outing. The trips become progressively more expensive: after the first two books, set in the United States, the group travels to Asia and Africa to hunt tigers and lions. The series appeared some years after Theodore Roosevelt's writings about his African expeditions but before Frank Buck helped popularize the concept of "bringing 'em back alive" for zoos instead of museums. Another Syndicate series from the same period, Don Sturdy (discussed earlier in this chapter), also reflects the trend toward hunting big game internationally.

Westerns   Long before the Bob Chase series premiered, Stratemeyer had introduced the first of his western series, the Saddle Boys (5 volumes, 1913–15). Written under the military-sounding pseudonym Captain James Carson, the Saddle Boys features two chums, Frank Haywood and Bob Archer. They live on neighboring cattle ranches in Arizona and face cattle rustlers, Mexican brigands, and other dangers. The timing again suggests Stratemeyer's awareness of popular trends, for the Saddle Boys appeared the year after Zane Grey's *Riders of the Purple Sage* (1912) achieved best-seller status (Mott 1947, 237). A second series, the X Bar X Boys (21 volumes, 1926–42), followed 13 years later. Perhaps coincidentally, the film version of *Riders of the Purple Sage* had been released the previous year. Like the Saddle boys, the X Bar X boys—Teddy and Roy Manley—live on a cattle ranch in or near Colorado. Series ads proclaimed that "the lads know how to ride, how to shoot, and how to take care of themselves under any and all circumstances." Cowboys, punchers, rustlers, and miners people the boys' world; almost everyone except the brothers speaks in a slangy western dialect.

Even when it was not the focus of a series, the West remained a popular place for series characters to visit. As early as 1908, a title in the Jack Ranger series heralded *Jack Ranger's Western Trip* (aptly subtitled *From Boarding School to Ranch and Range*). For the next few years, a flood of series characters traveled westward: Dave Porter (1910), the Moving Picture Boys (1913), Ruth Fielding (1913), the Moving Picture Girls (1914), Dorothy Dale (1915), the Rushton Boys (1916), the Fairview Boys (1917), the Motor Boys (1917), Bobby Blake (1918), Nan Sherwood (1919), the Bobbsey Twins (1920, with a return visit in 1935), the Six Little Bunkers (1921), the Rover Boys (1922), Sunny Boy (1924), Betty Gordon (1925), Frank Allen (1926), the Outdoor Girls (1928), and even little Honey Bunch (1928). The types of adventures vary: although both boys and girls go riding and find some type of puzzle to solve or hidden treasure to unearth, the boys also try their hand at roping, hunting, and camping out while girls and younger children content themselves with picnicking, exploring the ranch, watching rodeos, and marveling at the cowboys' abilities.

The Syndicate created its last two western series in the 1960s. Both combine westerns and mysteries, with the emphasis on detection. Written by the veteran western writer S. Omar Barker, the Bret King mystery series (9 volumes, 1960–64) contains smoothly written, fast-paced adventures. Eighteen-year-old Bret is a thoroughly modern cowboy living on Rimrock Ranch in New Mexico with his parents and younger brother and sister. In the first volume, *The Mystery of Ghost Canyon* (1960), Bret captures "a large gang of beef rustlers and bank robbers" and earns enough reward money to purchase an airplane, which he learns to fly in the second volume.[7] In keeping with the Syndicate's greater awareness of people of color, Bret's companions include a Navajo, Ace Tallchief, and Benny Ortega, a "Spanish-American" ranchhand (*SHP*, 14).

The second series, Linda Craig (6 volumes, 1962–64; 17 additional volumes, 1982–90), offered girls a chance to enjoy the western format, too. The orphans Linda Craig and her brother Bob live with their grandparents on Rancho del Sol in California. Linda's first love is Chica d'Oro, a highly trained palomino she acquires in the first book; her second is solving mysteries, aided by her brother and their two best friends.

With the advent of the Linda Craig series, the transformation of the outdoor adventure was complete. While the great outdoors retained its potential for excitement, the type of adventures and adventurers had altered. The genre had once been the province of gun-toting male protagonists tramping or skating through the wintery woods in the northeastern United States. Now girls and boys on horseback cantered over sandy southwestern deserts, more concerned with mysteries than with shooting at game. Demographic shifts, advances in technology, and new trends in recreational activities had reshaped the Stratemeyer Syndicate's offerings in the genre.

Themes and Traits

The three genres share a pride in America, although it takes slightly different forms in each type of book. The travel adventures and those historical fiction titles set in foreign lands compare Americans favorably with other countries and people. The historical fiction taking place in the past eulogizes America's heritage and the progress of civilization. The outdoor stories illustrate the richness of America's forests and wildlife— America the bountiful. The books contain contradictory attitudes toward the environment, occasionally sounding a somber note in their concern about vanishing wildlife, but overall they are designed to stir pride and patriotism in readers.

Stratemeyer's books appeared at a time when progress and patriotism—tinged by ethnocentrism and imperialism—suited the country's mood. During the latter half of the nineteenth century economic and social stresses facilitated changing attitudes in the United States. An influx of immigrants from southern and eastern Europe, often considered unassimilable, helped fuel nationalistic sentiments. The rise of social Darwinism, too, promoted a worldview that perceived Anglo-Saxons, especially Americans, as superior to other races and nationalities. Allied with these prejudices was the belief that Americans should not only set an example for other countries but also actively work to "uplift" and Christianize them. Concurrently, the closing of the American frontier, the Spanish-American War, and the need for new trade markets all encouraged Americans to look beyond their own borders. In 1898, the same year Stratemeyer started his historical fiction series, former Secretary of State Richard Olney summarized the United States' perception of its global role when he wrote that "the mission of this country . . . is not merely to pose but to act . . . to forego no fitting opportunity to further the progress of civilization."[8]

While young readers may not have been aware of Olney's statement, they received much the same message through Stratemeyer's works. The books proceed from the assumption that "civilization" or "progress" is— or should be—the goal of every country. Although the characters rarely define what is meant by civilization, their assorted comments suggest it is something technological (or industrial), economic, cultural, and moral—or, put more simply, a commerce and culture modeled after the United States. Competition and success, standard elements in Stratemeyer's fiction, also figure prominently in the stories but are expanded to include an implied or overt competition between America and other nations. Just as Stratemeyer's heroes are challenged by villainous characters, so, too, is America challenged by other nations. The protagonists function as both individual and symbol; their victories become not only their own but those of their race and their country.

Civilization and Conflict A necessary prerequisite for civilizing land is controlling it, and this provides the plot action in Stratemeyer's historical fiction. In series concerned with foreign wars, the characters enlist in the military to help the United States establish political control. In those set in pioneer times, the goal is physical control or actual possession of the land. Some characters join the army to defend their homes; others establish control by exploring the wilderness or facing the dangers of homesteading in newly opened territories. Whichever method they employ soon entangles them in economic concerns—trying to maintain farms or businesses in contested lands. Additionally, the characters face the hardships occasioned by life in the wild or a lack of technology. Triumph over these obstacles leads to progress—or the development of civilization—and the protagonists' actions toward this end receive praise. While such conflicts and favorable results become most apparent in the frontier tales, they also surface in the contemporary historical fiction and travel stories, in which the characters essentially repeat the same struggles their forefathers faced in settling America.

A common plot device is to incorporate a character's private quarrel into a larger issue, creating two related conflicts. The protagonist's struggle against his antagonists—be it a group of Indians, a brutish enemy officer, or a seemingly endless jungle—thus serves as a microcosm of the larger battles, and his eventual triumph ensures a personal and financial success and aids the advancement of the United States. Indeed, one book in the Mexican War series ends by noting that the next volume will tell what the protagonists "did to defeat both their personal enemies and also the enemies of their country."[9]

Depictions of Pioneer America   While the plots provide one method of presenting the struggle and eventual triumph of Americans and the American way of life, the books also use other techniques to convey the message. The United States, of course, is the standard by which other countries are measured and found wanting. As one character puts it, "There is no better place on earth to live than in our own dear native land."[10] The pioneer series serve a dual purpose: they not only chronicle the advance of American civilization but demonstrate that America was able to effect a massive tranformation in a relatively short time. Their underlying theme is not just the protagonists' victories over whichever opponent they happen to be facing but the triumph of an entire nation over the better part of a continent. The tales set in foreign lands are contemporaneous with the account and do not anticipate the snarled foreign relations these early military adventures would engender; by contrast the pioneer tales are colored by an awareness of the end result: America wins.

This knowledge shapes the perceptions of the settlers' trials and rugged living conditions, which are now long past. Rather than suggesting a primitive society, the hardships the characters endure serve to show just how far America has come. Scattered throughout the books are comments about life in the past. "In those days" is a favorite phrase, usually heralding a pronouncement of the difficulties of pioneer life: in those days "[letters] were not common," "visitors were far from frequent," "both telegraph and railroads were unknown . . . and everything moved slowly"[11]; "powder and ball were scarce," and even the weather was worse, for "the snow fell heavier in Kentucky than it does today."[12] Lest anyone miss the point, occasionally the narrator puts it more plainly: "How little do boys of today realize the perils and hardships of the years gone by!" (*WBF*, 287).

Although the stories are focused on the characters and their problems, Stratemeyer never forgets, nor allows his readers to forget, that these settings should be contrasted with modern-day America. A note of satisfaction sounds throughout the books as the omniscient narrator leaps forward in time to chart American progress. A typical passage appears after the battle at Fort Duquesne, when Stratemeyer announces, "To-day this ground is covered by the city of Pittsburg [*sic*], with its gigantic iron and steel works. What a mighty change from the lonely forest lands of less than a hundred and fifty years ago!"[13] One of Stratemeyer's own textual interjections best summarizes the books' message: "Reader, how quickly our great country has grown to be what it is!" (*WBF*, 81–82).

Civilization and Progress in Other Lands and Times   Having thus transformed their own country, Americans are eager to effect the same changes elsewhere. There is somewhat of a contradiction here, however, because the circumstances are not the same. The protagonists are not settling their own country, nor is the resolution a foregone conclusion. Instead, the boys are becoming involved in the current politics and cultures of other nations, yet they remain unresponsive to ways of life different from their own. Although the characters are working or fighting to improve civilization abroad, their inherent belief that America is superior means they never really expect that the inhabitants of a foreign land can achieve equal status.

One of the boys' first difficulties comes from their inability to understand the philosophy of living off the land without altering it and of producing just enough to sustain oneself instead of trying to make a profit. Even in the pioneer tales, characters remain perplexed by the Indians' reluctance to establish agricultural communities. Indeed, in several books the Indians are made to seem land hungry, while the poor settlers make do with small plots. One boy tells an Indian chief, "You ought to have the land just as well as the white man. But the trouble is, you won't cultivate it as we do. . . . A man who plants land can live on a few acres, but one who lives by hunting must have miles and miles of plains and forests for his roamings."[14]

The level of a country's industry and technology affects the characters' and the narrator's attitude toward the inhabitants. The Japanese, who receive the most favorable treatment in the books, have "a commerce that amount[s] to many millions of dollars annually," as well as an impressive army and navy.[15] When the texts carry generalizations about the Japanese, they take the form of praise for their endurance. Similarly, though the Russians are the antagonists in the Soldiers of Fortune series, the books contain few slurs against them. The boys understand the Russians' desire to build a trans-Siberian railway to aid commerce; their only objection is that it will "enlarge Russian territory and power . . . largely at ultimate expense to Japan" (*UMF*, 17). In contrast, the Chinese, who receive about the worst treatment of any nation or race, distrust modern technology and are said to be "so out of date that they are actually musty."[16]

The boys view the inhabitants' poverty almost as a character defect, which they perceive as an unwillingness to work. Noting the lush vegetation in Cuba, one boy observes, "[The Cubans] could raise [plenty of produce] if they tried. But the average Cuban . . . is rather lazy . . . and consequently, he doesn't grow any more than he actually needs" (*YVC*, 191–92). Traveling through Nicaragua, another character makes an almost identical statement about the Indians and blacks in that area.

These countries also provoke a paternalistic attitude from the boys. Their expectation is that it will take outsiders to change the country's standard of living, although they also expect that those outsiders should reap a significant portion of the profits. The beneficial effects of such intervention are already evident in Peru, where "[a] few years ago [the silver mines] were worked in a primitive manner, but now American and English capitalists are coming in with the very latest machinery, and the mines are being worked as never before."[17]

Some of the inhabitants' lack of initiative is attributed to the climate, which affects character. This attitude, common to many of Stratemeyer's predecessors and contemporaries, is repeatedly offered as an explanation for other countries' limited development. When a group of young hunters travel to Puerto Rico, they conclude that the "atmosphere would make the most active man in the world lazy sooner or later," while in Cuba and the Philippines the heat "take[s] all the starch out of a fellow" and makes the natives "lazy."[18]

Even when they are not inducing sloth, foreign climates have an adverse effect on productivity. When the soldiers are not fatigued by heat, they are mired in mud by torrential downpours or, worse yet, felled by tropical diseases. Such sickness reflected the very real dangers the American army faced in the Spanish-American War; at one point army doctors feared the United States could lose half its men during the summer if they were not evacuated. Such reports, as well as the battles with yellow fever during the attempts to build a Central American canal, undoubtedly influenced the books' depiction of foreign climates.

The deleterious effects of foreign climates contrast sharply with the invigorating air in the United States, another subtle reminder that even in matters beyond human control the United States is a favored nation. The pioneer tales introduce their protagonists by noting that, despite their youth, "a life in the open" makes them "appear somewhat older than [their] years," and they are able to work "almost as well as a man" (*WWW*, 3). In the Mexican War series, Ralph Granbury "had been a thin and delicate lad" when he moved to Texas, but three years there "had done wonders" for his strength and health (*FLT*, 16). The implication is clear: life in the wilds of America strengthens a person; life in the tropics weakens him.

American and Other Cultures   The books' preference for America and the American way of life extends far beyond the climate, however. Since the characters are stationed in foreign lands, occasional encounters with their cultures are unavoidable, but what little the characters experience of other life-styles usually leaves them dissatisfied or disapproving.

On the simplest level, foreign countries lack the cleanliness and cuisine to which Americans are accustomed. A standard incident is the hero's discovery of the former, to his dismay, when he tries sleeping in native quarters and finds them crawling with vermin. Whether the setting is a wigwam in the eighteenth-century United States or a hut in twentieth-century Cuba, Peru, Puerto Rico, or the Philippines, the scene is virtually the same: "Hardly had he dropped into a doze than he felt a nip on one limb, then a nip on another, and then what seemed like nips all over him. . . . Striking a light, he saw that not only his improvised bed, but the whole flooring of the house was alive with flees [*sic*], bugs, roaches, and other crawling things" (*YVC*, 193). The contrast between American and foreign standards is further heightened by the hero's realization that the natives seem impervious to these insects.

As for food, in all countries falling under Spanish influence the boys' main problem is with garlic, "the one vegetable that is never missing from the pot" (*SBD*, 110); garlic produces meals "fit for a dog" (*WSF*, 202). Even when they try dishes without garlic, the boys are either underwhelmed by foreign cuisine or, at best, occasionally surprised that it tastes all right. Lest Stratemeyer be faulted for creating a group of finicky eaters, one need only compare these reactions to a description of a colonial boy's dinner of freshly caught fish from an American stream: "Kneeling before [the fire, Fred] broiled one fish after another to his satisfaction. The smell was an appetizing one, and he could hardly wait until the last was cooked."[19]

With this as with other presentations of different cultures, Stratemeyer shared the ethnocentrism of his contemporaries and later series writers. One study of the series' attitudes toward foreigners remarked on the "continual comparison of American habits and attitudes with those of foreigners," as well as the presentation of foreign food as "unfit to eat" and foreign domiciles as "messy and dirty."[20]

The characters exhibit similar attitudes toward local customs. They find little to commend and expect that the American influence will soon eradicate some of the more distasteful activities. On learning that cockfighting is "the national sport" in the Philippines, one protagonist remarks, "It shows [the people] need education . . . that is all I've got to say."[21]

Local religions also wither beneath the characters' scrutiny. The books present non-Christian religions as curiosities or "tom-foolery," the products of ignorance.[22] In Hawaii and Cuba, the protagonists encounter or hear about voodooism and tribal religions, such as fire worshipers, and watch the latter ceremony with horrified fascination. The Chinese, repeatedly referred to as "heathens," are seen as victims of their misguided beliefs.

Soldiers and settlers alike, however, respect their own religion, observing the Sabbath and attending services whenever possible. *A Young Volunteer in Cuba* contains a lengthy passage in which the hero encourages a friend to attend the Sunday service, and a full page describing the service, complete with excerpts from the hymns (including, appropriately, "Onward Christian Soldiers") (*YVC*, 98–99). Although the characters' religion never plays a major role in the books, it is presented as a basic element in their lives.

Prejudice   Just as the books present the view that American beliefs and civilization are superior to those of foreign lands, so, too, do they suggest that Anglo-Saxon people—especially Americans—are innately better than anyone else in the world. In this, Stratemeyer's treatment of different racial and ethnic groups resembles that of his contemporaries, for nineteenth-century boys' adventure stories and twentieth-century series both promoted white, Anglo-Saxon males at the expense of all others. Several studies have examined the series' portrayals of Indians and foreigners, commenting on the "race consciousness, xenophobia, and imperialism," and a summary of their conclusions helps place Stratemeyer's works in perspective (MacDonald, 535).

Donald Colberg surveyed nineteenth-century boys' adventure stories, the predecessors for Stratemeyer's work, and found that the books included only a few ethnic groups. Almost all are presented negatively. Indians appear most frequently, generally in two guises: one or more friendly Indians help the protagonists, but the majority of Indians are depicted as "vengeful, ungrateful, cruel, and hideous."[23] Mexicans and Spaniards also figure in several plots, the former as "deceitful, cruel, and sinister-looking," the latter as sadistic and murderous (Colberg, 276, 298). Both nations, of course, had been involved in wars with the United States, a fact that contributed to the bitterness of the portrayal.

In the twentieth century, as the interests of the United States continued to expand beyond its borders, series books incorporated a more global cast of characters while retaining many of the same prejudices. MacDonald also examines the different forms of prejudice in the books. Like Colberg, MacDonald finds that the books frequently perpetuate negative images of Mexicans, "link[ing them] with filth, thievery, laziness, and general disorder," and that they usually extend this stereotype to include South Americans as well (540). In the Far East, the Chinese draw the strongest criticisms; however, most of the remarks MacDonald quotes focus on their "hideous" appearance, which suggests that characters distrust them as a matter of course rather than because of specific behavioral patterns. Prior to World War II the Japanese received mixed treatment in the series: although their "skin color and diminutive stature have been derisive themes," other traits are praised, and one book even calls them the "Yankees of the East" (542–44). Only the British receive fairly consistent positive treatment; indeed, MacDonald specifically cites Stratemeyer's works here, noting that he "was an Anglophile from the beginning of his career" (542).

Like the authors of the books examined in Colberg's study, Stratemeyer paints a harsh picture of the Indians, using the traits mentioned, although he, too, generally includes several friendly Indians as secondary characters in each book. His works contain unflattering characterizations of Mexicans but are even less tolerant of the Spanish. The overwhelming image, undoubtedly influenced by journalists' attempts to arouse sympathy for Cubans during the Spanish-American War, is of Spain as a greedy, cruel overlord, extracting wealth from Cuba and giving little in return.

Next to the Indians, the Chinese receive the most consistently negative portrayal, one that offers no friendly characters to offset some of the slurs. Although much of this attitude springs from the Boxer Rebellion, even before that Stratemeyer's books carried derisive references to the Chinese. His comments, too, suggest other bases for the characters' reaction to the Chinese: the "backwardness" and superstitiousness of the country were anathema to progressive Americans, and the Chinese religion further fueled the prejudice. The most common epithet directed toward Chinese in Stratemeyer's books is "heathens." Stratemeyer also clearly favors the Japanese, even more than do the authors in MacDonald's study. Except for infrequent references to size, Stratemeyer omits remarks about their appearance so that a reader unfamiliar with the race would have a difficult time picturing Japanese as different from Anglo-Saxons. Stratemeyer's depiction of Japanese traits such as cleanliness, industry, and endurance contributes to the positive image.

Studies have also noted the paternalism implicit in the treatment by Stratemeyer and his contemporaries of other races and peoples, and their assumption, bolstered by continual references to appearance, that "individual nationalities have immediately recognizable characteristics."[24] None too surprisingly, these authors treated foreigners—especially the United States' opponents—worst during wars (MacDonald, 538). These nationalistic traits remain evident in Stratemeyer and Syndicate series. Even with such studies, it is difficult to convey how thoroughly such attitudes permeate the texts. It is not just the occasional generalization or touch of paternalism but the entire fabric of the text that transmits these prejudices. A closer look at some of the methods shows the pervasive messages young readers encountered.

Sheer repetition of pejorative terms is one device. In the opening pages of *For the Liberty of Texas* Indians are referred to as "sneaking Comanches," "dirty Comanches," "bloodthirsty Comanches," "savage and lawless Comanches," and "treacherous Indians" (*FLT*, 12–16). Even the preface to *With Boone on the Frontier* speaks of "the jealous red men" and the many "outrages committed by the Indians" (*WBF*, iv). Such a constant stream of criticisms would wear at even an unbiased reader's perceptions. Additionally, many of these remarks are uttered by the protagonist or the omniscient narrator, giving them additional impact.

A more subtle form of prejudice is semantic. When the text introduces American-born white males, they are described once. Subsequent references use the character's name, "our hero," "the lad," or some such positive or neutral phrase. Characters from different ethnic or racial backgrounds, whether friendly or unfriendly, are initially identified by name and nationality, as if the latter were their outstanding characteristic. From then on the text alternates between using the character's name and his race (for example, "the German lad," "the Irishman"). If the character's physical characteristics differ from those of Caucasians, these, too, serve as substitutes for a proper name; even the protagonists use phrases such as "redskins" or "pigtails" (Chinese) in conversation. Such tactics semantically separate foreign characters from Americans and establish the hero as the norm.

This differentiation also extends to peripheral characters. When the hero meets a group of Americans, the characters are named even if they appear only briefly in the book. When he has similar encounters with foreign characters, however, they remain anonymous and are referred to by race or nationality, even when they are portrayed somewhat sympathetically. This presents Americans as individuals, dignified by names; foreigners become an amorphous group, lumped together by nationality.

The amount of text devoted to historical figures underscores this bias. The books spend one or more pages detailing the background and achievements of Americans such as Commodore George Dewey or Commodore Winfield Schley. Foreign leaders associated with America's allies receive a paragraph or two. Enemy leaders rarely merit even that much recognition; they are reduced to little more than empty names, temporary obstacles to American leaders.

The portrayal of "good" foreign characters also reinforces the sense of American superiority. Generally, foreign-born characters play secondary or supporting roles, not central ones. Even when they are not specifically servants, foreign characters—including men older than the hero—willingly perform menial chores for him or follow his instructions, but they never expect him to respond in similar fashion. The pioneer stories show good Indians not only siding with the English against the French and other Indians but also running errands and providing other useful services.

Good foreign characters are never as capable or intelligent as native-born white Americans. They may start the book on the same footing, but blood soon wins out. In *A Young Volunteer in Cuba* Ben Russell enlists in the volunteer army along with Carl Stummer, a German, and Dan Casey, an Irishman. None have military experience. By the end of their first set of drills Ben has "done better than any of the others," while poor Carl and Dan have earned some stern looks from the sergeant

(*YVC*, 73). At the series' end Ben has been promoted to major and Carl and Dan are only corporals, although they are now sharpshooters and have consistently shown courage and accompanied Ben on numerous sallies.

Finally, the heroes' treatment of people from other races also reinforces the philosophy that they are less important than white Americans—indeed, that they are sometimes less than human. Actions that would be unthinkable if performed toward a white person are treated matter-of-factly when done to those of other races, at times giving the impression their lives are worth little. In *The Campaign of the Jungle* (1900), when the hero, Larry Russell, and a friend are about to be captured by Philippine soldiers, Larry seizes a native woman and uses her as a shield while he runs for cover. *With Washington in the West* has settlers firing at the backs of retreating Indians because "they need the lesson" (*WWW*, 197).

Before concluding the discussion of prejudice in Stratemeyer's works, it is only fair to note that despite many of the negative images Stratemeyer does make some effort to present, if not a balanced view, at least a tempered one. Most books contain one or more noble or courageous characters from other nationalities or races. During the Spanish-American War Stratemeyer introduced courteous, honorable Spanish officers who capture the hero but do not mistreat him. *Under MacArthur in Luzon* (1901) has a brave and honest Filipino woman who stands up to the rest of her village to aid the injured Walter Russell because his brother helped her earlier.

Additionally, most of the books also use some Americans as antagonists, so not all Americans are painted as good. The stories set in the Philippines even mention and deplore some Americans' mistreatment of the natives and acknowledge that the truth behind some actions—such as the burning of Angat, which the Filipinos attributed to the Americans and the Americans attributed to the Filipinos—is not known.[25] While such inclusions cannot offset the negative depiction of foreigners, they at least begin to suggest that other nations and races, like America, contain good and bad people who should be judged individually.

Contradictory Attitudes about the Environment   One final aspect of the books deserves mention—those areas where statements or the characters' actions contradict other statements or actions in the text. These perhaps indicate cracks in a philosophy, or paradigm stress—places where past beliefs collide with the changing times. Given the present-day concern with endangered species and vanishing wildlife, some of the most striking contradictions occur in the historical fiction and outdoor series when characters' comments about the increasing scarcity of wildlife contrast sharply with their passion for developing the land and shooting almost every animal in sight.

Characters begin noticing the paucity of game as early as *With Washington in the West*, set in the 1750s. Early in the book, when Dave and his uncle kill a cougar ("painter"), Dave's uncle asks, "This is the first painter you've seen, isn't it?" Then he adds, "They are getting thinned out around here" (*WWW*, 78). Other titles in the Colonial series sound the same refrain. In *Marching on Niagara* Stratemeyer himself points out the change, even comparing it to the contemporary situation: "The buffaloes were now fast disappearing from this territory, as are to-day the deer, wolves, and other animals which were likewise numerous" (*MN*, 133).

The books mention two reasons for the loss: the cultivation of the land and the increasing population with its desire to hunt. However, the characters' awareness of these factors never seems to affect their actions. Their delight in "progress"—in settling farms and developing indus-tries—has been discussed earlier. Indeed, the contradictory concepts of "cultural primitivism," as embodied in the frontier, and the "myth of the garden," or the promotion of agrarianism, had figured prominently as themes in American literature and politics long before Stratemeyer's books appeared.[26]

Although the characters recognize hunting as part of the problem, they lay much of the blame for decreasing game stocks on the Indians and a few greedy white hunters rather than on themselves. After the protagonist remarks on the absence of game in *With Washington in the West*, a backwoodsman tells him, "In years to come game will be as scarce around here as it now is around the lower Potomac. . . . The majority of the redskins believe in bringing down everything in sight, jest as some foolish white men do. If the whites git out here in force, and hunt as they've been a-hunting, they'll kill off everything byme-by" (*WWW*, 175).

Despite these observations, Stratemeyer's books continue to glorify the hunt. The attitude of hunting for the sheer joy of shooting is typified by the characters in *Pioneer Boys of the Great Northwest* (1904), set in 1803–4. In one three-day trip early in the story two boys and their fathers bring down numerous birds and squirrels, six deer, and one lynx. As the foursome travels with Lewis and Clark into unspoiled territory, they encounter ideal conditions to inflame their hunting fever. At one point one of the boys even remarks, "This is a very Paradise for game." His father's response? "A well organized game company could make a fortune out here" (*PBGN*, 127).

In the outdoor stories, written in the 1890s and 1900s and set during that time period, the characters make similar observations about the shortage of game when they are forced to travel farther and farther for their outings. *Four Boy Hunters* (1906) contains this passage elaborating the boys' feelings about hunting and the attendant problems:

> "This day is opening finely," declared Whopper. "We [four boys] are bound to get about a hundred birds and animals, I'll wager."
>
> "That's right, pile it on," answered Shep with a grin. "I thought you had been keeping [your exaggerations] down lately."
>
> "Oh, a hundred is nothing," said Whopper, airily. "Maybe I'll get that many myself. I once heard of a man who shot two hundred wild turkeys in a day."
>
> "I don't call that sport," put in Grant. "I call that butchery."
>
> "So do I," answered Snap. "Even as it is, I sometimes think we are shooting too much."
>
> "Well, if we don't bring the game down, somebody else will," said Whopper.
>
> "Some day they'll have to pass some more laws, protecting game," was Shep's comment. "If they don't there won't be anything to shoot inside of the next fifteen or twenty years."
>
> ". . . Well, I am going to shoot what I can . . . ," said Whopper.[27]

Once again, the characters attribute part of the problem to overzealous hunters—while a possible solution, legislation, is left to an ambiguous "them"—and the protagonists' response to the situation is to go on with the hunt.

The boys have stated that game is scarce, but the number of animals they find suggests otherwise, just as their actions belie Snap's concern over the problem. A tally of their kills reveals that in the course of the trip the boys down 44 birds (4 quail, 2 ducks, 9 wild turkeys, 21 partridges, 8 unspecified), 34 fish (1 trout, 3 catfish, 7 pike, 1 muskellunge, 1 sucker, 1 sunfish, 4 perch, 16 unspecified), and 79 mammals (44 rabbits, 2 foxes, 17 squirrels, 5 deer, 2 beavers, 4 wolves, 1 wildcat, 2 bear, 2 mink, 1 muskrat). The story ends with Whopper announcing his goals for the next hunt: "sixteen deer, twenty bears, two hundred wild turkeys and about a thousand [rabbits]" (*FBH*, 235).

Stratemeyer's own hunting series never resolve this problem, although later Syndicate series deal with it by increasingly using cameras instead of guns, by moving the characters' trips abroad, and by having them hunt for animals for museums.

Stratemeyer's historical fiction, travel adventures, and even some of the outdoor stories offered readers a chance to sample experiences far different from their own. The books portrayed boys shouldering man-sized responsibilities and confronting and overcoming dangerous obstacles while championing patriotism and progress. In the process, they devalued other cultures and races, comparing them unfavorably with the United States. But if the boys who read these stories sometimes longed for glamorized glimpses of their own world, Stratemeyer was prepared to accommodate them as well. Stratemeyer's school and sports stories, presenting challenges closer to home, offered readers a chance to savor vicariously the hero's triumphs on the schoolgrounds and on the playing field.

5

School Stories

By the turn of the century Stratemeyer had already successfully combined action and adventure with the career story and historical fiction and was ready to tinker with another popular formula, the school story. Beginning with the Rover Boys, Stratemeyer took the school story one step further, incorporating formulas from other genres like travel stories, mysteries, sports, and even romance. One volume might relate a traditional school tale, full of pranks and sporting competitions, while in the next characters toured the South or the West or hunted for hidden treasure. No longer were working boys the focus of the books. Instead, heroes shed their adult responsibilities and financial worries. They went off to expensive schools and colleges and chartered yachts or bought cars for fancy vacations. The series offered stories imbued with the cozy familiarity of continuing characters—and more affluent, boyish characters, at that—but spiced with adventures from different genres.

Stratemeyer's school stories went through several changes. Those for the story papers resemble dime novel tales: they were hastily written and are packed with exaggerated adventures. Early series, like the Rover Boys, still show vestiges of the nineteenth century in style and theme but also incorporate current trends, varied locales, and a lively pace for the adventures. The characters are fairly affluent and attend boarding schools. The boys still face some adult adversaries and threats to their lives, but they also participate in many adolescent activities—attending classes, playing sports, joining clubs, even calling on girls.

In these early works the characters progress through high school and college. By the end of the series they are adults with wives and careers. The Stratemeyer Syndicate altered this formula after about 1912. Later school and sports stories gradually adopt a narrower focus and time frame. Characters no longer age. They attend public schools rather than private ones, and they usually do not make the costly cross-country jaunts their predecessors take for granted. Later series became more specialized, with the athletic hero flourishing. Although these books also contain mysteries and some of the other escapades found in early series, sports victories often serve as the unifying element.

Like Stratemeyer's other stories, the school and sports stories deal with idealized situations, and their most common motif is the continuing success of the hero. Stratemeyer modeled most of his protagonists on the same pattern, giving them similar traits and attitudes. While the heroes are, ostensibly, schoolboys, their victories actually occur in a number of spheres; they triumph not only in school and in the outside world but over adults as well. Different locales and genres offer even more scope for the heroes to demonstrate their abilities. The stories are perhaps the ultimate in wish fulfillment, masquerading as quasi reality.

Stratemeyer's School Stories

First Story-Paper Fiction: Establishing a Formula   Stratemeyer's earliest school tale, "The Schooldays of Fred Harley; or, Rivals for All Honors," was serialized in *Good News* in 1894, under the pseudonym Arthur M. Winfield, and later published in book form. It mirrors such established stories as Thomas Hughes's *Tom Brown's School Days* (1857) and indicates the direction many of Stratemeyer's stories would take. Sent off to Maplewood School, Young Fred Harley meets two boys en route: Leroy, an affable lad who is already a student there, and Carl Schoenberg, a chubby German boy who provides comic relief. Leroy warns Fred about the resident bully, Hugh Dawson, and his toadies, and Fred announces in true heroic fashion that he will not be intimidated by anyone. He soon proves this by defying, then outwitting Dawson when the latter tries to haze him. Despite troubles with Dawson and with a mean-spirited farmer, Fred enjoys life at school and demonstrates considerable athletic ability. He and Leroy successfully outrun the "hounds" in a game of hare and hounds. Fred also plays a key role in Maplewood's football victory over a rival institution, in his team's intramural hockey victory, and in the school's baseball victory over another academy.

Throughout the story Fred and Dawson continue to quarrel, until Dawson and his friends frame Fred for an act of vandalism. Fred knows the identity of the culprits but is unable to prove their guilt or his own innocence. While Fred is awaiting the headmaster's judgment, Dawson and his cohorts have a boating accident. Risking his life, Fred rescues the boys, who then confess to their crimes, reform, and become his friends. At the end of the school year Fred finishes second in his class scholastically and also receives the school's highest honor, the True Hero award.

"The Schooldays of Fred Harley" established the pattern used for most of Stratemeyer's subsequent stories. The hero is accompanied by several faithful friends throughout the series. They include the likable lad, who is usually already acquainted with the school; the fat or foreign boy, usually German, who is never as clever or capable as the rest of the group and who good-naturedly endures teasing and readily accepts inferior status; and the boy with an academic or literary bent (absent from this tale), who is sometimes used as another figure of fun. It also introduced the standard figure of conflict: a bully, already enrolled in the school, who is unpopular with many of the better lads but supported by a few toadies. The protagonist quickly quarrels with this boy, refusing to acknowledge his leadership. His action arouses such an unreasoning hatred that for the rest of the book, and sometimes for several books, the bully embarks on extreme and often implausible schemes for revenge. Eventually the protagonist's noble nature effects a reform.

Sports and other extracurricular activities hold an important place in the stories; the hero is wondrously adept at almost all games and thus able to drive in the winning run at baseball, kick the winning goal at football, and make the winning dash in track or the winning spurt in boating or skating. In addition to competitive sports, heroes often engage in other athletic activities, such as gymnastics and iceboating. The latter provides a sure guarantee of excitement since the boat almost invariably either crashes through a hole in the ice or runs ashore. Rarely does an iceboat survive more than one book—or, sometimes, more than one ride.

The heroes also plan late-night feasts and play pranks on other characters, generally the bullies, any sanctimonious or overly strict teachers or townspeople, the hired help, or the comical schoolboys—but not the headmaster, the affable close friends, or any siblings. Most scenes occur outside the classroom and are built around outdoor activities or after-hours pranks and parties in the dormitory. Although the protagonists are rarely seen in the classroom or engaged in study, they usually finish at or near the top of their class.

Later Story-Paper Fiction   Several of Stratemeyer's other works for story papers used elements that would resurface in series fiction. Three of his stories ran in *Bright Days* in 1896. "The Schoolboy Cadets; or, Fun and Mystery at Washington Hall" introduced the prototype for Tom Rover in the form of a mischievous but popular boy from a wealthy family. This also appears to be Stratemeyer's first tale set at a military academy, and the first school story to include a touch of romance, two elements found in the Rover Boys and subsequent series.

The two other stories, "Tom Fairwood's Schooldays; or, The Boys of Riverdale" and "The Schoolboy's Mutiny; or, Lively Times at Riverdale," are actually one tale that ends in midstory in one issue, then resumes under the new title in the next. The stories show a boarding school out of control. The schoolboys are mistreated, poorly fed, and frequently punished, while the schoolmaster, his daughter, and his son-in-law (also on the staff) enjoy elaborate meals and absolute authority. Such misman-agement, which escalates until the headmaster's son-in-law actually shoots one of the boys, presages the type of episode that occurs with Josiah Crabtree in the Rover Boys and Putnam Hall series.

After these few narratives, almost three years went by before Stratemeyer did anything more with the genre other than preparing his serialized tales for publication in cloth covers. Then, in 1899, he pub-lished the first volume in what was to be the longest and most successful series actually written by Stratemeyer—the Rover Boys.

The Rover Boys and Series Fiction   Much has been written about the Rover Boys (30 volumes, 1899–1926), both the series and its relevance to Stratemeyer's career. Originally intended as a trilogy, the series ran ten times that length and became one of the best-selling series of its era, spawning imitations and parodies. Articles about Stratemeyer dubbed him "the father of the Rover Boys" as if that alone were suffi-cient claim to fame. A nostalgic reader called the Rovers "the imperish-able friends of our boyhood . . . they seemed to satisfy the appetite of young America as no other boys' series has since."[1]

Many surveys of the Syndicate place the Rovers as the foundation of Stratemeyer's empire, the pattern on which later series were modeled ("For It Was . . . ," 86–87).[2] One analysis notes that the books "demon-strate Stratemeyer's unique status as a transitional writer who, on the one hand, worked squarely within the kind of simple and moralistic adventure story he inherited from Alger and, on the other, experiment-ed with new patterns of suspense."[3] While the books still retain some of the overt didacticism of the nineteenth century, they also contain "'up-to-date' action and characters who enjoyed the freedoms and privileges of a new era" (Billman, 5, 41).

The series relates the adventures of Tom, Dick, and Sam Rover from adolescence to adulthood. Like most Stratemeyer heroes, the Rover brothers begin the series with the same qualities they will have when it ends: honesty, intelligence, strength, fortitude, courage, charisma. As the blueprint for many of Stratemeyer's and the Syndicate's later series, the Rover Boys provides the most striking example of the variety of adven-tures and challenges the heroes face, as well as of their continual tri-umphs. The pattern of the Rover boys' lives is an unqualified success story, filled with enough adventure and rewards to satisfy any reader's most extravagant daydreams.

When the series begins, in *The Rover Boys at School* (1899), the Rover boys are about to be sent off to a military academy by their exasperated aunt and uncle, who are unaccustomed to the antics of three "wide-awake, funloving" boys.[4] En route to Putnam Hall the trio meet several of their friends and learn that they, too, have just enrolled there. The boys also overhear a bully, Dan Baxter, annoying three young ladies (Dora Stanhope and her cousins, Nellie and Grace Laning). The Rovers intervene, and the girls, who had shunned the bully, allow the boys to introduce themselves. The boys discover that the girls live near Putnam Hall, a convenient situation for all. Dick is quite taken with Dora; Sam and Tom find Nellie and Grace rather pleasant. Upon the boys' arrival at Putnam Hall, Tom clashes with Josiah Crabtree, the overly stern and crabby first assistant, but the headmaster supports Tom, admiring his wit and spirit.

At Putnam Hall the Rovers make friends, demonstrate their proficiency in sports, engage in numerous practical jokes, and foil Josiah Crabtree's attempt to marry Dora's mother, the widow Stanhope. When school lets out, their uncle charters a yacht for them, and they journey down the Hudson River and into Long Island Sound in *The Rover Boys on the Ocean* (1899). No sooner have they returned to school than Dan Baxter and Josiah Crabtree join forces to kidnap Dora Stanhope, and the boys set off in pursuit, rescuing her during an ocean battle. In the third book, *The Rover Boys in the Jungle* (1899), the boys and their uncle search for their father in Africa. Along the way they are captured by a fortune hunter and the inimitable Dan Baxter, and Dick is almost killed by Josiah Crabtree. (Series villains have a talent for turning up in the most obscure corners of the world, providing the heroes are there.) Eventually the trio find their father, who had discovered a rich gold mine, and return to the United States.

The series having proved successful, Stratemeyer added *The Rover Boys Out West* (1900), in which Dick, Tom, and Sam interrupt their schooling in midsemester because their father's interest in another lucrative mine is in jeopardy. Their father and uncle have been injured and are unable to travel, so the boys convince their adult relatives that they are capable of managing the investigation themselves and proceed to Colorado to reestablish the claim.

The brothers' adventures and incredible luck continue in *The Rover Boys on the Great Lakes* (1901), in which they not only take a trip through the Great Lakes but also stumble across a cave holding a treasure. Part of the treasure, a money casket, provides the challenge for *The Rover Boys in the Mountains* (1902). Before leaving on a hunting and camping trip in the Adirondacks, the trio find a map hidden in a secret compartment in the casket, showing a treasure located in the area they plan to visit. Even though Dan Baxter steals the map, the Rovers reach the treasure first, rescuing one of Baxter's injured cronies along the way. The next volume, *The Rover Boys on Land and Sea* (1903), opens in San Francisco with the brothers and Dora, Nellie, and Grace planning an outing on a friend's yacht. After a storm sends the boat out to sea, they are picked up by a ship that, with typical Rover luck, is soon shipwrecked, leaving the sixsome and a sympathetic captain and mate to reenact *Swiss Family Robinson* on a small island and later to fight off a scavenging, drunken crew.

After that, the schoolboy plots during the annual encampment of Putnam Hall, covered in *The Rover Boys in Camp* (1904), seem almost tame, but the melodrama returns in *The Rover Boys on the River* (1905). The Rover boys, their school chums, and their girlfriends take a cruise down the Ohio River on a houseboat with Mrs. Laning as chaperone. The trip proceeds nicely until Dan Baxter and Lew Flapp, another of the Rovers' enemies, steal the houseboat with Dora and Nellie aboard, precipitating a frantic—and eventually successful—chase. Undaunted, the Rovers et al. plan to continue their trip in *The Rover Boys on the Plains* (1906), until the boat is grounded for repairs, leaving the boys to make the journey on horseback. Along the way they clash with a group of counterfeiters and help capture them. The houseboat is again stolen and recovered in *The Rover Boys in Southern Waters* (1907), set in Florida. More surprisingly, in this volume Dan Baxter reforms, later to reappear as a friend and admirer of the Rovers.

The boys return home and finally matriculate from Putnam Hall in *The Rover Boys on the Farm* (1908), but they start traveling again in *The Rover Boys on Treasure Isle* (1909). This time, a relative of the Stanhopes and Lanings has hidden a treasure on an island in the West Indies, and two new enemies, Sid Merrick and Tad Sobber, are after it.

First days at college—filled with sports and hazing and, of course, old and new friends and enemies—occupy most of *The Rover Boys at College* (1910), but the boys' studies are interrupted in *The Rover Boys Down East* (1911). Josiah Crabtree, aided by Tad Sobber, again kidnaps Mrs. Stanhope, hoping to mesmerize her into marrying him so he can control part of the fortune from Treasure Isle. After rescuing Mrs. Stanhope, the brothers purchase an airplane and spend most of *The*

Rover Boys in the Air (1912) aloft. Their aerial adventures end when the plane crashes in *The Rover Boys in New York* (1913), and they journey to the city to find their kidnaped father and prevent business rivals from ruining his company. In the course of a fight, Sam receives a serious head injury, but this does not keep him from attending Dick and Dora's wedding at the end of the book.

It does, however, set the stage for *The Rover Boys in Alaska* (1914), the most serious of the books, and an inspired climax to the series. While Dick goes into business with his father, Tom and Sam return to college, but Tom complains of headaches and acts more and more erratically. After seeing a movie about the gold rush, he runs off to Alaska, thinking he is a character in the movie. Badly shaken, Dick and Sam follow his trail to Alaska, fearing that he may be dead, or that his madness may be permanent. At last the brothers are reunited and Tom begins his recovery.

Tom and Sam briefly return to Brill College but soon head for New York in *The Rover Boys in Business* (1915), this time to help retrieve stolen bonds. In the final chapter, Tom weds Nellie Laning. Sam's activities at school and his graduation occupy half of *The Rover Boys on a Tour* (1916), the twentieth volume of the series; the other half takes the brothers, their wives, Sam, Grace, and two of Grace's friends on an auto tour out west and concludes with the marriage of Sam and Grace.

After that, readers must have wondered what more could possibly be left for the Rovers. Stratemeyer soon showed them. Between the twentieth and twenty-first books of the series, the brothers buy three adjacent houses on Riverside Drive in New York and sire six children (Jack and Martha for Dick; Fred and Mary for Sam; and the twins, Andy and Randy—perpetually referred to as "a great surprise"—for Tom). Volume 21, *The Rover Boys at Colby Hall* (1917), opens with a summary of the trio's activities, then introduces their sons, who are about to be sent off to Colby Hall, a military academy run by one of the Rover's former schoolmates. (Putnam Hall had been destroyed by fire, and Captain Putnam had decided to retire rather than rebuild.) The series then recounts the adventures of the four Rover sons for ten volumes as they, too, hunt, camp, sail, survive shipwrecks, and search for treasures. Although at first the Rovers *peres* tend to participate more frequently than most series fathers, their role gradually decreases as the series progresses.

The Rovers were Stratemeyer's tour de force. So popular were they that apparently readers asked for more information about Putnam Hall. Stratemeyer, able to recognize a ready-made market when he saw it, cre-

ated the Putnam Hall series (6 volumes, 1901–11), setting it at Putnam
Hall shortly before the Rovers' arrival. It contains few of their friends
but most of their enemies, notably, Josiah Crabtree and Dan Baxter. The
series differs from the Rover Boys in that the stories are set at Putnam
Hall, thus omitting adventures during vacations. A second school series
from this period, Dave Porter (15 volumes, 1905–19), resembles the
Rover Boys but has a more personable hero. The series again combines
school adventures and searches for missing relatives and chronicles the
hero's growth to adulthood and eventual employment.

Syndicate School Series

Development of Syndicate School Series   By 1907 Syndicate
writers were already assisting with some series. Jack Ranger (6 volumes,
1907–11), a clever, mechanically minded boy, is almost a humorous pre-
cursor of Tom Swift. He first upsets his hometown by inventing a
machine that stencils the town sidewalks with footprints for an advertising stunt, then unmasks a charlatan and sabotages his props immediately before a performance at Jack's aunts' home. As happens to the Rovers,
Jack's mischievousness prompts his relatives to send him off to school.
Also like his predecessors, Jack divides his time between school and
vacations: in the second volume he journeys west to search for his father;
in subsequent volumes he takes an ocean voyage (complete with obligatory shipwreck) and the requisite camping trip.

Other school series soon followed: Dorothy Dale, the first girls' series;
the Darewell Chums (5 volumes, 1908–11), the first series set at a public school; the Up and Doing series (3 volumes, 1912); the Racer Boys (6
volumes, 1912–14); Tom Fairfield (5 volumes, 1913–15); the University
series (2 volumes, 1914); and the Rushton Boys (3 volumes, 1916).
Stratemeyer also adapted the form for young readers with the Bobby
Blake series (12 volumes, 1915–26), featuring a ten-year-old boy and his
friend.

Most combined stories set away from the campus with those set at
school: roughly three-fourths of the boys' series published after 1906
have at least one volume whose the title or subtitle refers to hunting or
to camping outdoors; another, to boating or taking an ocean or sea voyage; another, to a trip west or time on a ranch. And, of course, all contain at least one story set at school. The degree of similarity becomes
even more apparent when one considers that many of these series only
ran five or six volumes. Although there is some variation, the general

pattern sets the first volume at school, the third and/or fifth outdoors or camping, and the fourth on or near water. This is essentially a condensed version of the early escapades of the Rover Boys: their yachting trip and ocean voyages in volumes 2, 3, and 5; their trip west in volume 4; and their camping expedition in volume 6.

Sports and School Series   Sports had been part of Stratemeyer's school stories since their inception. In 1910, however, the Syndicate created a series that made the connection even more overt. The College Sports series (6 volumes, 1910–13) was the first to highlight the emphasis on sports through the series' and the books' titles. The first four books alternate between baseball and football. The last two cover track and field athletics and boating. These, incidentally, comprised the four major college sports.[5]

Similar series soon followed: the Boys of Columbia High (8 volumes, 1912–20), led by Frank Allen, try baseball, boating, football, skating, track, iceboating, and camping. Some series, such as Tommy Tiptop (6 volumes, 1912–17), use younger boys as protagonists.

Sports series experienced one more change, a concentration on one sport. This began with the Baseball Joe series (14 volumes, 1912–28), which follows the meteoric rise of a young pitcher. Baseball Joe is apparently unique among sports series in that the character "actually moves from amateur to professional athletics."[6] The titles alone summarize Joe's success. He begins as *Baseball Joe of the Silver Stars* (1912) (his local team), then plays . . . *on the School Nine* (1912), . . . *at Yale* (1913), . . . *in the Central Leagues* (1914), . . . *in the Big League* (1915), . . . *on the Giants* (1916), . . . *in the World Series* (1917), and on a special tour . . . *around the World* (1918). Having established his skill as a pitcher, he then becomes . . . *Home Run King* (1922), . . . *Captain of the Team* (1924), and . . . *Champion of the League* (1925), until an arm injury forces him into a temporary retirement as a baseball . . . *Club Owner* (1926), after which he returns triumphant as a . . . *Pitching Wizard* (1928). Joe's adventures coincided with the growing popularity of baseball and the World Series. So closely did the Syndicate monitor current events that the year after the Black Sox scandal, it published *Baseball Joe Saving the League* (1923), in which Joe defeats a plot to throw some games.

Although the series did well, it was not until it had almost ended that another began along similar lines. The Garry Grayson Football series (10 volumes, 1926–32) takes Garry from grammar school to technical college. Oddly, after the other school and sports series had long been discontinued, the Syndicate revived this format with the Mel Martin

Baseball Stories (6 volumes, 1947–53) about yet another baseball whiz pitching his way through high school and college games.

The titles and ads for these later sports series show their increasing reliance on mystery as a plot element. While Baseball Joe is plagued with numerous enemies to outwit, the volume titles and the promotional materials focus on Joe's sports career. The final sentence of one ad summarized the thrust of the books: "In this series, Baseball Joe advances, step by step, from playing on a country town team until he becomes the leading pitcher of the Big League." The Garry Grayson series, too, employs titles that direct attention toward the game (for example, *Garry Grayson at Lenox High; or, The Champions of the Football League* [1926] and *Garry Grayson's Winning Kick; or, Battling for Honor* [1928]). The ads introduced two other elements, boyish activities and mysteries, and wrapped up their description of the series with the comment: "Good clean football at its best—and in addition, rattling stories of mystery and schoolboy rivalries." By the Mel Martin series, however, it is hard to tell whether mysteries or sports provide the main attraction. Volumes carry titles such as *The Mystery at the Ballpark* (1947) and *The Southpaw's Secret* (1947), and the concluding paragraph in the series ads proclaimed: "While baseball is Mel's main interest, somehow mystery and danger seem to follow him and his friends in whatever they do. Mel and the Wright twins constantly find themselves in ticklish situations as Mel's detective work involves them in skirmishes with crooks and mysterious strangers."

In later years, the Syndicate moved away from boys' school stories. While school-age characters, especially young children like the Bobbsey twins and the Hollisters, continued to appear in Syndicate series, schools no longer played an active role in the stories. More and more of the books followed the trend toward mysteries.

Themes and Traits

The Stratemeyer and Syndicate school series chronicle the continuing success of boys against external obstacles. They present young readers with idealized characters, all cast from similar molds, facing a variety of challenges. Character development is not the issue: even at the start of the series the protagonist's fully developed and near-perfect character is already in place. Instead, the stories show that it is possible to be an all-around hero.

The school series contain instant gratification and total victory, beginning as early as the boy's arrival at school. Characters start the series by entering a new school away from home and friends. Their identities, however, are not subsumed within the greater one of the institution. Rather, the reverse occurs: upon arrival, they demonstrate their ability to maintain their autonomy whatever the surroundings.

The Rover boys provide a striking example of the confrontation between school and scholar. When the boys first reach Putnam Hall, Tom sets off a firecracker, immediately breaking one of the school's rules. In the absence of the headmaster, the assistant tries to discipline him, over the Rovers' objections, but Tom runs away and spends the night at the home of some newfound friends. The next morning he confronts the headmaster and his assistant, insisting that since he was not yet officially enrolled the school has no right to punish him. He threatens to withdraw from school unless the incident and all punishment are forgotten. Although Tom has created a disturbance, repeatedly defied the assistant headmaster—even knocked him down—and spent the night away from campus, the headmaster agrees to his demands and welcomes him to the school, admiring his spirit. Tom's first actions and the official response demonstrate that he, not the authorities, is in control. This stance is echoed throughout this and other series as the protagonists challenge the actions of teachers and instructors, even causing some to be dismissed.

Other series extend the boys' influence to the school itself. In *The Racer Boys at Boarding School* (1912) the boys not only demonstrate their independence but are actually responsible for reshaping the institution. The Racer brothers enroll in a run-down academy lacking in school spirit and considered inferior to a newer institution nearby. As the omniscient narrator predicts, "though Riverview Hall did not know it, the dawn of a better day was breaking with the advent of the Racer boys."[7] The boys begin renovating some of the athletic paraphernalia, encourage their classmates to participate in sports, win a boating race against the rival academy, and bring the school favorable publicity—thereby encouraging a wealthy alumnus to give the school the financial support that saves it from closing at the end of the term. When the headmaster announces his plans for the new year, the renovations and increased emphasis on athletics have turned the school into the type the Racers had initially wished it to be.

The boys' impact on the school also includes a collision with a school bully; in these series such contact is often the start of a long-running feud. The school bully is an older and bigger boy, well known and feared, who wants all newcomers to recognize his authority. The hero states his readiness to stand up to any bullies and does so, sometimes even before he arrives at school. His quick wits and courage allow him to humiliate and squelch his opponent in early encounters, although in many series the bully serves as a recurring villain and institutes repeated clashes. The hero bests him in several ways: verbally, by refusing to obey or respect him and by making a clever riposte that leaves others laughing; physically, in a contest of skill such as a race; and morally, by unmasking him as the perpetrator of a major misdeed, sometimes causing the boy to be suspended or expelled.

The hero also cheerfully participates in the school's social life. In general, his lowly status as a newcomer is not a cause for humility or for assimilation into the framework of the school and its classes but for triumph. With his arrival, his class becomes the best in the school, winning contests against other classes and earning recognition. In *The Rover Boys at College* the trio enroll in a school where the sophomores and juniors traditionally seize the freshmen's neckties on one hazing day; losing them deprives the freshmen of the right to wear the school colors that year. Learning of this, the Rovers devise a counterplot and enlist the rest of their class, who successfully unite to foil the older boys. Their efforts do not go unrecognized: afterwards, "because of his work during the necktie rush Dick was chosen as the leader of the freshmen's class."[8] Rather than fitting in, the hero thus stands out.

The hero also excels at sports. In the Stratemeyer and Syndicate series, as with other sports stories, skill at the game does equate with fame in the school. For the series hero, however, success is rarely a matter of gradual development and recognition but rather an early demonstration of superior skill. When the protagonist tries out for team sports, he either immediately makes the team or else is placed as a substitute because older, more experienced students have prior claim to his position. In the latter case, events quickly conspire to bring him into the game, and his performance earns him a permanent spot on the team. Competitions and athletic contests are scattered throughout the story, and the hero is almost always the agent of victory. Each hero excels in at least one sport; some seem able to manage them all.

Sports contests illustrate the hero's success against near-impossible odds; he brings himself or his team to victory, but rarely against equal or honest opposition. Opponents are bigger, tougher, better trained, or older than members of the hero's team. Rival teams try to injure, drug, or kidnap players; disloyal schoolboys give away football signals and strategies; biased umpires rule in favor of opponents. As with other kinds of contests in the dime novels and series books, sports offer a message for life: "Watch out for treachery." Yet despite the inequality in the contests, the heroes play on and usually win.

Although the boys love their alma mater, there is rarely any sense that it has shaped them or that they will serve as mentors to instill its values in younger students. Unlike British schools, which are often a family tradition, the schools in the American series are relatively new institutions, often selected because the boys' parents or guardians know the headmaster or have seen impressive advertising brochures. Many of the American schools are also transitory, as is most evident in the Rover Boys series, the one instance where alumni might have had the opportunity to demonstrate second-generation loyalty to a school by enrolling their sons: by the time the Rover boys' sons reach school age Putnam Hall no longer exists.

This difference also reflects an American delight in the new. When the Racer boys are sent to an older school with a prestigious reputation, they find it in a state of disrepair—"old and out-of-date"—and clearly inferior to the "real, live, up-to-date" school that has recently opened nearby (*RBBS*, 5). It thus seems appropriate that these American heroes do not shape younger students to carry on their school traditions, for tradition is not a part of the series. The school is of secondary importance to the heroes.

Girls and romance also play a part in the stories. The boys protect and rescue them from ruffians and school bullies; they participate in school contests with more perseverance and pride when the girls are watching; they temper their behavior when they accompany girls on outings. The girls' presence originally served the practical purpose of attracting more female readers. In a 1927 interview, Stratemeyer remarked that he "receive[d] a great many letters from the boys and girls who read [the series] books. . . . The boys want to know what the hero is going to do in the next book. . . .The girls, with scarcely an exception, want to know how soon the hero of that particular story is going to marry his best girl" ("Newarker"). Although girls play progressively smaller roles in the later school series—perhaps because by then the Syndicate was already creating numerous series specifically for female readers—many of the boys continue to have a special girlfriend. The girls' presence also contributes to the emphasis on the world beyond the school: they involve the boys in outside activities and allow the boys to show their mastery of the social graces as they escort their dates about the city and countryside.

Although they are schoolboys, the protagonists spend a considerable amount of time away from school. No matter what the setting, they demonstrate competence and confidence. They face the personnel of everyday life—shopkeepers and clerks, fellow travelers and officials—with determination and equanimity. When they travel west, they learn to ride horses with ease; on shipboard, they never suffer from seasickness; in cities they enjoy the sights and cope with the complexities of urban transportation; in the wilds they prove adept at shooting and camping. A friend of the Rushton boys sums it up when he remarks, "They're right on the job in whatever they set out to do. They'd make good at anything."[9] The competence and cheerfulness heroes demonstrate at school thus extends to the world beyond—which they are fully capable of facing long before they graduate.

The Character of the Hero

Physical and Personality Traits   Just as the Stratemeyer and Syndicate stories spend little space on the development and maturity of the central characters, so, too, do they expend little time on complex characterizations. Although there are a few individual differences, most protagonists have the same basic personality, the standard equipment for a series hero as it were. Some traits are plainly stated, through either authorial comments or other characters' observations; some can be deduced through a protagonist's actions and conversations; a few are implied. What emerges is an assertive hero, determined to make his mark on the world.

One of the implied messages in the books is that superiority and leadership are innate abilities. Heroes never become leaders in the course of the series: they start out that way, and the rest of the book and series only serves to demonstrate their superiority. In the preface to the first volume of the Dave Porter series Stratemeyer himself points out to young readers these gradations of ability:

> [Dave's school] represents a type of institution to be found by the score in many of our states, and the scholars attending the school are no better or worse than are the boys elsewhere. Each lad has his peculiarities: one is bright and clever, another dull and slow; one upright and manly, another low and cunning; one full of life and merriment, another given to look on

the dark side of things. Taken as a whole, such a school represents the world at large, for "men are but youths of larger growth."

It may be thought by some that Dave is an unusually bright and clever boy. Such, however, is far from being the fact. *In every school there are certain lads who stand head and shoulders above those who surround them. As among men, they are natural born leaders, and they show this leadership at the first opportunity given to them.*[10]

The initial volumes in a series usually include the most detailed description of the hero, highlighting his finer traits. Voracious or astute readers may have noticed that Stratemeyer heroes not only resemble each other in character but also in appearance, sometimes even in the words and phrases used to describe them.

The generic Stratemeyer or Syndicate hero is a white American boy, usually aged 14 to 17, with a healthy body and spirit. He is apt to be tall, with brown hair and brown eyes. Favored traits include a pleasant disposition, as evidenced by the hero's "merry eyes" or "cheery face"; an open, active nature, variously described as "fearless and frank" or "frank and friendly," and "lively" or "full of life"; and a love of and ability at sports.[11] A hero also possesses a strong sense of self-worth and self-confidence, a readiness to stand up for himself and others, and cheerful determination, which is perhaps another aspect of his good nature. The former two traits are usually central to his advancement as well as to his troubles. His determination underlies many of his actions and responses to life and adversity. In addition, a hero is courageous and honest, although the latter trait is not quite as straightforward as it sounds.

The hero's self-confidence forms an integral part of his personality. The standard hero believes in himself; he willingly accepts challenges and tries new activities, supremely confident he will manage a good showing. When Tom Fairfield learns he is to be sent to boarding school, he cries, "Say, that's all right. I'm satisfied! . . . When can I start for Elmwood? Have you got a catalog from there?"[12] Tom and other series heroes respond to new situations with enthusiasm and anticipation—and with no uncertainty about how they will fare in unfamiliar circumstances. This attitude extends to all upcoming events, whether the heroes are entering a contest, enrolling in a new school, preparing to visit a classmate in a distant state, or setting sail for foreign lands. And, on almost all occasions, the outcome justifies their optimism.

Closely allied to this confidence is the hero's expectation that he will be treated courteously and fairly and his forthrightness in demanding such treatment if it is lacking. This precipitates numerous clashes when characters fail to accord him proper respect. The school bully, accustomed to dominating new students, provokes one of the first encounters, but other characters, including adults, also collide with the hero's self-esteem. For example, in *The Rover Boys in New York* a section boss on the railroad mistakenly carts off the wreckage of the Rovers' plane. When they try to claim it, he growls and storms, telling them to leave. The Rovers refuse to back down and end up not only with their plane but also with the railroad company's agreement to move the wreckage free of charge to a site of their choice. Afterwards, Dick Rover even remarks, "It pays to put on a front . . . if I had been weak-kneed about it that fellow wouldn't have done a thing."[13]

This readiness to insist on respectful and honest treatment also extends to a concern for others unable to defend themselves, such as the very young, the elderly, or the naive. When a bully tries to intimidate a little newsboy, Dave Porter intervenes, declaring, "I am not going to stand by and see you abuse this boy or anybody else" (*DPSR*, 83). Girls and women, of course, also receive the hero's ready assistance. The Rovers' initial clash with Dan Baxter in aiding Dora, Nellie, and Grace has already been mentioned. (In another book, *The Rover Boys at College*, this type of gallantry backfires when Dick Rover helps rescue a young lady from the amorous attentions of two of his schoolchums and her resulting gratitude causes a misunderstanding between him and Dora.)

The third characteristic of the hero is his good nature and continued optimism, even when facing difficulties or setbacks. Heroes rarely grumble but instead remain determined to enjoy themselves and make the best of things. This essential trait becomes more evident through the adverbs used to describe the heroes' actions than through overt authorial statements. Heroes do things "cheerfully" and without complaining, an attitude that contrasts sharply with that of the antagonists, who are often described as "sneering," "grumbling," or "whining." On a few occasions, the protagonists themselves voice their philosophy. After the shipwreck in *The Rover Boys on Land and Sea*, Dick "cheerfully" remarks, "Well, as our situation cannot be helped, let us make the best of it."[14]

In addition, the hero's behavior supports his personal code of ethics. He is courageous, sometimes even foolhardy. More frequently, however, the hero asserts his bravery in a more constructive fashion, by helping others despite the potential danger to himself.

A Complex Code of Honor   Although heroes are often described as honest, open, and frank, they follow a more complex code of behavior than these simple qualities imply. While heroes do not steal or lie, they do play schoolboy pranks and break rules. Their victims can be other boys, staff, townspeople, or even schoolteachers. When the mischief is discovered, even if another person's property has been damaged, the hero's code of ethics does not require him to admit his involvement unless others are wrongly accused. In some cases, the heroes make restitution anonymously; in others, especially if the target is an unpopular teacher or schoolmate, the victim bears the cost of replacing damaged articles. The assumption, sometimes reinforced by the behavior of those in authority, is that such activities form a natural part of boyhood. Often, the headmaster treats these incidents as natural high-spiritedness and does not even pursue a serious investigation. Sometimes he even has difficulty hiding a smile over the cleverness of the prank.

Some of the pranks that go undetected or unpunished are retaliatory, aimed at the hero's enemies. The books rarely question their somewhat vengeful nature, instead adopting the philosophy that unpleasant characters deserve to be treated unpleasantly. The hero's actions are criticized by neither other characters nor the omniscient narrator; rather, they are condoned.

Other pranks punish characters, some of them adults, for past actions or injustices. On an overnight stop, the Rovers discover that they are staying at the same hotel as Josiah Crabtree, the former teacher at Putnam Hall whom they all dislike. Tom purchases six crabs, and the boys sneak into Crabtree's room and put the crustaceans in his bed. That night, after he goes to bed, the crabs attack, whereupon:

> Crabtree leaped straight out of bed, one crab hanging to his left knee, several on his feet, and one, which he had caught hold of, clinging to the back of his hand. . . . Then came a crash as the washstand went over, carrying with it a bowl, a soap tray, and a large pitcher filled with water. . . . The noise soon aroused the entire hotel and the clerk, several bellboys, and finally the proprietor rushed to the scene.
> . . . "Take them off!" shrieked Josiah Crabtree, and kicked out right and left. One of the crabs was flung off, to land on the hotel proprietor's face and to catch the man by the nose. . . . Safe in their own room, the boys laughed until they cried. (*RBAS*, 197)

Although the boys have disrupted the hotel, it is Josiah Crabtree who is asked to leave, and the next morning the clerk, who suspects the Rovers' involvement, winks and tells them, "It served the old crank right" (*RBAS*, 199).

The Rovers are not at all disturbed that the hotel proprietor, who has done them no disservice, becomes an unwitting victim of their plot. In this and similar situations, the prank also illustrates the stratified society in the books. Certain types of characters serve as convenient targets for mischief or mistreatment—most notably, foreigners or members of the working class, especially those employed at the school or in establishments patronized by the schoolboys. Although the heroes would be incensed were they, their girlfriends, or their immediate families to receive such treatment, all of their victims are expected to endure these tricks good-naturedly as their due. Failure to do so only makes them targets for further mischief.

If the heroes are asked directly about their involvement in more serious cases involving pranks or other misbehavior, they will not lie or disclaim responsibility, but they will refuse to incriminate anyone else. They are usually admired for this stance. This attitude seems predicated on the assumption that a gentleman will own up to his wrongdoings; naming him deprives him of the opportunity to do the honorable thing himself. As Dave Porter tells the headmaster when asked to identify participants in a schoolboy initiation, "I would rather you would not ask me to mention any names . . . I think every fellow ought to speak up for himself. He will if he has any honor about him."[15] (And, to their credit, some of the other boys do.) Only in unusual cases does the hero reluctantly name the guilty party—usually when the latter has committed a fairly serious offense and seems unlikely to confess. Even so, it takes much deliberation and urging before the protagonist will identify the wrongdoer, and even then only if he has solid proof of guilt.

The school stories offer young readers a chance to triumph vicariously over situations encountered in their own world: sports competitions, bullies, harsh teachers, and similar obstacles. They also provide more glamorous material for daydreams, since few readers can expect to have the chance to travel across the country or over the ocean to rescue relatives or discover treasure. The stories present readers with ready-made heroes who include numerous school victories among their many successes.

The heroes are often described in prefaces or series ads as "lively" or "wideawake," a characterization supported by their behavior. Even though the hero occasionally indulges in mischief, such actions are not treated as character flaws but merely as expressions of his assertiveness or high spirits. The hero bears some traits that readers can emulate, such as self-respect and optimism, but the books also imply that most heroes are born not made. Courageous and confident, the schoolboy hero is a natural leader and winner, receiving the ready admiration and loyalty of his friends as he triumphs over obstacles to success. His idealized life, which tantalizes young readers with its worlds that are readily conquered and its many victories, is intended to be not a portrayal of reality but an escape from it.

6
Girls' Series

The Syndicate's girls' series were a logical outgrowth of Stratemeyer's penchant for experimentation in juvenile fiction. They offered a chance to reach a different market by using female characters in modified versions of school and career stories. Like the boys, the girls go off to boarding schools and plan trips to visit friends; they cope with school rivals, participate in athletics and other extracurricular activities, and sample the new technology. However, unlike the boys they rarely chase professional criminals or face threats of physical violence at others' hands. Girls' hardships center on emotional and social crises, their own or someone else's, and their goals relate to resolving those problems—and to filling an ample supply of free time.

Despite Stratemeyer's willingness to try the genre, the Syndicate's girls' series remain secondary to its boys' fiction. From 1908 to 1930, when the emphasis switched to mysteries, Stratemeyer created only 17 girls' series, less than half the number issued for boys during that period. Moreover, while the boys' series encompass many types of stories, those for girls have narrower horizons. Girls stay firmly within their own time period and in everyday surroundings—their stories are not historical or science fiction, and there is almost no foreign travel for them. Even the patterns of their lives are more limited. Most Syndicate girls' series developed along one of two lines: a single character gradually triumphing over her surroundings, or a group of girls in search of casual adventures.

The single-character series—that is, those named after their heroine—follow a fairly common formula for the early volumes. An orphan or half-orphan, with an older male as a relative or guardian, arrives in new, usually unsympathetic surroundings. Naturally kindhearted and cheerful, she works to improve or brighten her surroundings, help the unfortunate, and otherwise demonstrate her noble nature. She meets one or more other girls, who become her best friends and loyal admirers for the remainder of the series. Although adversity or straitened circumstances delay her entrance to boarding school for one or more books, she eventually enrolls and spends the next few books there or vacationing with school chums. Her extracurricular adventures include outings similar to those in the boys' series: one winter trip somewhere snowy, one summer trip near water, and a visit to a ranch "out west," almost all involving a minor mystery or problem to resolve. However, rather than proving herself through physical prowess—on the athletic field or capturing wrongdoers—the heroine's struggles demonstrate her emotional stamina in overcoming various losses or unjust accusations. Alternatively, she helps others with these difficulties. Whatever the circumstances, she adheres to her beliefs and maintains her morals and manners. Her natural goodness and determination eventually set matters right. Upon graduating (if the series lasted), she goes to college and sometimes gets engaged and even marries.

The group series are more difficult to characterize, for the nature of each series depends on the group. Several girls of varying dispositions unite to participate in a shared interest, usually involving outdoor activities or technology. Though the group is the title character, one girl emerges as the leader: she is the most poised, courageous, and competent. Her companions admire her and tacitly acknowledge her superiority. The other girls have minor flaws, whether in appearance (plumpness), manners (tomboyishness), or mettle (recklessness or timidity); however, they play strong supporting roles. Boys take strong secondary parts in several series, frequently accompanying the girls on outings. The greatest difference between single-character and group series is occasioned by the nature of the group: a close, supportive unit, the group satisfies each member's emotional needs, so the characters rarely undergo the same type of suffering or psychological hardship as the heroine of a single-character series. Additionally, the girls usually come from well-to-do families and are frequently seen away from school.

It is difficult to trace shifts in the two types of series because of their limited number. Most series differ from each other primarily through variations in the heroine's circumstances. Over time each type of series tended to adopt characteristics from the other. Girls in the early single-character series are more wrapped up in domestic and nurturing activities; those in the later series become more carefree, an attitude closer to that found in the group series. The early group series portray girls traveling about the countryside using different methods of transportation or seeking leisure activities; later series feature girls from less wealthy families who are more concerned with home and community affairs.

The Syndicate's girls' series have a fairly clear cutoff date: all but two ended by or in 1932. In 1930 the Syndicate began developing girls' mystery series, with a different type of heroine and a clear emphasis on mystery; those series and their protagonists are discussed in a later chapter.

Syndicate Single-Character Series

Dorothy Dale (13 volumes, 1908–24), the Syndicate's first single-character series, shows the typical blend of emotional and social crises. In the initial volume Dorothy's widowed father, Colonel Dare, falls ill, and his livelihood is threatened when he is unable to keep publishing his newspaper. Dorothy bravely carries on, shouldering financial and occupational responsibilities as well as the emotional strain of his illness. In the second book, the emphasis shifts: Dorothy and her friend Tavia go off to boarding school and face the more typical problems of arrogant girls and initiation ceremonies for secret societies. Subsequent stories follow Dorothy and Tavia at Dorothy's aunt's home for winter vacations, back at school, or traveling west. The books stress Dorothy's common sense and ladylike qualities, contrasting her with the often irresponsible, untidy Tavia, who, nonetheless, remains a sympathetic character. The characters age as the series progresses, and the penultimate volume sees Dorothy's engagement.

The Syndicate's next single-character series, Ruth Fielding (30 volumes, 1913–34), proved one of its most durable until Nancy Drew. W. Bert Foster probably started the series and authored most of the early volumes; Mildred Wirt Benson wrote seven of the final eight books.[1] This was the Syndicate's first use of the cheerful orphan, and Ruth Fielding's popularity may have encouraged it to stay with the formula, especially for series assigned to Foster.

Ruth Fielding faces a bleak situation when she moves to the Red Mill to live with her miserly Uncle Jabez. Coldhearted and unsympathetic, Jabez tolerates Ruth but offers no affection or comfort. The only kindness Ruth receives comes from Uncle Jabez's housekeeper, "Aunt" Alvira, and two wealthy neighboring children, Helen and Tom. At first it seems Ruth will spend her days trapped in the confines of Jabez's crabbed world, but when Uncle Jabez loses a money box—the only thing dear to his heart—and Ruth's ingenuity restores it, he gratefully finances her stay at boarding school with Helen. There, after troubles with a snobbish club, Ruth forms an alternative and more humane society, the Sweetbriers, which becomes the most popular group in the school.

Ruth's situation differs from that of many other heroines, for she never forgets that her uncle is paying for her education and that she is thus subsisting only on his sufferance. Consequently, even early in the series she watches for ways to become self-sufficient or to contribute to her upkeep. She also develops her talents for screenwriting and, while still in school, writes a screenplay whose performance earns enough to help rebuild the school's dormitory when it is damaged by fire.

Ruth's courage and independence emerge even more strongly in books from the middle of the series. During World War I she goes to Europe and helps Tom with intelligence work. (By now, their relationship has progressed to romance.) She returns home after being wounded and takes up a career writing, directing, and producing movies, and even marries the faithful Tom. Surprisingly, the series does not end there. Instead, Ruth continues her career and also becomes a mother. Thus, while the first half of the series depicts Ruth's adventures as a schoolgirl and young woman, the second half focuses on her career and the attendant problems.

Ruth is far more adventurous and self-reliant than most series heroines. Carol Billman calls Ruth Fielding a "no-nonsense, unsentimental, independent, aggressive, ambitious, assertive" heroine, the string of adjectives serving to underscore the great difference between Ruth and most of her contemporaries, in or out of books (67). Ruth is also a heroine who "likes activity and mental challenge" (70). The Ruth Fielding books were among the earliest Syndicate girls' series to incorporate mysteries, although these frequently relate to Ruth's situation as a schoolgirl or career woman. Moreover, Billman notes that the series "cohered," showing a "sense of direction" (a characteristic of Foster's series) rather than random adventures (66).

Billman observes a change in the formula after Ruth's marriage, "stem[ming] from the tension Ruth's two lives, the personal and the professional, created. . . . She repeatedly proclaims her complete submission to Tom and family life . . . [yet] she passionately defends her work." While Billman attributes this to "irreconcilable structural— actually genre—differences" (74–75), that is, the conflict between the adventure story and the romance, it is also noteworthy that Ruth's character change occurs shortly after Mildred Wirt Benson took over the series. The final volume (not by Wirt Benson) actually concludes with Ruth deciding, "I'm home never more to roam. . . . If there are any more adventures in our little family, they will be passed on to [our daughter] June."[2]

The year after Ruth Fielding began, the Syndicate started an unusual single-character series, the closest it came to outright didacticism. In the first volume of the Do Something (Janice Day) series (5 volumes, 1914–19), young Janice Day arrives to stay with relatives in aptly named Poketown while her father tends to business in Mexico. She is appalled by the town's slovenliness and carelessness. Energetic and cheerful, she revolutionizes and reforms the entire town, persuading shopkeepers to wash store windows and develop enticing displays; homeowners to fix fences, mow lawns, and trim hedges; and the town to organize a rubbish drive, start a boys' reading room, move the school to a new building, and institute new educational theories. The people even discover that the town should have been named after its founder, and they change the name to *Polk*town, showing they are no longer "poky." In this, the series echoes themes found in Stratemeyer's Progressive boys' career series, although Janice's reforms predominantly affect the domestic sphere—homes are tidied, the town is "prettified," and the schoolchildren are helped. She receives no financial benefits, only the satisfaction of living in an attractive town, improving the children's future, and inspiring the young schoolteacher—with whom she becomes romantically involved.

Later volumes continue Janice's drive for reform. In *How Janice Day Won* (1916) she leads a battle for temperance in Polktown; the situations presented are as melodramatic as any from T. S. Arthur's *Ten Nights in a Bar-Room* (1854). Unless the last volume in the series has an undiscovered earlier publication date, it actually is a "pre-quel" to the first story, describing Janice's life with her father before her stay in Polktown—an atypical end to a series.

Betty Gordon (15 volumes, 1920–32) seems an attempt to repeat Ruth Fielding's success but marks a shift toward emphasizing the protagonist's girlhood. Well written and entertaining, it stands as one of the Syndicate's most enjoyable series. The orphaned Betty is left to the care of a wealthy uncle, who sends her to Bramble Farm to board with a woman he knew long ago; he is unaware of the character of her husband. Like Ruth, Betty finds herself in harsh, rural surroundings, in a home dominated by a brutal, miserly man. Josiah Peabody tyrannizes the farm, reserving his worst treatment for Bob Henderson, a "poorhouse boy" taken in for his work value. Unable to change Peabody or reach her uncle, Betty leaves Bramble Farm in the second book to search for her uncle in Washington, D.C., the last place mentioned in his letters—a variation on the theme of the lost father. A case of mistaken identity allies her with a kind, wealthy family that shelters and helps her. Betty finds her uncle in Oklahoma in the third book, and he conveniently adopts Bob, too.

In subsequent books, Betty and several characters from earlier books attend boarding school, while Bob enrolls in a nearby military academy. During vacations, they, too, travel about the country, planning outings to Ocean Park, Rainbow Ranch, mountain camp, and other typical series locations. Bob plays a strong role as Betty's counselor and friend. The series lasted 15 volumes, but the penultimate book still finds Betty at school.

The third series for 1920 changed the pattern, introducing a character who was neither an orphan nor facing hostile surroundings. Billie Bradley (9 volumes, 1920–32), a cheerful schoolgirl, inherits a house from her great-aunt and, at the book's end, finds it contains a trunk filled with valuable coins and stamps. This wealth, of course, enables her to go to boarding school. There she finds a situation almost straight out of Stratemeyer's earliest boys' school series. When the headmistress is called away, two schoolteachers with unreasonable and unrealistic ideas about discipline and meals cut rations until several girls actually become sick, whereupon Billie convinces all the students to leave the school. The headmistress, who has just returned to town, is understandably astonished to discover her entire school checking into the local hotel, but, commendably, she forgives the girls and dismisses the two teachers. In later volumes Billie solves minor mysteries at school and during vacations. The greatest difference between Billie Bradley and other single-character series, however, is in tone. As her actions with the schoolteachers demonstrate, Billie is more apt to be angered by mistreatment or to rebel against it than to suffer docilely. The plots still involve helping others, but the series focuses on Billie and her friends' carefree activities rather than on emotional distress.

Syndicate Group Series

In contrast to heroines in single-character series, none of the group heroines attend boarding school. Instead, the stories emphasize their extracurricular activities and shared interests. The title of the first such series, the Motor Girls (10 volumes, 1910–17), conveys its obvious emphasis: a group of girls—and sometimes their brothers and boyfriends—use their autos to tour the countryside. Lillian Garis, whose husband Howard Garis wrote many volumes in the Syndicate's Motor Boys series, authored several titles.

Like the Motor Girls, the Outdoor Girls (23 volumes, 1913–1933), the most popular group series, is about a group of friends traveling and pursuing good times. The original foursome, aged "about sixteen" at the series' start, are an eclectic group: Betty Nelson, the unofficial leader, practical and vivacious; Grace Ford, stately and fair, and never without a box of chocolates; Mollie Billette, half French and temperamental; Amy Stonington, quiet and younger than the rest. In the first book, they plan a walking tour about the countryside with a goal of covering 10 to 20 miles per day and making evening stops at the homes of relatives. Boys play more prominent roles in later volumes. Betty begins with two suitors: flashy, wealthy Percy Faulkner, whom she does not care for, and the law student Allen Washburne, whom she does. Grace's brother Will, who is fond of Amy, appears regularly, as do Will's friends.

Betty acquires a motorboat, *Gem*, in the second book, and the girls travel down the river and compete in several races. In the third book Mollie gets an auto, and the group take a motor tour. After several books at scenic spots, a more serious note intervenes when three of the boys enlist as the nation begins preparing for World War I. Readers expecting the Outdoor Girls to emulate Ruth Fielding's courage by going to Europe were in for a disappointment, however. In *The Outdoor Girls in Army Service; or, Doing Their Bit for Uncle Sam* (1919) "their bit" consists of knitting for hours on end, fretting over the boys (who have been sent to training camp some miles away), and finally helping to set up a hostess house near the boys' camp. The war dominates the next few books, although the girls' part is frequently limited to worrying about their boyfriends and relatives.

After the war ends, the boys return home and the girls resume their jaunts. The writers, however, faced a dilemma: Betty had practically promised to marry Allen before he left for the war—several books back—and Amy and Will had been getting steadily more serious. If readers wondered when the pairs would ever wed, Stratemeyer must have wondered what would happen to the Outdoor Girls if they did. In *The Outdoor Girls on Cape Cod* (1924) he hit upon the happy solution of having the group encounter two new girls, Irene Moore and Stella Sibley, who are about to move to Deepdale, the Outdoor Girls' hometown. Betty and Allen marry at long last, and Stella and Irene join the group. The next two books continue the romantic trend, with a wedding apiece. Although the books include visits to the married members, perhaps some readers protested the loss of their favorite characters, for the seventeenth book brings all the girls together for a vacation. This reunion provides a nice prelude to the next story, in which Mollie, the last of the original quartet, marries. Two new girls join the group, which, in a gesture reminiscent of the first story, plans a walking tour with stops at the homes of the married members. The series lasted for three more books but ended without further nuptials.[3]

Healthy outdoor activities remain a central feature for the Girls of Central High (7 volumes, 1914–19). Patterned after the Syndicate's Boys of Columbia High series, it recognized the growing interest in athletic activities for girls. As one character explains, "We girls should have some interest in athletics besides our loyalty to the boys' basketball and football teams. I want the girls of Central High to organize for our own improvement and pleasure."[4] The four central characters begin with basketball and rowing shells; later volumes add track. The final volume, written after a four-year hiatus, shows the girls supporting a patriotic cause by staging a play to raise money for the Red Cross.

W. Bert Foster was the shaping force behind a different type of group series, the Corner House Girls (13 volumes, 1915–26). Four young orphans and their aunt live in poverty in a small city apartment, trying to be cheerful in straitened circumstances. They find a benefactor in their late uncle's lawyer, who explains that they are apparently their uncle's sole heirs. Even though a will has not been found, the lawyer encourages them to move into their uncle's home, a comfortable house on the corner of a sizable lot (hence, the series title). The first book describes the girls settling into their new home, their worries about the will and difficulties with a rival claimant, and their sense of responsibility for several families living in tenements that are also part of the estate; the second covers their friendship with a runaway boy, Neale O'Neil, and their further involvement with their tenants.

Even these synopses suggest some of the differences between these books and most of the Syndicate's other series. The girls' common bond is their family relationship, and this forms the core of the books. They are younger than most group characters: at the start Ruth is 16, Agnes is 12, Tess is 10, and Dot is 6 or 8. While they have some measure of independence—Ruth practically runs the house, even though their aunt lives with them—an adult accompanies them on their travels and takes responsibility for their safety. They possess a far greater social conscience than most heroines. Indeed, the series ads described the girls as "always eager to have a good time, also anxious to help other people and to alleviate the sufferings in the world."

The series is also unusual in that its initial audience is slightly younger girls. In many volumes, the three younger girls have more active roles than Ruth does, and many chapters describe Agnes's activities with Neale or Dot and Tess at play. Foster apparently delighted in the antics and speech of young children, for the books abound with anecdotes, told by the children, of small pranks and incidents at school, and the text is peppered with jokes springing from their misunderstandings or misuse of language. Part of the series' charm stems from Foster's careful attention to detail and continuity. As the series progresses, the reader becomes acquainted not just with the girls but with their neighbors, tenants, and all their families, and with a veritable menagerie of pets. The girls age little in the series: the last book opens with Tess and Dot still playing and Agnes only beginning to realize her relationship with Neale may be more than friendship.

Themes and Traits

In an essay titled "Plucky Little Ladies and Stout-Hearted Chums" Jane S. Smith summarizes the mixed messages contained in the genre. The books were written at a time when technological and social changes were transforming society, and when children were enjoying greater amounts of unsupervised leisure time with their peers. Accordingly, one facet of the books "showed the adolescent years as a glorious era of independence and discovery" with stories that moved "away from the family and toward a society of friends united by age and common interests."[5] However, while the protagonists' activities display a newfound freedom, their value systems and struggles suggest more traditional mores. Girls still worry about proper attire and tidy surroundings and observe the conventional social graces. Smith captures the essence of girls' series when she notes that they blend "escapist and didactic fiction," essentially "grafting onto the formulas of the adventure story many of the preoccupations of both the romances and the novels of manners" (161, 163, 165).

Thus, the Syndicate's girls' series offer a split vision of the world. It is not just that girls have less independence than do boys but that the structures of their world take on a different shape, that of the heart. If boys prove themselves through physical fortitude and courage in the face of danger, girls prove themselves through emotional stamina and perseverance in the face of social slights or cruelty. Boys chase and capture villains, often receiving some form of financial recompense; girls aid the lost or heartsick, reuniting them with their families or bringing them into a circle of warm friends, and are rewarded by seeing their happiness.

Like their male counterparts, the girls generally begin the series with all the qualities necessary for success. They do not need to become good:

they are already. Rather than improving their characters, the situations they encounter test their inner strength by either allowing them to demonstrate their kind hearts or contrasting them with others who lack their fine qualities.

The formula for the single-character series is especially appropriate for allowing the heroine to prove her mettle right away: after moving into a new environment, she immediately begins to try to improve it, initially through cleaning, tidying, or otherwise making the place more comfortable. Ruth Fielding, arriving at the Red Mill, walks in the door, has a good cry in Aunt Alvira's lap (she has had a particularly trying time en route), and announces, "I am going right to work to help you."[6] She then seizes the brush and promptly sets to work cleaning the floor. By the time her uncle comes in for dinner Ruth "had learned a great deal . . . about the work Aunt Alviry had to do [and] was of much assistance" (*RFRM*, 54–55). Similarly, on Janice Day's first afternoon with her relatives in Poketown, she starts weeding the much-neglected carrot patch. The next day she helps clean house, and by the third day she has coaxed her cousin into helping her give the front lawn "such a cleaning as had not happened within the memory of the oldest inhabitant along Hillside Avenue."[7]

For many of the girls in single-character series, their initial struggle is twofold: enduring both physical and emotional deprivation. One aspect of this deprivation is learning to accept a different—and often less pleasant and less comfortable—way of life than that to which they have been accustomed. Improving their surroundings can counteract some of their physical deprivation, but not all. The rest requires a sunny disposition, a certain amount of resignation, and endurance. Billman identifies the prototype for this situation as Cinderella, for like Cinderella the heroine must begin her story unappreciated in dismal, loveless surroundings before she can attain the life of a princess (69–70).

Ruth Fielding and Betty Gordon find themselves in about the worst circumstances. Betty has not been at Peabody's Bramble Farm an entire day before she wonders aloud, "Is there [even] one pleasant, kind thing connected with this place?"[8] Meals, which are already scanty, inexpensive, and unappetizing, are made more unpalatable by Peabody's constant rudeness. Her bed is "the hardest thing she had ever lain upon," and the room is filled with mosquitoes, for Peabody will not allow his wife to spend money for netting to screen the windows (*BGBF*, 69). Betty is constantly faced with suffering she cannot alleviate: Peabody bullies and verbally abuses his wife, beats Bob, the young farmhand, and rules the house with threats, repression, and rage. At first Betty is thoroughly miserable. At the end of the first day she "flung herself on the bed . . . sobbing uncontrollably and more unhappy than she had ever been" (*BGBF*, 64). As the story progresses, her attitude changes. The narrator explains, "Conditions did not improve, but Betty developed a sturdy, wholesome philosophy that helped her make the best of everything" (*BGBF*, 96).

Even though the girls' physical surroundings improve in later books, initially they face the same emotional trials. Dorothy Dale suffers during several different terms at school. In one, she is the victim of a whispering campaign and "one miserable day . . . [finds] all her friends, at least those who had claimed to be her friends, suddenly lost to her. Those who were not openly rude enough to deliberately turn their backs upon the astonished girl, made some pretense of avoiding conversation with her."[9] Dorothy is wretched for several weeks and considers leaving school; but then she decides that "surely [she] should display better courage than to let a crowd of foolish girls drive her from Glenwood!" (*DDGS*, 180). Her endurance is rewarded as, one by one, the girls weigh Dorothy's character against the false accusation and renew their friendship.

Although the heroines show determination in such circumstances, it is a blend of active and passive response. They do not give up and go home; they do not creep around cringing or crying openly; they do not let themselves be cowed—at least visibly—by others' behavior. However, they also do not fight back or confront the ringleaders. In short, they act as what might be considered the ideal passive woman—if they are neglected, unloved, or mistreated, they put on a cheerful face, remain affectionate, and do good, determined to endure.

In boys' series, the hero's troubles at school frequently spring from a perceived threat to another's authority. Girls, however, make enemies by encroaching on domestic and social spheres: their antagonists' place and popularity. The first trouble usually occurs when they are assigned a room or space another girl covets. Poor Ruth Fielding's problems at the local school begin when the teacher assigns her to share a desk with a girl who had expected to sit with her best friend. The angry girl becomes the ringleader of those who ostracize Ruth. Although the scenes are probably designed to show the self-centered nature of the antagonist, it seems ironic that, in one sense at least, the heroine is ousting her female antagonist from her "home" or (literally) separating her from her loved ones—that is, her friends.

The girls' second difficulty is somewhat similar to one that the boys face: their opponent is accustomed to having her own way and expects to be admired or fawned over. The heroines truckle to no one and respect only those whose characters merit it. Sometimes the trouble springs from a perceived threat to another's position. In *Dorothy Dale at Glenwood School* Dorothy tries to be kind to Viola, her antagonist, but her attempts to reach out have little effect, for Viola has recognized Dorothy as a potential rival: "It had been [jealousy] from the first, from the very first moment she set her eyes on Dorothy Dale [and her] beautiful face. . . . Dorothy had made friends with the best girls in Glenwood, she had been taken up by the teachers, she had been given the very best part in the play" (*DDGS*, 200). The antagonist usually plays a continuing role in the series, but as the heroine gradually gains a close circle of friends she is less anguished by the antagonist's attacks—and less vulnerable to ostracism because of them. Instead, she can afford to overlook or laugh at barbs directed at her.

In addition to coping with their own problems, the girls frequently help others. Indeed, a girl's passiveness disappears if another is the victim. Characters who will not speak out to defend themselves do so readily to defend their friends. More often than not, however, the heroine's role lies in comforting others or improving their lot. Some subplots use an early version of the mystery story: a new girl, obviously troubled or sorrowful and frequently secretive about her past, joins the school but remains outside the social circle. The heroine brings her into the group, cheers her up, and resolves her problem. In *Dorothy Dale and Her Chums* the headmistress actually calls on Dorothy to ask her to welcome and befriend a new girl, Miette. Dorothy not only does so but also learns Miette's secret—her only relative has disappeared, apparently abandoning her—and sets in motion a chain of events that result in the girl's relative, her family lawyers, and her fortune being found. Miette's lawyer praises Dorothy and her actions; he is "very glad indeed to have met this little heroine," adding, "Our young girls of to-day often display a more commendable type of heroism than characterized the Joans of former days . . . the results of their work are more practical, to say the least."[10]

Like *Dorothy Dale and Her Chums*, many plots deal with discovering loved ones or helping others to do so. Sometimes the protagonists benefit: Janice Day finds her father, and Betty Gordon her uncle; Ruth Fielding finds her boyfriend, who had been missing in action in World War I. Even in group series, where the girls are less concerned with others, reunions among secondary characters are frequent. The Corner House Girls seem forever to be involved in aiding lost souls: in one volume they trace Neale O'Neil's father, in another their lawyer's runaway wards, in a third two long-lost sisters, and in the final volume their own lawyer, who has had a breakdown from overwork, forgotten his identity, and wandered off.

Sometimes the discovery seems more accidental than planned. The Corner House Girls provide the catalyst for reuniting two sisters, separated since early childhood. Although the girls have much of the information necessary to uncover the connection, they do not see it. Their conversations with each sister about the other finally prompt one sister to make further inquiries, revealing the relationship. Other times the girls' deductive ability or intelligence unlocks the mystery. Billie Bradley notices the similarity between a drawing by Huldah, an abused girl she and her friends have been sheltering, and a picture painted by a famous artist. She asks the artist to meet the girl and learns that Huldah is the woman's daughter, stolen in childhood.

Helping others can also involve personal sacrifice, and the heroines readily give their own money to those in greater need. After saving a little girl named Lottie from falling off a pier, Janice Day learns that the child is blind and slowly going deaf. Lottie's father cannot afford an operation to restore her sight, nor can he pay the tuition at a school for the deaf. When Janice's father sends her a check to buy the automobile she has longed for, Janice spends it on the operation instead. Learning of her action, Janice's aunt says, "But you've talked so much about your automobile, deary. . . . Ain't you most disappointed to death, child?" and Janice shows where her heart lies: "Oh no, Aunty," returned Janice cheerfully. "You know, I could be just awfully selfish, *in my mind!* But when it came to running about the country in an automobile, with poor Lottie blind and helpless because of my selfishness—No, no! I could not have done it" (*JDP*, 292–93). People, not material things, are most important.

As can be seen, the girls receive few material rewards from these endeavors and expect none. Their happiness lies in helping others. The narrator of *Betty Gordon at Bramble Farm* summarizes the typical heroine's goals: "For your girl dreamer always plans for her friends and for their happiness, and she seldom dreams for herself alone" (*BGBF*, 140).

Although many of the plots deal with aiding others, the books also send other messages about behavior and appearance. Girls in most single-character and some group series are expected to be not only generous but also industrious and capable in domestic matters. Part of the girls' energy can be attributed to their good health and physical fitness, and the books stress the importance of exercise and outdoor activities. Ads for the Outdoor Girls described them as "fun-loving girls who have a common bond in their fondness for outdoor life." In *The Girls of Central High* an older man tells the group, "When *I* was young, girls didn't have athletics—and yell like Indians while they were at it" (*GCH*, 171). One girl responds with a passionate defense of their activities: "Why, even my mother says that we girls are much better physically than the girls of her day. We work much harder in school, but we do not get nervous and 'all played out.' . . . She believes it is due to our physical exercises and our outdoor lives. The games and exercises we have in this athletic field are making us stronger and abler to meet the difficulties of life" (*GCH*, 172).

Although they are athletic, girls rarely acknowledge competition, much less the value of winning. They have far fewer athletic contests than boys do, though the heroines usually win those in which they participate. Even the Girls of Central High series, which, according to ads, tells of "many contested matches on track and field, and on the water," contains remarkably few matches and stresses noncompetitiveness. Before the girls' first basketball match, their team captain tells them, "Good nature wins more games than anything else," and the athletic director cautions, "Play the game for the game's sake—not so much to win" (*GCH*, 153, 149).

Girls are also concerned with outward appearances. While boys' books rarely mention attire—except for a passing delight in the military uniforms of the academy—girls' books include many descriptions of the heroine's outfits and often those of her friends. *Dorothy Dale at Glenwood School* details all of the articles Dorothy receives from friends at a going-away party: "fourteen beautiful dainty little handkerchiefs, four handmade collars, and a darling pink and white linen bag . . . with Dorothy's name done in a tiny green vine, with dots of pale lavendar violets peeping through" (*DDGS*, 121).

Moreover, the girls are quick to appraise the appropriateness of their own and others' attire, and the books speak out against excess. Dorothy Dale's aunt explains to Dorothy's father that "the best dressed girls do not, by any means have more clothes than others. They simply have what is needed" (*DDGS*, 69). In *Betty Gordon at Boarding School* Betty and her friends are highly amused when one girl arrives with five trunks and another with three. They are glad to learn that the headmistress has enough "sense" to insist the girls "send all the trunks home except one apiece."[11] Indeed, the experienced reader can usually identify a book's antagonist by her attire: she is "an expensively dressed girl—almost flashily dressed" or "rather over-dressed" or "dressed up like a little Christmas tree."[12] In contrast, heroines like Dorothy Dale dress simply, as do women presented as role models. At Betty Gordon's school "the exquisitely groomed principal, though always dressed very simply, set them all a high standard."[13]

Some of this criticism of elaborate attire stems from another cause: an injunction against growing up too soon. The protagonists and even the narrator comment adversely on some girls' eagerness to try to be adults while they are still young. The narrator of one book observes that some characters who behave in this fashion "were about as fresh as is a dried prune. They had jumped from childhood into full-blown womanhood (or thought they had), thereby missing the very best and sweetest part of their girls' life."[14]

The Syndicate's girls' series, then, encourage girls to be girls—but with a confused definition of girlhood. On the one hand, the series endorses traditional feminine values: domesticity, concern for appearance, noncompetitiveness, an emphasis on internal (or emotional) matters. Especially in single-character series, a girl's success comes first from weathering her own emotional trials and gaining friends and a more secure place through her endurance, then from helping her friends or the less fortunate. In both types of series, the wrongs girls set right are frequently social or domestic rather than criminal, and their rewards are inner peace and the satisfaction of watching others' joy. At the same time the girls enjoy a generous amount of independence, going away to school, visiting chums on vacations, planning trips about the country. Their activities involve an acceptance of contemporary concerns—everything from athletics to automobiles. The series thus blend the conventional and the contemporary, the everyday and the adventurous—creating the old-fashioned modern girl.

7

Tots' Series

Stratemeyer developed his series for younger children (sometimes called tots' series) in the mid-1910s, and they flourished for a little over a decade. Here Stratemeyer faced an audience with different needs: books that could tell an engaging story without the life-threatening situations common to boys' books or the emotional distress found in girls' series. Instead, tots' series create a cozy world, replete with friendly animals, marvelous toys, and delightful vacation spots. If the protagonists are smaller than their counterparts in other Syndicate series, so are their trials and adventures. Falling into a flour barrel or snowbank, losing a doll or kite (or even oneself)—such misadventures frequently constitute the extent of these children's troubles. Protagonists romp through relatives' homes and farms, stage their own circuses and plays, celebrate birthdays and national holidays, and visit picturesque sites. Tots' series exalt happy families, happy homes, happy lives—and material values. Like other Syndicate series, they offer vicarious success and wish fulfillment, but in the domestic realm; they paint the everyday world as delightful.

Nine of the 14 Syndicate tots' series were developed during the years between 1914 and 1920. Except for the Bobbsey Twins, Stratemeyer's first few series were gender specific, usually had only one protagonist, and could be classified as series for boys or girls (but not both) rather than tots' series. Two of his last creations adopted a variation of this format. The remainder, advertised for both boys and girls, used multiple protagonists, usually an equal number of boys and girls. Unlike Stratemeyer's other works, not all the tots' series use humans as central characters. Animals and even toys act as protagonists, and, accordingly, a few series move into the realm of the fantastic.

The series experienced few changes in the short time they lasted. During their heyday, from 1915 to 1920, the series were most often launched by issuing the first five volumes in one year and two or three volumes annually for the next year or so, so that even short-lived series could run for ten or twelve volumes. As with the girls' group series, the tots' series gradually shifted from having wealthy protagonists to featuring those in families with more moderate incomes. This change does not directly affect the children; they simply have fewer expensive playthings and take less elaborate vacations. The only other distinguishing features between series could easily be attributed to the different ghostwriters rather than to design. Many series draw on conventions Stratemeyer had used before, most notably, the use of siblings as protagonists, travel and different settings, and the concept of helping others by locating lost items or solving minor mysteries.

Syndicate Series

The Bobbsey Twins   Stratemeyer's first series, the Bobbsey Twins (115 volumes, 1904–92) was an auspicious start and stands as one of the Syndicate's most successful creations. In 1937 George Dunlap, cofounder of Grosset & Dunlap, noted that the series had sold 5,600,000 copies, second only to sales for Tom Swift.[1] The early volumes set the tone for the first 30 or 40 years, both in theme and style. The stories overlay wish fulfillment and ego gratification with a veneer of realism, creating a tantalizingly plausible world with the Bobbsey children at its center. This magical-realistic world begins with the twins themselves—two sets, ages four and eight. Flossie and Freddie, the younger pair, are blond and blue-eyed—thus, fluffy and cherubic in appearance, despite their occasional innocent scrapes. The elder two, Nan and Bert, are more responsible and capable and, accordingly, have a more serious aspect: dark-haired and dark-eyed. (No one questioned the genetics involved.)

Using two sets of twins was a brilliant tactic. First, as Bobbie Ann Mason has observed, the use of even one pair of twins "stroke[s] the deepest longings of a child for a soulmate . . . capital[izing] on this desire children have for a mirror-image that talks."[2] Moreover, two sets of twins meant double appeal: younger readers could identify with one set; older readers could be amused at Flossie and Freddie's pranks and misunderstandings, while simultaneously admiring Nan and Bert's calm competence. The younger twins also assume a role similar to that of the best friend in other series—less adept than the protagonists, in need of occasional guidance, and ready to admire or follow the elder children's lead.

The Bobbseys live in an ideal world. They have two parents, as do almost all protagonists in tots' series. Mr. Bobbsey owns a lumber company nearby, next to Lake Metoka, and willingly provides Bert with materials for building iceboats and other contrivances. Mrs. Bobbsey, a housewife, keeps busy with social and charitable activities and also teaches Sunday School. The family employs two live-in servants, a black married couple named Sam and Dinah Johnson. Partway through the first book the twins acquire a cat, Snoop; in the fourth book they find a circus dog, Snap, who, like Snoop, has remained with them throughout the series. All of the adults treat the children with affection and respect, allowing them a great deal of freedom and presenting them with special treats. They are the darlings of the household and possess numerous toys, although they frequently make their own as well. Many children their own ages live in their neighborhood, though, again, they are equally happy with each other and play together cheerfully. Indeed, the heart of the series lies in the twins' enjoyment of whatever activities they are engaged in. Like youngsters in toy commercials, they radiate enthusiasm. Whether they are building snow forts or pasteboard cities, planning a party or a picnic, they set to with an energetic cheer and determination, as if it were the most absorbing activity in the world.

The Bobbsey Twins; or, Merry Days Indoors and Out (1904) introduces the twins and tells of their "haps and mishaps" at home and playing with friends. The second and third books of the series, published three years after the first, extend the twins' idyllic world by adding two sets of relatives. Uncle Daniel and Aunt Sarah have a farm in the country and a son Nan and Bert's age, providing the locale for the second book. Uncle William and Aunt Emily, who live by the seashore with their daughter Dorothy (also Nan and Bert's age), play host to the family in the sequel.

After those trips, six years passed before the next title, *The Bobbsey Twins at School* (1913), appeared: again set in the twins' hometown of Lakeport, it describes their activities during the school year. It also reintroduces a character from the first book, Danny Rugg, the Bobbseys' nemesis. Danny is the typical bully, lifted straight from boys' books; he torments *all* the Bobbsey twins, frightening the younger children, bullying Nan and her friends, and fighting with Bert. He and his friends provide the disruptive elements in the Bobbseys' world—hiding their dog, enticing the young twins into the woods and abandoning them there, stealing ice cream meant for a Halloween party, framing Bert for smoking cigarettes. From then on Danny became a regular in the series, for the Ruggs have an uncanny talent for turning up wherever the Bobbseys go.

Despite Danny, the Bobbseys continue their good times, taking trips to every place imaginable. As Bobbie Ann Mason notes, "The Bobbseys got to do not just one or two thrilling things . . . but *all* the thrilling things" (29). The obligatory snow adventure comes in the fifth volume, when they travel to Snow Lodge. Although the series already included one trip to a water locale, the next volume introduces another—but with typical Bobbsey flair. Rather than journeying *to* water, they travel *on* it, taking a houseboat trip down a river and reuniting a runaway with his family in the bargain. As the series grew more extensive, so did the twins' jaunts and experiences. They sample new technology, going on an airplane trip in 1933 and taking part in a radio play four years later. They travel to Washington, D.C., the West, the Deep South, Plymouth Rock, London Tower—as well as to such picturesquely named spots as Tulip Land, Indian Hollow, Rainbow Valley, and Sugar Maple Hill. In all of these stories, they find places to see, people to help, and usually puzzles to solve.

Even at home the twins' adventures are rarely mundane. In *The Bobbsey Twins at the Circus* (1932) the Bobbseys adopt Waggo, another lost dog—which turns out to be a trained animal that can stand on its forepaws, beat a drum with its tail, play dead, climb a ladder, and "rescue" dolls from a tub of water. After watching the trick dogs at the circus—and refusing a lucrative offer for Waggo—the Bobbseys are ready to stage their own performance, delighting friends and family in true Bobbsey style. In *The Bobbsey Twins' Own Little Railroad* (1951) the twins acquire a toy railroad—not a model train, but an actual miniature railroad with several hundred feet of track—which they are allowed to set up and run on an empty lot. Is it any wonder Bobbie Ann Mason and thousands of others enviously devoured their every adventure?

In later books, the tone changes. The world around the Bobbseys has become faster paced and more sophisticated, as have the Bobbseys. By the 1960s the children have aged slightly—Nan and Bert are 12, and Flossie and Freddie are 6 (even the laws of nature bow to Bobbseys), and like the other Syndicate characters they have become amateur detectives. Earlier books were extensively rewritten or allowed to go out of print; newer titles downplayed domestic adventures in favor of tracking clues or glamorous activities—by the 1980s the twins were even occasionally playing in a rock band. The earlier books were designed to show the quality of the Bobbseys' life; the newer titles, by contrast, concentrate on episodes that advance the mysteries. Rather than moving smoothly between a child's world of play and more grown up situations, the Bobbseys are now obsessed with clues and mysteries. As Mason notes, "There used to be a lot of simple fun in the childlike defense of innocence, but nowadays the twins are super-serious" (46). Some elements from the earlier series remain: the continual traveling, family activities, and phenomenal success—Bobbsey trademarks.

Other Tots' Series   The Kneetime Animal Stories (17 volumes, 1915–22) marked Stratemeyer's first use of animal protagonists. It appeared under the pseudonym Richard Barnum (adults could hardly fail to make the connection with P. T.) and followed the adventures of an anthropomorphic group of animals. Stratemeyer linked titles in the series by adapting a technique used in his Boys of Business books. Although only one creature is the main character of each story, during the course of the narrative he or she meets characters from several of the other books. Thus, in the first book of the series, when Squinty the Comical Pig runs away from the farm, he finds Slicko the Jumping Squirrel (the title character of the next book) in the woods and plays with her for a chapter, before teaming up with Mappo the Merry Monkey (the protagonist of the third book) for another chapter's escapades. Children with good memories or a concern for detail may have found these encounters puzzling, for, at least in the case of Mappo and Squinty, the same meeting is described in both books but many of the details do not coincide.

In a sense, the plots compress the formula used in series with human protagonists. Traditional tots' series frequently start with one book at home, then move the children to different locations in succeeding stories. In the Kneetime Animal series several of the books begin with chapters showing the protagonist at home with his or her family, after which he or she is sold or otherwise changes owners and has several adventures— frequently involving children—in these new surroundings. The animal then runs away and experiences life on her or his own. After a time in the wild, the animal is recaptured or manages to wander back to a former owner and settles down, delighted to have had so many adventures and now to be safe at home. The protagonists thus offer a curious mixture of self-sufficiency and dependence—they are capable of surviving without others' supervision yet eventually they end up back in someone's care, thus underscoring the value of homes and belonging.

Stratemeyer returned to human characters with Bunny Brown and His Sister Sue (20 volumes, 1916–31), near clones of Freddie and Flossie Bobbsey, but introduced a different type of child protagonist in another family series, the Six Little Bunkers (14 volumes, 1918–30). Like the Bobbsey twins, the six little Bunkers are a group of siblings of varying ages and interests. Most of the similarities, however, stop there. The writer behind the Bunkers apparently subscribed to the theory that mischievous, realistic children would be appealing and shaped the six accordingly. Where the Bobbseys are industrious, intelligent, and well behaved, the Bunkers could be aptly renamed the six little terrors—or at

times the six little whiners. The Bobbseys usually play together cheerfully and unselfishly; the Bunkers want to do the same thing at the same
time and require adults to make them share. They seem incapable of
managing for long without causing trouble.

The beginning of *The Six Little Bunkers at Aunt Jo's* (1918) offers an
example of their propensity for misbehavior. At their grandmother's the
children quarrel over who will ride on their raft until their mother tells
them to let the little ones go first, at which suggestion Rose, the eldest
girl, complains. When they learn they have been invited to visit Aunt Jo
in Boston, they are uncertain whether they want to go, since there will
be no pond or farm there. (The Bobbseys always delight at the chance
for new adventures—and never worry about a possible lack of things to
do.) On the boat to Boston, Margy Bunker wanders off to play with a
strange dog and crawls into a stranger's berth to sleep, causing conster-
nation until she is found. No sooner has the family arrived at Aunt Jo's
than Mun Bun (Munroe) and Margy, the two youngest children, put her
dog in the bathtub and turn on the shower. They are discovered when
they begin fighting over whose turn it is to pull the chain and wet the
dog again. Not to be outdone, Russ and Laddie dig a hole in Aunt Jo's
backyard and stick the hose in it for a fountain, soaking the gardener
and making a muddy mess of themselves, the dog, and the yard.

Even the Bunkers' parents seem less pleased with them than Mr. and
Mrs. Bobbsey are with their offspring—understandably so. They frequently tell the children to quiet down, stop asking questions, or leave
them in peace. (To be fair, there are six Bunkers—ages four to eight,
including one set of six-year-old twins—and only four Bobbseys, and the
Bunkers frequently travel without their housekeeper or another adult to
help with the children.) The Bunkers do resemble the Bobbseys in one
respect, however: they have numerous relatives willing to tolerate visits.
Their series is a perpetual round of trips, distributing chaos from one
household to another.

In later series, Stratemeyer continued using siblings as protagonists,
although he apparently decided—rightly so—that six children were too
many. The Four Little Blossoms (7 volumes, 1920–30) reduced the
number by two, and Sunny Boy (14 volumes, 1920–31) used a single
protagonist, a five-year-old dubbed Sunny Boy because "he was nearly
always cheerful."[3]

Three years later Stratemeyer created the female equivalent of Sunny
Boy in Honey Bunch (34 volumes, 1923–55), a long-running series for
young girls. Honey Bunch's real name is Gertrude Marion Morton, but

her adoring parents—and everyone else—prefer to call her Honey Bunch, a tribute to her sweet nature. Simply put, Honey Bunch is a perfect child, leading a perfect life. Bobbie Ann Mason describes her as a "little girl with grown-up manners and goldilocks {who} never {gets} her chambray and challis dresses dirty" and who "is capable and serious at age five—the 'grandest' little housekeeper and a 'capital little nurse.'. . . . She does everything an ideal child is supposed to do, and she follows all the rules" (3, 20–21). Not only do her parents dote on her but so does everyone else—friends, relatives, even people she meets while traveling. On her first visit to New York, in book 2, she chats with a train conductor who still remembers her affectionately six books later when she and her parents embark for Bermuda. Honey Bunch's life is—literally—a continual series of firsts: all but the initial and last two titles in the series begin *Honey Bunch: Her First . . .* (*. . . Auto Tour, . . . Days on the Farm*, etc.).

As Mason notes, in many ways Honey Bunch is already closer to being an adult than a child, despite her youth. She carries her domestic world with her wherever she goes, so that even the unfamiliar becomes a backdrop for routine activities. On an auto tour, she takes pleasure in caring for the toys she has brought along, helping her mother set the table for meals, and playing with children she has met at previous campsites. She is even the perfect tourist: wherever she travels, she remembers to send postcards to all her friends back home.

Like the Bobbseys, Honey Bunch is able to make simple activities seem entrancing, bathed in a special light. Washing her dolls' clothes, packing for a trip, playing zoo with her friends—all seem the most engaging pastimes imaginable. Sometimes the ordinary actually does become extraordinary: in *Honey Bunch: Her First Little Garden* (1924) Honey Bunch is busily preparing her own litle garden plot when a stranger, charmed by the sight, promises her some seeds to plant. They turn out to be prize winning snapdragons, leading to Honey Bunch's first little ribbon at the flower show.

Part of the special aura surrounding Honey Bunch comes from the narrator's tone, presenting a child's-eye view of life. Bobbie Ann Mason points out that the books capture the seriousness with which children view themselves and their world and their attempts to make sense of unfamiliar words and adult situations (26–27). While grown-ups occasionally laugh at Honey Bunch's misconceptions, the narrator presents them as logical conclusions. Moreover, people in the books—even adults—take Honey Bunch very seriously, paying attention to her comments, explaining puzzling things, treating her respectfully, and including her in their activities. She, in turn, responds by emulating them and participating in their world. Honey Bunch rarely misbehaves: her adventures lie in her daily activities, her inclusion in an adult world (and her misunderstandings of same), her efforts to help others, and her peripheral involvement in others' mischief.

Honey Bunch was an unusual series, for it not only lasted over 30 years, long after all but the Bobbsey Twins had been discontinued, but two years after its conclusion it underwent a metamorphosis and reemerged as Honey Bunch and Norman (12 volumes, 1957–63). Norman, the mischievous boy next door, had played a part in most of the original series, even becoming a title character for the last two volumes, *Honey Bunch and Norman Ride with the Sky Mailman* (1954) and *Honey Bunch and Norman Visit Beaver Lodge* (1955), which were reissued as part of the new series.

Stratemeyer's last tots' series was his most unusual and least successful, although at least some of the fault lies with the unknown writer. The Flyaways (3 volumes, 1925)—Ma and Pa and their two children, Susie and Tommy—are "part real and part fairy" and thus can travel to fairyland and meet characters from fairy tales. Advertisements for the first volume explained that it tells "how the Flyaways went to visit Cinderella only to find that Cinderella's Prince had been carried off by the Three Robbers, Rumbo, Hibo, and Jobo. 'I'll rescue him!' cried Pa Flyaway and then set out for the stronghold of the robbers." The idea may have been charming; the execution—an all too apt term in this case—is not.

The description indicates one problem: the adults play prominent roles in the plots, with the children assisting rather than initiating the action. Poor writing only makes a bad situation worse. Ma and Pa Flyaway are, at best, absurd caricatures. Ma "loved three things": children, cooking, "and dress[ing] in silks and satins and pretend[ing] she was a Fairy Godmother or a Queen."[4] Pa likes "carpentering" and what he calls "'fairylanding'. . . hop[ping] astride his motorcycle, perhaps with Tommy and Susie on the rear seat, or [taking] the whole family in his motorboat, his airship, or his automobile, and [going] to some fairyland" (*FC*, 5).

Kept in check, these could have been character traits, but the writer exaggerates them—and everything else—to unbelievable proportions. Even the preceding excerpt shows one example: Pa Flyway owns not just an auto but also a motorcycle, a motorboat, and an airplane. Similarly, in the first scene Ma's idea of baking is making "four more chocolate cakes, seven lemon pies, five pans of pudding, and three dozen doughnuts" (*FC*, 5). The foursome rush about in hastily described adventures, dominated by Ma's culinary activities and Pa's efforts to rescue people or do carpentry. The stories suffer from excess—too much food, too many possessions, too many fairy tale characters jumbled together, too many quick adventures. Ironically, what ruins the tales is an overdose of the same element that makes Stratemeyer's other series so successful—wish fulfillment, catering to the reader's desire for exotic adventures and material goods. Here, everything comes so fast and so effortlessly that the reader is sated long before the story is over. Rather than elevating the formula, it reveals the underlying greed.

The series was a sad finale to Stratemeyer's excursions into tots' series. Although he added titles to some existing series, no new series for children appeared during his lifetime, and all but two had ended by the year following his death. After 1930, the few tots' series the Syndicate developed all stressed mystery.

Themes and Traits

Tots' series offer contrasting images of the world. The predominant image is of cheerful, contented families leading lives bounded on all sides by security and abundance. Children have all they could wish for and more: loving families, ample food and possessions, numerous vacation spots, and the leisure to enjoy them. Adults exist to make their lives easier and more pleasant, a task aided by the children themselves, who are almost chronically incapable of being bored or out-of-sorts. They fill their days with toys and travel and seem surrounded by a special radiance, blessed by fortune. Their success, if it can be called that, lies in the nature of their existence. They are born into lives that guarantee them three things: emotional security, or being loved by family; material bounty, or having and perpetually receiving good things; and continual activity, or doing interesting things and visiting different places.

However, not everyone in series books leads such a rosy life. The protagonists regularly meet or hear of others whose lives differ radically from their own—orphans, families living in poverty, working children. Living lives shaped by want and loss, these characters appear regularly in secondary roles or brief mentions. Never do the books suggest that such misfortunes could befall the protagonists. Instead, the role of the less fortunate characters seems twofold: they subtly reinforce the protagonists' good fortune, and they serve as recipients of their assistance or charity.

Happy Families   To begin at the simplest level, tots' series apotheosize families—happy, secure families. Considering the time period when the books were written, it is not surprising that no divorced parents appear in them; however, given the typical family in series for older children, it is noteworthy that no protagonists in tots' series come from single-parent families. They have two healthy parents, devoted to their well-being. Moreover, once a series has begun its nuclear family remains the same throughout: parents never alter the family structure by separating or dying or even having babies.

Life within the family is, if not idyllic, quite near that. Series parents are usually all-wise, all-patient, all-good, and all-accommodating. They neither belittle their children nor view them with anything except loving tolerance; they grant requests readily and take care to avoid disappointing them. The books are filled with examples of parents striving to please children. After the Bobbseys see a merry-go-round being transported to the county fair, the younger twins excitedly plan to ride it. Nan intervenes, saying, "The Bolton fair is a long way off," but Flossie trustingly responds, "Daddy will take us."[5] Even though doing so involves taking a trip lasting several days, Mr. Bobbsey agrees.

Indeed, at times parents seem almost too tolerant. In *The Six Little Bunkers at Cousin Tom's* (1918) the Bunkers are hurrying to board a ship when Margy Bunker spots a kitten, lets go of her sister's hand, and rushes off to chase it. The kitten darts under a fruit stand, and Margy kneels on the dirty sidewalk to follow. Her mother calls, "Margaret Bunker, get right up off your knees this instant! You'll spoil your clean white stockings! Get up!"[6] Deliberately ignoring her, Margy follows the kitten and is retrieved only when her father reaches under the stand and pulls her out. She insists on keeping the kitten and cries when told it does not belong to her. Rather than punishing her, her parents allow the man in charge of the fruit stand to placate her with an orange. Margy never apologizes for her behavior or gives any indication she realizes her actions were wrong, nor do her parents reprimand her.

Siblings also coexist harmoniously. Children occasionally disagree but never go beyond minor squabbles, which are quickly resolved. Younger children acknowledge the authority of their older siblings and view them as surrogate parents, problem solvers, and protectors. Older children, in turn, accept responsibility for younger ones. Bunny Brown's mother has often told him to "take good care of little Sue," and he takes this charge very seriously.[7] He "always watched over and protected her when they went out in wintry weather"; indeed, "you seldom saw Bunny without seeing Sue not far away."[8] The Bobbseys have a similar relationship. The older twins, especially Nan, automatically assume responsibility for the care and amusement of their younger siblings, even when it limits their own activities. When the foursome attend a church picnic in *The Bobbsey Twins at the County Fair* (1922), Nan forgoes playing with girls her own age to stay with Flossie and Freddie. Bert, heading off for a game of baseball with his friends, promises he will return later and take the younger children on the lake.

The sense of family, however, goes deeper than that, for protagonists belong to large families. Aunts, uncles, grandparents, and cousins all welcome them into their homes for extended visits, plan special outings to amuse them, and readily forgive minor and major transgressions. Visiting his grandparents, Sunny Boy uses paper from his grandfather's desk to make a kite and learns—after it is lost—that the "paper" was two $500 Liberty bonds. Grandpa is distraught over the loss of the money, a significant part of his savings, but tells Sunny Boy, "Never mind, Sunny. . . . You didn't mean to lose the bonds . . . so we'll just stop crying over spilled milk and cheer up and be happy again" (*SBC*, 125). No matter what the children do, they are certain to receive gentle treatment and continuing love. (The kite is eventually found in the last chapter, undamaged, the writer apparently having forgotten about the rain four chapters before.)

Material Values   A significant part of the children's security comes not just from having families but from their comfortable financial status. Bobbie Ann Mason notes that series books "celebrate materialist values" (25). The families operate within a white, middle-class ethic and endorse traditional values, including consumerism. A more than adequate income makes their lifestyles and vacations possible and shelters them from the type of misfortunes others face. Parents never lack funds and, at times, seem to buy their way across the country, stopping in hotels and restaurants and paying farmers for fresh milk, produce, and baked goods. Several of the series children—most notably, the Bobbsey twins, Bunny Brown and his sister Sue, Honey Bunch, and Sunny Boy—have all they could possibly want and more.

The basics, food and clothing, are always available, with replenishments in reserve should they be needed. When Sunny Boy starts kindergarten, his mother takes him downtown to purchase a lovely winter coat, which is stolen from school the first day he wears it. No matter—

she soon replaces it with another. After Honey Bunch's cousin Stub ruins two dresses in one day, Honey Bunch's mother arranges a shopping trip and buys her two more.

As for food, parents and housekeepers provide not only regular meals but afternoon snacks—usually milk and freshly baked cookies, pie, or cake. Holidays signal especially lavish celebrations, complete with detailed descriptions of meals. The Bobbsey twins' Halloween party, which is combined with a birthday party for Flossie and Freddie, boasts "two large cakes—one at either end of the table. . . . On one cake was the name *Flossie*. The other was marked *Freddie*. The names were in pink icing on top of the white frosting that covered the cakes."[9] Before tackling cake and ice cream, however, the children eat "platefuls of delicious creamed chicken, mashed potato, and peas" (*BTS*, 106). Just as children's families are always happy, so, too, are meals always tasty. No series child sits down to a dinner of spinach or leftover meatloaf, or ever leaves the table hungry.

Acquisition—that is, being given nice things by other people—figures largely in the books. Food and clothing are one part of this, presents another. Sometimes the pleasure seems to come not in consuming but merely in receiving. In the first Honey Bunch book, Honey Bunch's fifth birthday is a momentous occasion: the celebrations cover two full chapters. Her day begins with five kisses apiece from her parents and a "brand new blue [cereal] bowl" from Mrs. Miller, the housekeeper. Her mother tells her, "Daddy and I decided you would have a better time if you didn't have all your presents at once. They are hidden around the house."[10] In the course of the morning, she finds a gold locket and chain, a doll's trunk with a small doll and numerous doll clothes, "a set of doll's furniture," hair ribbons, and "a glass jar of candy" (*HBJLG*, 148–53). Friends of the family send her a "pretty blue sweater" and a sweater and cap for her doll (*HBJLG*, 150). Her best friend gives her "a set of celluloid animals" and "a rag dog, a rag cat and two rag puppies and two rag kittens" similar to a set Honey Bunch has admired (*HBJLG*, 155–56).

In addition to birthdays and Christmas celebrations, children acquire presents for no particular reason or as special treats. At the start of *Four Little Blossoms and Their Winter Fun* (1920) the younger children are eagerly awaiting their mother and aunt's return from town, for, as Twaddles tells his older siblings, "They're going to bring us something nice. They promised."[11] The day before Sunny Boy starts school, his father brings him a "shining silver pencil with [a] box of leads."[12]

The children must own a truly overwhelming assortment of toys; ironically, however, they are rarely seen playing with them. Instead, they make their own playthings or play games requiring simple objects. Honey Bunch and her cousins play hide-and-seek and pretend-zoo and use rags from the scrap bag to cut out cloth figures of animals. Sunny Boy hauls out an old box to stand on to play traffic policeman. Indeed, *Sunny Boy and His Games* (1923) is not about Sunny Boy's toys but about a series of different games he invents, most involving wordplay or imagination rather than material objects. The unimportance of toys is underscored each time children go on vacation: several books include a scene where a child brings out numerous playthings and is told to select one or two small items—and after doing so never misses the rest.

The trips themselves suggest both the children's importance to their relatives and the adults' concern for their happiness. Unlike nineteenth-century characters, who travel extensively to learn about other countries, children in Syndicate series go on trips to have fun and to enable relatives to see them. Each of the first four books in the Six Little Bunkers series contains a specific statement about how the children will enjoy themselves on their visits. When the children wonder whether they will enjoy visiting their aunt in the city, their mother reassures them that "Aunt Jo wouldn't ask us to spend two weeks or more at her house if she didn't know you children could have fun."[13]

A related reason for travel is the parents' reluctance to be separated from their offspring, a feeling that, again, is connected with their desire to please the children. Many of the Bobbseys' trips occur because Mr. Bobbsey is called away and brings the family. When business summons him to London, it is unthinkable that he would go alone. Instead, he brings the entire family so they can enjoy foreign sights, although they spend considerably more time sleuthing than absorbing British culture. Similarly, when the Lumber Association decides to hold its convention in San Francisco, the children ask if he will take them along, and he and Mrs. Bobbsey willingly agree. The scenery in and around San Francisco receives only cursory mention—one and a half pages for commentary on the sequoia trees, followed by the comment, "These giant trees, together with many other interesting sights, kept the Bobbseys entertained while their father was busy at the convention."[14] After that, the convention concludes and the family travels to an Arizona ranch where technology—in the form of a motion picture being filmed—absorbs the twins' interest.

Along with an ample supply of material goods the protagonists have generous amounts of leisure time. None of the protagonists are employed—or even have regular household chores, music lessons, or other commitments that preclude or interfere with their hours for play. The exception, of course, is school attendance, and even that can be flexible. Apparently none of the six little Bunkers go to school, even though the elder two are seven and eight, for the first four books span July through December and the family spends the entire time visiting different relatives.

The Less Fortunate   Throughout their travels, series children encounter and sometimes help others who have experienced misfortune. One such set of troubles involves family problems, a sharp contrast to the protagonists' happy lives. In *The Bobbsey Twins at Snow Lodge* the twins stay at a winter lodge owned by a man who believes his nephew, whom he has loved like a son, stole from him. Uncle and nephew have not spoken for years, nor will either enter the lodge, which held so many happy memories. They finally reconcile when the Bobbseys discover the missing money. In such cases, the protagonists resolve the adults' problems, but more by chance than by design. At Snow Lodge a tree falls during a snowstorm, smashing a wall and revealing the lost money.

Other children lack—or only belatedly acquire—the supportive family networks that series characters possess. The Bobbseys, especially in the early books, befriend other children whose lives differ drastically from their own. In the second book, when the twins visit their aunt and uncle in the country, they meet city children at a fresh air camp who have no such relatives to host their visits. The family even considers adopting one little boy whose father has had to give him up because he cannot afford a housekeeper to care for him. In the sixth and seventh books of the series, as well as in several others, the children shelter runaway orphans who have fled harsh guardians.

The necessity for helping others through charity is a recurring motif in the books, sometimes occupying a large part of the story, other times consigned to a few paragraphs. The world's poor provide the incentive (or excuse) for the children to stage numerous fund-raising activities. *Bunny Brown and His Sister Sue Giving a Show* (1919) centers on Bunny's efforts to stage a children's show for charity—though he is less concerned with which organization receives the money than with the excitement of planning and acting in the affair; he even changes the designated charity partway through the book.

Holidays also prompt benevolent acts. Thanksgiving, especially, is regularly associated with gifts of food. In *The Bobbsey Twins at School* the Bobbseys' mother tells them,

> "When daddy heard about several families in Lakeport who have had hard luck this winter and weren't going to have the kind of Thanksgiving dinner we are, what do you think he did?"
> "Bought them turkeys," guessed Nan.
> "Yes," said Mrs. Bobbsey, "and celery, cranberries, sweet potatoes, onions, turnips, everything! And we'll send them mince pies made by our own Dinah Johnson." (*BTS*, 132)

When children in Sunny Boy's kindergarten are asked to bring food for Thanksgiving baskets, Sunny Boy selects an assortment of vegetables from his parents' cellar, then decides to bring some coal, too, so the recipients "could sell it and buy a turkey" (*SBSO*, 154). None of these donations, however, involves the protagonists' deprivation. They do not have less to eat because of their contribution, nor, in fact, do they actually pay for the food.

Occasionally, the children do make some sacrifices to help the less fortunate. Vacationing in New York, Honey Bunch spots a neighbor's runaway monkey at the zoo and insists on giving the $50 reward to the zookeeper's children. She explains to her uncle that the children "don't have much fun" and have to wear secondhand clothes; she and her cousins already have nice things, so it is better that the other children should have the money.[15]

Working children also appear regularly in series books. The Bobbseys always have a grand time at the county fair, and during each visit they stop to see Bob, a boy they met earlier. He, too, is at the fair—working full-time running the merry-go-round. Although his job might sound exciting, the book makes it clear that Bob's life is an unhappy one. His guardian is a cross, greedy man; Bob even tries running away, but his guardian finds and reclaims him, not from affection but for the boy's work value. Sometimes such children are eventually helped. (The Bobbseys' uncle adopts Bob and takes him to live on a farm.)

In other cases, however, these children continue to work, without question. Bunny and Sue Brown's mother takes in two child actors, orphans who were left stranded when their company folded. Doing so is certainly a charitable act; nevertheless, Mr. Brown puts the boy to work at his boat and fish business, and the girl assists Mrs. Brown with the housekeeping. Eventually the Browns trace the children's aunt and uncle, also traveling performers, and the two children plan to join them, presumably as members of their troupe. The difference between these children and those who are helped by the protagonists is that they apparently have kind or sympathetic employers. Indeed, in tots' and other Syndicate series the nature of the employer rather than the age of the child usually determines whether the child remains employed.[16] Although the books rarely make a direct comparison, it seems ironic that the only thing standing between the protagonists' lives and those of other characters is the continued health and financial success of their parents.

The books clearly portray a class society, with the protagonists in one group and numerous needy people, including children, in another. Sometimes this division serves as a convenient plot device. In early series books, unlike more contemporary ones, the children's role is more restrained: they do not track adult criminals or engage in sleuthing that could place them in dangerous situations. Encountering others who are in need or suffering thus adds drama to the story while still insulating the protagonists. It also allows them—in conjunction with the adults in their family—to help others and resolve problems, providing a plot or subplot as both a dramatic and a unifying device.

Such plots were occasionally necessary to add spice to the series, for tots' series depict a cozy world, one designed to cater to young readers' dreams of having fun and to avoid disturbing them with the kind of menacing characters and situations found in other Syndicate series. The near-idyllic environments filled with loving relatives, caring strangers, and countless material pleasures offer readers security and wish fulfillment. There are always good things to eat, nice presents to open, interesting games to try, novel places to see. The protagonists lead busy lives, traveling, playing, and occasionally helping others, while readers vicariously share their fun. In addition to the satisfaction derived from the stories themselves, tots' series provided younger children with an introduction to series fiction—including watered-down versions of older characters' concerns—and prepared them for more adventurous books as they grew older.

8

Mystery Series

In retrospect, the most surprising thing about Stratemeyer's mystery series is the late date at which they emerged, for Stratemeyer had toyed with the genre from his dime novels onward. Boys in his early career stories regularly set out to restore their family fortunes by finding proof of others' deceit, and those in later series track villains who abscond with their possessions, inventions, or girlfriends. Girls and children locate lost items, unearthing everything from family heirlooms to missing relatives. However, it was not until 1927 that Stratemeyer introduced a juvenile series that placed mysteries at the core of the story, laying the foundation for the works that would keep Syndicate fiction a household product for well over half a century.

Focusing on mysteries allowed Stratemeyer to continue a number of themes he was already comfortable with—perpetual travel and excitement, helping others, confrontations with villainous types, tangible success—and simultaneously to justify it with detection. Rather than stumbling on mysteries or informally investigating for a friend, mystery series protagonists eagerly seek puzzles and develop reputations as amateur sleuths. Each case adds to their renown and brings further requests.

For the boys, sleuthing entails the same hazardous situations found in other series; the characters themselves do not alter appreciably, except for their stated interest in solving mysteries. For girls, detecting permits an advance into slightly more dangerous terrain, although they still face lesser menaces than do their male counterparts. Accordingly, female characters display more independence and assertiveness than their predecessors. They also no longer begin in misery or poverty but in comfortable surroundings that allow ready access to the resources needed for their sleuthing.

The Hardy Boys

In 1927 Stratemeyer began the first of two series that would introduce three generations of readers to the joys of mystery stories and outshine and outsell all his previous creations. That series, of course, was the

Hardy Boys. In conjunction with Nancy Drew, the Hardy Boys series accounts for over half of the Syndicate's estimated sales of roughly 200,000,000 copies. Both inspired countless imitators (none of which have attained similar success) and made their characters household names. Scholars have analyzed the books, examining everything from cultural messages to reasons for their popularity; children simply read them and return to the library or bookstore for more.

Leslie McFarlane was the ghostwriter behind most of the first 25 volumes of the Hardy Boys series (117 volumes, as of 1992, 1927–). In his autobiography, McFarlane explains that although he had penned many of the Dave Fearless volumes quickly, he adopted a different approach with the Hardys, striving for a better quality of writing and incorporating humor and other touches to reach boys. His efforts were successful, and many older readers consider the McFarlane titles the best in the series.

As reviewers have noted, the Hardy boys lead lives designed to thrill young readers; their everyday lives are filled with exciting mysteries to solve. The protagonists are two brothers, Frank Hardy, "a tall, dark-haired boy of sixteen," and 15-year-old Joe, "pink cheeked with fair curly hair and blue eyes."[1] Frank is sometimes described as the leader and the more serious of the two, typical of older siblings in Stratemeyer's fiction, but this trait is more evident in the narrator's descriptions than in the boys' actions. The brothers live with their parents, the "internationally famous detective" Fenton Hardy and his wife, Laura, in the town of Bayport, on Barmet Bay near the Atlantic Coast.

Frank and Joe first ride into sight on a pair of motorcycles, introducing a trademark of the series—mobility via fast, modern transportation. The Hardy boys own their own motorcycles, car, speedboat (appropriately named *Sleuth*), and iceboat; in later books they hop aboard planes to track cases across the country or around the world.

The vehicles alone would have been enough to inspire envy in bicycle-bound readers, but they were only one element of the Hardys' life. Far more important and alluring were the mysteries and adventures encountered at every turn. The first sentence of the first book introduces the boys' interest and, more crucial, their skill at detecting: Frank announces to Joe, "After the help we gave dad in that forgery case I guess he'll begin to think we *could* be detectives when we grow up" (*TT*, 1). These traits—the desire and ability to detect—remain a central part of the Hardy Boys books and subsequent Syndicate mystery series.

The Hardys' connection with crime comes largely through their father's work. Bayport plays host to droves of criminals, a situation exacerbated, of course, by Fenton Hardy's fame—those in need of help come to Bayport seeking him out, bringing their pursuers along with them. Although the Hardy boys are still in high school, they are kept busy investigating some of their own mysteries and aiding their father with his work. The two often fortuitously dovetail; no sooner do the boys uncover a suspicious character than they learn he is also a suspect in their father's current case.

In *Rascals at Large* (1971), a nostalgic look at series books, Arthur Prager summarizes the five stages of a typical Hardy Boys mystery. First, the boys either notice a suspicious character or are asked to handle a case for their father. Next comes a warning to stay out of things, a common event in juvenile mystery series. Phase two, marked by "fortuitous coincidence," such as spotting suspicious characters or otherwise acquiring additional information (but not evidence to convict), leads them to phase three, which Prager simply calls "trouble."[2] The boys pursue the criminals, occasionally engaging in violent confrontations as the villains try to evade them. After gradually closing in on them or their hideout, the fourth stage unfolds: the Hardys are captured by those they have been pursuing. The final stage covers the boys' escape, the capture of the criminals, and the reward (Prager, 116–22). This last stage involves a triple triumph: moral victory, with wrongdoers punished for their misdeeds and property or other items restored to their rightful owners; emotional gratification, with friends, family, and former victims gratefully and enthusiastically praising the boys' talents; and financial acknowledgment, usually in the form of a monetary reward.

Carol Billman concurs with Prager's outline but adds that the Hardy Boys mysteries are generally more complex. They involve multiple plots, which Billman calls a "trademark" of the series (88). Early chapters gradually introduce several different puzzles—Billman notes that *The Mystery of the Chinese Junk* (1960) contains five mysteries—all of which eventually dovetail. As Billman puts it, "What keeps readers guessing . . . is not so much the outcome of each as the interconnection that will inevitably tie together the disparate threads" (88). Billman also explains that the series combines elements of the adventure story with those of the mystery. Unlike Nancy Drew's environment, the Hardy boys' world is often an outdoor one filled with caves, islands, cliffs, and forests.

A synopsis of the first book of the series, *The Tower Treasure* (1927), gives an idea of the types of criminals the Hardys encounter and the way the series blends adventure and mystery. The story begins when a red-haired man in a speeding car practically forces the Hardys over a cliff on a narrow road. Later, they find the car wrecked in a ditch. When their friend Chet Morton announces that his roadster has been stolen, they theorize that the red-haired man took it. The only problem is that witnesses claim a man with *dark* hair used the yellow roadster for an abortive robbery at the local steamboat office.

While the boys are puzzling over this contradiction, they learn that the Applegate mansion outside of town has been robbed. The caretaker, the father of another of their friends, is the only suspect. Hurd Applegate hires Mr. Hardy to find the thief, and the boys accompany him on a fruitless search of the mansion. Later, picnicking outside of town with their friends, the boys spot Chet's abandoned roadster and uncover a red wig hidden in the brush.

Mr. Hardy traces the wig and finds that it was stolen by Red Jackley, a dark-haired thief with a penchant for wearing red wigs. Mr. Hardy pursues Red, who, while fleeing, is mortally injured in an accident and hospitalized in another town. The town's inept policemen decide to interview Jackley, hoping to solve the mystery and claim the $1,000 reward offered by Applegate. As police, they have first rights at interrogating the prisoner, but Mr. Hardy worries that they will botch the interview and the prisoner will die without giving any useful information.

The Hardy boys tell their friends of the situation, and Chet devises an ingenious—albeit morally questionable—plan. He distracts Rocco, an Italian vendor, while Tony Prito places a box with a ticking clock under Rocco's fruit stand. Chet and Tony convince Rocco he is in danger from the Black Hand just before he discovers the package. Panicked, Rocco summons Chief Collig and Detective Smuff—neither of whom will touch the ticking box. At length they find Officer Con Riley, who is blissfully unaware of the imagined danger, and order him to dunk the package in water. By this time the police have missed the train and Fenton Hardy is able to question the dying man.

The mystery is not over yet: Jackley claims he hid the stolen items "in the old tower," yet a search of both the old and new towers in the Applegate mansion fails to turn up anything. Despondent, the Hardy boys decide to relax with a picnic out in the country. There Frank spots an old railroad tower and recalls that Jackley had worked for the railroad. He looks at Joe, who has just had a similar idea. The two clamber up the tower and discover the treasure, solving their first case, exonerating their friend's father, and claiming the $1,000 reward.

While the case lacks some of the stages in Prager's summary—it is one of the few in which the Hardys are not captured by criminals or even actively menaced—it does illustrate the use of lesser mysteries to contribute to a larger one, as well as the tremendous amount of action and touches of humor typical of this series. Incident follows incident as the boys stumble on yet another puzzle or uncover promising clues, while the reader races toward the solution. Additionally, as the synopsis shows, *The Tower Treasure* may take its title from the robbery at the mansion, but much of the action occurs in and around the country-side—on narrow roads near cliffs, in tangled underbrush, and in fields outside of town.

The Tower Treasure also introduces a number of regular characters in the series. The Hardys' most constant companion is Chet Morton, the traditional overweight chum who serves as a comic figure. The Hardys' other friends include "Biff" Hooper, so named "because of his passion for boxing"; Phil Cohen, whose surname suggests Semitic ancestry (although the books never specifically make the connection); and Tony Prito, who is "the son of a prosperous Italian building contractor" and has "not yet been in America long enough to talk the language without an accent," but who is also "quick and good-natured" (*TT*, 130). (Given the criticisms leveled at the Syndicate for negative racial and ethnic stereotypes, this is a surprisingly multicultural group.)

In 1959 the Syndicate began revising its top two series. By then advances in technology and changes in the culture had left the early volumes outdated. The revisions encompassed all titles written prior to 1959 (1957 for Nancy Drew); the project ran through 1973. The newer versions removed many of the racial and ethnic slurs and updated the styles, landscapes, and characters' life-styles and possessions to appeal to a new generation of readers. The stories were also streamlined: their length was reduced by 15 to 20 percent, making many older readers nostalgic for the older versions. In some cases, the revisions resulted in entirely new texts because the entire plot premise was deemed obsolete, as in *The Flickering Torch Mystery* (1943), which originally concerned the development of artificial rubber.

In commenting on the new versions, one critic noted a "toning down of excess," whether it be violence, eccentricities, or ethnicity.[3] Guns and references to violence have decreased, as have unflattering descriptions of many supporting and peripheral characters. Fenton Hardy, who is some-what aloof in the early books, becomes more genial; Tony Prito loses his accent; Joe's girlfriend, Iola Morton, loses weight. Joe, who previously had "mumbled and muttered" while talking to Iola, finally becomes comfortable with girls and "dated her regularly." Sadly, the revised versions, though commendably devoid of offensive stereotypes, suffer from an appalling blandness in everything from characters to writing style.

In 1987, in an attempt to woo older readers, Simon & Schuster, which had purchased the Stratemeyer Syndicate, issued a second Hardy Boys series, which ran concurrently with the original series. The first book in the Hardy Boys Casefiles (70 volumes, as of 1992, 1987–), *Dead on Target* (1987), introduced more changes for the boys. They begin on the first page of the book when the brothers' car explodes sky-high—instantly killing Iola Morton. The greatest change, however, is in the boys themselves. The books no longer mention specific ages, although Tony Prito, their high school chum, now manages a pizza parlor, implying that the boys have graduated at long last. Their actions on cases—and the type of danger they encounter—are as sophisticated and adult as those that characterize the adventures of James Bond or any other agent, except that the Hardys do not kill people and generally avoid carrying guns. Although the boys remain amateur sleuths, they now help Network, a U.S. intelligence unit, on some cases. However, their lives outside of their cases still suggests adolescence: they live at home, their relationships with girls never go beyond kisses, they do not drink, and their attitude toward recreation and vacations suggests, at best, the interests of college-aged boys.

As Iola's death indicates, violence in the stories has escalated; the brothers are now tracking murderers, members of international terrorist groups, and the like. High technology abounds, and it is used by both sides. In the first book, a stranger gives the brothers his business cards, which turn out to be sophisticated tracking devices. Frank has become a computer hacker and uses his skills to break into the enemy's computers.

Despite the changes, or perhaps because of them, the stories are highly readable, at least to readers unaccustomed to the original series. (Those who remember the early series with affection sometimes find the new one a shocking change; after it appeared, a number of newspaper articles came out discussing the radical difference between the two series.) Some are actually true mysteries, that is, the brothers' instincts are not enough to solve the crimes. No longer do criminals look the part. While fast action and continual pursuit—now international—remain integral parts of the series, the identity of the criminal remains undetectable until the mystery is solved. Others resemble adventure stories: the boys are repeatedly captured and the reader waits to see what ingenious plan they will devise to escape. Whichever approach the books take, they present a pair of thoroughly contemporary boys who retain their courage, quick wits, and love of mysteries, though they have traveled a long way from the motorcycling pair who discovered the Tower Treasure.

Nancy Drew Mystery Stories

Like the Hardy Boys, the Nancy Drew Mystery Stories (110 volumes, as of 1992, 1930–) have proved astonishingly popular and long-lived. By the 1980s over 80,000,000 copies of the books featuring the "venerable sleuth," as she is often called, had been sold, with sales in the 1970s and 1980s of close to 1,000,000 copies annually (Billman, 100). Her adventures have been translated into various European and Scandinavian languages (as has the Hardy Boys series), and articles about her appear on both sides of the Atlantic. Most of the first 25 volumes were ghostwritten by Mildred Wirt Benson; those she did not write were handled by Walter Karig. Harriet Adams and an assortment of ghostwriters worked on later titles.

Nancy Drew first appeared in *The Secret of the Old Clock* (1930) as "a pretty girl of sixteen" with a "curly golden bob," which, in later books, turned to "titian hair," despite most cover artists' determined portrayal of her as a blonde. She lives with her father, Carson Drew, "a noted criminal and mystery-case lawyer" in the midwestern town of River Heights.[4] Ironically for a series that began in the 1930s, Nancy Drew has greater freedom than the Hardy boys do. She is already out of school; she still lives at home, but since her father is often away and the household is run by the housekeeper, Hannah Gruen, Nancy is left largely in control of her own time and activities.

Like the Hardys, Nancy's connection and assistance with mysteries comes partly through her father. He frequently provides her with background information on cases, suggests areas for further investigation, and refers cases to her that he is too busy to handle. He also treats her with great respect, discussing cases and allowing her to sit in on sessions with clients, assuring them of her ability to keep information confidential. His status also serves her well: upon learning that she is Carson Drew's daughter, officials regard her with respect and allow her entry into areas closed to others.

Nancy's career begins in *The Secret of the Old Clock* when she foils a group of thieves robbing summer houses and discovers a will, hidden in the clock, that bequeaths a sizable inheritance to a number of deserving, courteous folk instead of a wealthy, ill-bred family. She accepts the clock as a souvenir of the case, which is an excellent start to her career and leads to her second mystery, *The Hidden Staircase* (1930), classic Nancy Drew.

A synopsis of *The Hidden Staircase* shows the type of mystery Nancy typically encounters. She is alone in the house when Nathan Gombet, a man with an "unpleasant face," "sharp, piercing eyes," and "ill-fitting," out-of-date clothing enters and pushes past her to Carson Drew's room, ignoring her protests and insisting that Carson has papers belonging to him.[5] When Nancy springs to the phone, ready to call the police, he leaves, telling her, "Your father ain't seen the last o' this" (*HS*, 10). Immediately afterwards, Allie Horner, one of the beneficiaries from *The Secret of the Old Clock*, stops by. She knows Gombet and tells Nancy he is a dishonest man.

That evening, Gombet returns, claiming that the land commission underpaid him for property he had sold them and demanding $10,000. He is still uttering threats when Carson puts him out, after vainly trying to explain that Gombet had received a fair price.

The next day, visiting another of the beneficiaries from her previous case, Nancy meets an old woman, Rosemary Turnbull, who has heard of Nancy's detective work and begs for her help. Rosemary and her sister Floretta live in a mansion, "not unlike a ruined castle," that recently has exhibited signs of being haunted (*HS*, 42). Nancy agrees to investigate but refuses payment. Since Carson Drew will soon be going out of town for a week, she decides to stay at the Turnbull mansion during his absence but tells no one of her plans. Consequently, she is astonished to receive a warning in the mail, telling her to "keep away from the Turnbull house" (*HS*, 63).

Undaunted, Nancy moves into the mansion, and her "presence . . . [has] a wholesome effect" on the sisters, who had been unnerved by the strange goings-on. She begins examining the "fifteen large rooms" in the house, looking for secret passages or evidence of recent entry, and spends the next few days in a fruitless search. A "blood-curdling yell" awakens her one night, and she and the Turnbulls find that a family heirloom, a valuable silver urn, has disappeared from the library (*HS*, 79). No one is in sight, and there are no clues to the identity of the thief or to his method of entry.

Nancy also has another worry: she has not heard from her father. Hannah tells her he has not returned, and a telegram to Chicago brings the troubling response that he left two days earlier. While she is rereading the telegram, a shriek draws her to Floretta's room upstairs. An almost hysterical Floretta exclaims that three of her dresses have been stolen and two canaries have inexplicably appeared in the room. Another vain search for a secret entryway ensues.

Nancy questions the sisters about offers for their property. They tell her that Nathan Gombet claims he has an option to purchase their home for a ridiculously low price; the sisters fear they may have to accept this price, since a haunted house is almost unsalable. Nancy is "now convinced that Nathan Gombet had some connection with the mysterious things which had been going on in the old house. Perhaps he was trying to frighten Rosemary and Floretta so that they would be glad to sell at his price" (*HS*, 101).

The next two chapters use a flashback to follow Carson Drew, an unusual tactic. On his return from Chicago, he finds Gombet at the railway station, waiting with the news that Nancy has been badly injured in an accident. Gombet tricks Carson into accompanying him to his home, a stone house next to the Turnbull mansion. Locking the attorney in a small room, Gombet tells him he will remain a prisoner until he signs papers paying Gombet $20,000 for the land previously sold to the land commission and agreeing not to prosecute. Carson refuses.

Nancy continues to worry about her father but stays on at the mansion. Finally, she decides to question Gombet about the Turnbull mansion and learns that he is the next-door neighbor. When the sisters remark that Nathan also keeps birds, including canaries, Nancy resolves to investigate his house secretly. Late that evening she creeps to Gombet's home, arriving just as he is leaving.

Entering through a cellar window, Nancy barely evades the housekeeper and makes her way upstairs, where she hides in a small closet to escape detection. She feels a small knob on the wall, opens a secret passageway, and topples headlong down a flight of stairs. When she recovers consciousness, she bravely follows a dank, stone passage through twists and turns, reaching an exit just as her flashlight fails. She emerges in the Turnbulls' attic. The next morning she leads the sisters on a tour of the passageways, and they find additional exits in other rooms of the house.

Nancy and the Turnbulls call the police and rush to Gombet's house, where his housekeeper bars their entry with a gun. At Nancy's suggestion she and two officers use the secret passageways to sneak up on the woman. They capture her, then discover Gombet and Carson Drew upstairs. Gombet confesses, Carson is freed, and the sisters present

Nancy with the silver urn as an expression of gratitude. She tells them she will keep it on the mantelpiece, next to the old clock from her previous case.

This case illustrates many standard features in Nancy Drew stories. As with the Hardy Boys books, the plot involves several interrelated mysteries. In an analysis of Nancy's cases, Prager lists several common elements, all of them evident in *The Hidden Staircase:* a warning to stop the investigation; violence or bodily injury to Nancy, frequently a blow to the head; and the kidnapping of Nancy, her friends, or her family (79–80). The ghostly aspects of the plot—and Nancy's refusal to believe the house is haunted—are also typical. Nancy frequently deals in cases that appear to have supernatural elements, but she demystifies them by tracing the phenomena to human agents.[6] Moreover, many of her cases have Gothic overtones: crumbling, near-deserted mansions, secret passageways, and the like (Billman, 115–16). The victims fit neatly into this framework: they come from good families but no longer possess the wealth of bygone days. Their loss frequently involves something connected with the family heritage: in *The Hidden Staircase*, a few small items, the urn, and, most important, the reputation—and increased value—of the sisters' ancestral home. In contrast, the criminals come from a different background, evidenced by their behavior (coarse, greedy, and rude), their speech (rough and ungrammatical), and their appearance (slovenly or tastelessly flashy). Even the use of a pair of criminals is typical; Prager notes that Nancy Drew mysteries frequently feature a man and a woman as the antagonists. Finally, Nancy's refusal to take money for her work—unlike the Hardys—and her acceptance of some object involved in the case as a souvenir are trademarks of the series.

Harriet Stratemeyer Adams took a strong interest in Nancy Drew and was responsible for a number of changes that were made after the first few volumes.[7] Nancy's mother died when Nancy was three, so Nancy has had much experience running the household and does so capably. The first books depict Hannah Gruen as "an elderly maid," a minor character. Later books enlarge her role and promote her to a "housekeeper" who is "regarded almost as a member of the family."[8] Nancy now confides in her and treats her more like an older aunt. Nancy initially works solo; the fifth book introduces the blunt, boyish George Fayne and the feminine, timid Bess Marvin, who frequently accompany her on cases. Both girls were Adams's idea, as was Nancy's boyfriend, Ned Nickerson, who appears in the books when he is not away at Emerson College.

Her detection skills alone do not account for all of Nancy's popularity. Anne Scott MacLeod has analyzed the series and its competitors and notes that although many others adopted the pattern of "one parent, two chums, one boyfriend, and comfortable middle-class girl sleuth," none ousted Nancy from her position at the top.[9] According to MacLeod, Nancy's success springs from several sources, including her personal and financial independence and her strong character. The books demonstrate "Nancy's straight thinking, remarkable competence, and unshakable dignity." Moreover, the series is "focused[:] A Nancy Drew mystery is only that, never a school story or a romance or a career novel with a bit of mystery thrown in" (314). However, the key to Nancy's success, MacLeod believes, lies in her "autonomy" and in the books' "steady, profound, but largely covert . . . feminism" (442).

Her autonomy, of course, is occasioned by Nancy's situation: no school or employers to restrict her movements, no mother to fuss, no siblings to watch over, and an indulgent and famous father who grants her ample freedom—and, presumably, an equally ample allowance for car maintenance, travel, and needed supplies. Her feminism is more subtle, consisting of numerous character traits repeatedly mentioned throughout the series. The narrator not only stresses Nancy's capability but attributes it to "self-training," not chance or intuition; Nancy's actions and character "counter every stereotype of 'feminine' weakness" (MacLeod, 444–45). Emotionally strong and self-assured, Nancy stands ready to lead or take action as needed, without quailing or hedging. She is also serious, less interested in parties and frivolity than in sleuthing and improving her mind. Even romance is clearly secondary—Ned is a convenient boyfriend but rarely absorbs her thoughts (445–49). These feminist elements work, however, largely because they are hidden under "layers of conventional propriety" (449). Nancy is well mannered, well dressed (usually in skirts or "frocks"), and well versed in social graces; she avoids slangy speech, treats others with courtesy, and displays modesty. Nancy is thus able to adopt many characteristics traditionally associated with male protagonists without seeming masculine.

MacLeod does not comment on Nancy's cases, but they, too, contribute to the series' aura of conventionality. Although Nancy Drew may not be a fragile, romantic heroine, the elements of her mysteries are highly romanticized, the stuff of which Gothics are made. Her "clues" are dainty mementos—scarlet slippers, ivory charms, and the like—rather than evidence providing information about the criminals (Craig and Cadogan, 155). While the Hardy boys do their sleuthing in the outdoors, Nancy Drew's world is more closely tied to society and culture, traditionally the domain of the female. The feminist Bobbie Ann Mason has commented that a number of Nancy's cases seem based in a Victorian world full of tea shops and tidy manners (57–61). Accordingly, many of Nancy's mysteries deal with restoring heirlooms or estates to their rightful (and well-bred) owners, or, as some have interpreted it, with maintaining the status quo and old order.

Nancy has been alternately praised and panned by feminists. The series has been, perhaps unfairly, criticized for failing to come to terms with women's roles: although Nancy is independent, that freedom does not extend to other females in the series. Nancy herself lives in a kind of postadolescent limbo; the series writers have always carefully ignored her future. Unlike the Hardy boys, who plan careers as detectives, Nancy is often described as an "amateur sleuth," and no indication is given that she plans on pursuing this line of work—or any other career—in the future. Her girl companions, the tomboy George and the frilly Bess, have been cited as the two extremes of a female personality, one renouncing femininity, the other overindulging in it; only Nancy unites them. On the other hand, the series has also received praise from women who believe it offers a positive role model for girls by showing a capable, fearless heroine well able to cope with the world, one who relies on her wits, not her appearance, to resolve problems.

Some of Nancy's feminist character changes in later books. Ironically, as women have gained freedom and independence Nancy has gradually lost hers. By 1965, in *The Phantom of Pine Hill*, she repeatedly bows to others' requests to avoid dangerous situations and spends much of her time dining and dancing instead of sleuthing. Ned is ever-present and always insisting upon protecting her—at one point, when she wants to take a short walk through the woods, he even tells her, "You'll be safer if I go with you."[10] It is timid Bess who actually captures the criminals, Nancy and George having been rendered unconscious by knockout gas. Many of the elements MacLeod praised have diminished or vanished entirely, including the focused approach. *The Phantom of Pine Hill* tries to blend school life, romance, and detection, with Nancy, Bess, and George visiting Ned and two of his friends at Emerson College. The story shifts from college parties to mysteries to dates to mysteries, and surprisingly little is accomplished on any front.

Books from the 1960s and later alter Nancy's character in other ways as well. By then Wirt Benson had left the series, and the books were being ghostwritten by an assortment of others and extensively edited.

The writing is weak, at best, with a puzzling emphasis on insignificant details. Scenes begin and end abruptly, and characters and settings remain woefully undeveloped and underdescribed. The bland style—short, noncomplex sentences and simple words rather than more sophisticated ones—also makes the mysteries seem more simplistic, almost as if they were written for a beginning reader. While this style may make the books more accessible to a younger audience, it also renders the plot less engaging and decreases the impact of Nancy's skill at sleuthing.

By the 1980s, when the books appeared in paperback, the stories had again changed. The writing style had improved, with greater emphasis on dialogue. Nancy is livelier, more chatty, and more sociable with her peers and young children, but less dignified and mature. She has, however, regained her courage and composure and is able to hold her own against an assortment of antagonists, from snippy rivals to villainous thugs.

Nancy's greatest transformation, however, occurred in the Nancy Drew Files (78 volumes, as of 1992, 1986–), a series running concurrently with Nancy Drew Mystery Stories. Designed to appeal to teen readers who find the original series too simple for their tastes, the new line produced a radical change. The traits that made Nancy what she was originally are gone. The opening chapter of *Secrets Can Kill* (1986), first in the series, is almost entirely devoted to a discussion between Nancy, Bess, and George of clothes, boys, and romance. While the Hardy boys face international terrorists and work with adult agents from Network, Nancy moves amid a younger set, filled with adolescents, and has adopted many of their values. The adult world, which once interested her, now bores her. In *Secrets Can Kill* Nancy is asked to solve a mystery at the local high school, but while the principal explains the situation Nancy is more interested in Daryl, the handsome senior assigned as her guide: "The attraction between them crackled like electricity. . . . As Nancy tuned out the principal's voice, she tuned into the beautiful face before her."[11] The girl who, in earlier works, discusses Shakespeare knowingly with college professors and translates quotations from Chaucer now finds school tedious and remembers "why she'd been happy to leave [it] behind" (*SCK*, 25). Nancy also becomes more vulnerable. When she begins undercover work in the high school, she "felt exposed and self-conscious, and like all new kids, she wished she had a friend nearby" (*SCK*, 14). This is a far cry from the independent, self-reliant Nancy of the 1930s and 1940s. While the Hardys have matured during the intervening years, Nancy seems to have regressed—or belatedly discovered adolescence.

Syndicate Series after Stratemeyer's Death

Although Stratemeyer was responsible for creating two enormously successful mystery series, a look at Syndicate series from 1927 through 1930 shows that he did not intend to concentrate solely on the genre. Of the nine series initiated during those years, only Nancy Drew and the Hardys were mysteries, although a third, Roy Stover (4 volumes, 1929–34), is about a reporter whose talent in detection helps his paper get better stories. The others continued existing trends: aviation, sports, career series. It is probable that the four series issued in 1931 were also carryovers from Stratemeyer. Only two of these were mysteries, one for boys, one for girls; both were short-lived. It remained for Harriet Stratemeyer Adams, assuming control of the Syndicate after her father's death, to alter the shape of Syndicate fiction gradually, making mysteries their mainstay.

The Doris Force series (4 volumes, 1931–32) showed Nancy Drew's influence already emerging. A pert 16-year-old with a "curly red bob," the orphaned Doris lives under the guardianship of her uncle, Wardell Force. He is a wealthy, retired businessman prominent in the community through his work for charity. Doris's constant companion, Kitty Norris, serves as her unofficial admiration society. The two are less independent than Nancy Drew; they usually travel under the chaperonage of Mrs. Mallow, the owner of the estate where Doris and her uncle reside. Doris Force still shows traces of the old girls' series. She begins detecting while trying to settle her own claim on an inheritance; the first three books relate the various complications from this situation. The last volume, set at Doris's boarding school, reverts to the typical girls' series pattern: Doris uncovers a fortune and lost relatives for a school chum.

Boarding school also provides the locale for the opening chapters in Perry Pierce Mystery Stories (4 volumes, 1931–34). The first book, *Who Closed the Door* (1931), introduces Perry Pierce, president of the Skull Mystery Club. To join the club, "each prospective member must have solved or help [*sic*] solve one mystery, either by himself or in the company of his chums. And to stay in the club each member must turn in one solved mystery each year."[12] The book begins on a light note with initiation rites, a series of pranks designed to test the mettle of prospective club members. However, things soon become more serious. On their summer vacation, Perry and three of his friends decide to solve a mystery at a storage warehouse. The elderly caretakers claim to have seen lights flashing and "strange figures movin' in some of the old rooms and corri-

dors" at night (*WCD*, 48). During the investigation all of Perry's friends
are injured, leaving only Perry to continue the hunt. At last he discovers
a group of thieves robbing the warehouse of the more valuable items.
After a wild pursuit culminating in a gun battle between the police
(aided by Perry) and the thieves, the criminals are caught, ensuring
Perry's and his friends' membership in the club for another year. Other
volumes follow this pattern: schoolboy high jinks preface a turn toward
more serious affairs.

After Perry Pierce, three years elapsed before the Syndicate tried more
new offerings. Both new series for 1934 featured girl sleuths, undoubtedly triggered by the popularity of Nancy Drew, by then the Syndicate's
best-selling series ("For It Was . . . ," 88). Kay Tracey (18 volumes,
1934–42), another schoolgirl detective, was in large part the work of
Mildred Wirt Benson, who ghostwrote volumes 3 through 14. The
Dana Girls (34 volumes, 1934–79), published under the same pseudonym as the Nancy Drew books, combined elements from the Hardy
Boys and Nancy Drew—hardly surprising since ghostwriters from both
series worked on the Danas. The protagonists are two sisters, 17-year-
old Louise, who is dark-haired and serious (like Frank Hardy), and 16-
year-old Jean, who is fair-haired and more impetuous. Another pair of
orphans, they live with their Uncle Ned, a ship's captain, and his sister,
Aunt Harriet, a clone of Hannah Gruen. The first three books were
authored by Leslie McFarlane, the next eleven or twelve by Wirt Benson.

Like Nancy, the Danas solve cases in a seemingly Victorian world,
with characters out of Gothic or romance novels: gracious, genteel
ladies, temporarily impoverished; old women living alone in stately
mansions, with nephews or doctors dancing attendance; hardworking
folk in tidy cottages with flower-filled gardens. However, the Syndicate
had apparently opted for school settings: like Doris Force and Perry
Pierce, the Danas attend boarding school, the elegant Starhurst
Academy. Because they are in school, they never achieve the same independence as Nancy; they may venture into an adult world to solve mysteries, but the girls are drawn back into the confines of adolescence each
time they reenter the supervised world of the school grounds. Numerous
scenes set at school also reinforce their connection with an adolescent
world and the accompanying problems, most notably, the stereotypical-
ly unpleasant wealthy girl who is jealous of the Danas and eager to make
trouble for them. Schoolgirl clashes undercut the attempts to present
Louise and Jean as equal participants in adult matters, and the pair seem
forever caught between the two worlds.

During the years Adams controlled the Syndicate the number of
series decreased and the proportion of mysteries increased. The last series
created before a long hiatus was one aimed specifically at younger children. By then existing tots' series had gravitated toward mysteries. The
Bobbsey twins' adventure for 1934 was titled *The Bobbsey Twins Solve a
Mystery*, and the following year saw *Honey Bunch: Her Own Little Mystery*.
Consequently, the Mary and Jerry Mystery Stories (5 volumes, 1935–37)
seemed a natural development. Ads explained that the protagonists, 12-
year-old Jerry Denton and his 10-year-old sister Mary, "have an interesting hobby—they love to solve mysteries. Between school hours and on
weekends they follow clue upon clue, each more puzzling than the last,
through a whole series of strange adventures."

Although the ads suggested that some serious sleuthing occurs in this
series, in actuality the books are far closer to traditional tots' stories than
to mysteries. In *The Mystery of the Toy Bank* (1935) Jerry's bank disappears after a grouchy sailor visits the family's home. The children devote
some time to tracking the sailor but also spend a number of chapters
renovating an old boat, outwitting a local bully, and trying to get a
replacement bank. When they eventually confront the sailor (quite
politely and almost apologetically), he turns out to be a nice man, a contradiction of information found in earlier chapters. The bank is found,
the sailor gives Mary, Jerry, and their friends a dollar each as a gesture of
goodwill, and the book ends. Other stories in the series also rely more on
the children's episodic adventures than on detecting.

From then until 1947, when the Mel Martin baseball series appeared
(and incorporated mystery into its plots), the Syndicate developed no
new series, relying instead on adding volumes to a few old favorites,
including Nancy Drew and the Hardy Boys. After Andrew Svenson
joined the staff, he created and wrote the Happy Hollisters, a mystery-
adventure series for tots.

The Happy Hollisters (33 volumes, 1953–70) are a bouncier version
of the Bobbsey Twins. A lengthy blurb on the back of the books' dust
jackets introduces readers to the entire group, making them sound like a
cross between a 1950s television show and display models for an adver-
tiser's version of the ideal American family. Mr. Hollister, who "owns the
Trading Post, a combination hardware, sports, and toy shop . . . likes to
take his family on exciting adventures." Mrs. Hollister "is always ready
to meet any sudden need—for a surprise picnic or a helping hand";
along with Mr. Hollister, she "share[s] in the play and the mysteries the
children always solve." As for the children, "Pete, the oldest, is a sturdy

boy of twelve, with sparkling blue eyes" and a "love of sports," which "is shared by his sister Pam, who is ten . . . [and] is kind to everyone and loves animals." Ricky, a red-haired, freckled, "seven-year-old package of perpetual motion . . . is full of fun and sometimes teases his six-year-old sister, Holly," a tomboy. "The baby of the family," Sue, "is only four, [but] she romps in all the fun the Hollister family enjoys day in and day out." That's not all, though; the family also owns a "peppy collie dog, Zip," a cat, White Nose, "which [Holly] carries under her arm like a fluffy purse," and White Nose's five kittens, which Sue "likes to cuddle."

As the blurb suggests, the Hollister children inhabit an ideal world, one that makes characters in the Syndicate's earlier tots' series seem almost impoverished. The word *happy* is crucial here: whatever happens, the characters remind each other that "we're going to stay happy," and they do, tackling mysteries with zip and cheer.[13] In the first book, their toys, some household items, and important papers belonging to Mr. Hollister are stolen from a van while they are moving to a new home. Nonetheless, they keep their spirits up, immediately make many new friends, and eventually locate the stolen items.

The Hollister children tackle assorted mysteries in the series; they frequently look for lost or hidden treasures rather than for stolen items, though, alternatively, they sometimes combine the two quests. In *The Happy Hollisters at Mystery Mountain*, for example, they befriend two children who own a "very, very old storybook about Mexico" illustrated with a map showing "the Cave of the Dollmakers on Mystery Mountain," a site containing ancient dolls and other artifacts.[14] When the book is stolen, the Hollisters and their friends track the thief, who is also a sheep rustler. Eventually they find him, the sheep, the book, and the cave (complete with ancient artifacts), ensuring an appropriately happy ending.

In the 1960s a spate of new series came out, none lasting more than four years. (The Bret King and Linda Craig series are discussed with outdoor adventures, and Chris Cool with career series.) The Tolliver Adventure Stories (3 volumes, 1967) seem modeled after the Happy Hollisters, with one significant difference—the Tollivers are a black family, the Syndicate's attempt to reach minority readers.

These marked the last mystery series featuring new sleuths. In 1978 the Syndicate tried a two-volume picture-book series using Nancy Drew. Then, in the late 1970s and early 1980s, it issued Kay Tracey and Linda Craig, two of its earlier girls' series, in revised editions. The only continuing series for which new volumes were written were the Bobbsey Twins (which by then had become mystery oriented and even carried the legend, "A Pre-Hardy Boys/Nancy Drew Mystery" on the cover) and the Syndicate's three key mystery series—the Hardy Boys, Nancy Drew, and the Dana Girls (whose last volume was published in 1979).

Many of these newer books heavily emphasize what the Stratemeyer Syndicate once described as "the Stratemeyer Syndicate formula"—a mixture of action and educational material. While early series titles included some informational tidbits worked into the narratives, many of the newer books use informational material as a replacement for background or character development, weakening the narrative flow and turning some titles (especially those set in historic or scenic locales) into travelogue-mysteries.

After Adams's death, Simon & Schuster purchased the Syndicate and marketed Nancy Drew and the Hardy Boys in every combination imaginable. It offered Nancy Drew and Hardy Boys Ghost Stories, Nancy Drew and the Hardy Boys Be a Detective Mystery Series (interactive fiction—readers determine which clues the trio will follow), and Nancy Drew and the Hardy Boys Super Sleuths (short stories that team the three detectives). As mentioned earlier, in 1986 Nancy Drew became two separate series—Nancy Drew Mystery Stories, continuing the digest-sized series, and Nancy Drew Files, a line of mass-market paperbacks. The following year the Hardy Boys followed suit, and 1988 saw yet another series, Nancy Drew/Hardy Boys Super Mysteries, more mass-market paperbacks uniting the three sleuths. These last offer an interesting twist: "The Nancy Drew/Hardy Boys Mystery Hour" television series (1977–79) had gradually introduced a romance between Nancy Drew and Frank Hardy, and the Super Mysteries continually toy with the idea but refuse to commit to it, probably because of the complications it would cause in the individual series. Instead, Nancy and Frank spend a great deal of time looking at each other admiringly, then remember they love other people. In *Double Crossing* (1988) the two actually kiss but afterward decide to pretend it never happened, resuming their friendship instead. The books are published under the pseudonym Carolyn Keene, and while the point of view alternates between Nancy's and the Hardys' Nancy's perspective frequently prevails.

Although the mystery series was the last major genre Stratemeyer introduced, it has been the longest lasting and most successful. In a sense, much of his earlier work was moving in that direction, for his protagonists had been solving problems and pursuing criminals as far back as his dime novels and story-paper fiction; the greatest difference in the mystery series is that protagonists no longer need to rely on family or friends for mysteries. Instead, their growing reputations as amateur sleuths convince outsiders to ask them for help. Being amateur sleuths allows the protagonists to engage in many of the same activities as protagonists from earlier series, such as traveling extensively and using new technology, but the mystery series combine these activities with investigation. Detecting also ensures action and a unified plot, gives protagonists challenging competition, and guarantees them visible success, complete with plentiful accolades.

The major series—the Hardy Boys and Nancy Drew—have somewhat similar plot formulas, but elements in each series are geared to their readers' gender and expectations. The Hardy Boys employ outside settings and a plethora of motorized conveyances; Nancy Drew's is a more genteel world. Both series adapted with the times, changing everything from their writing styles to their characterizations. The Syndicate's willingness to revise dated titles and create spinoff series has enabled it to continue offering old favorites in new forms, to appeal to new readers. Although the new sleuths may differ radically from the originals, one thing has not changed—their continuing popularity. Judging by that success, future generations of readers will also be able to enjoy sleuthing with Stratemeyer Syndicate characters.

9

Conclusion

Like the characters he created, Edward Stratemeyer enjoyed phenomenal and unprecedented success. An article in *Fortune* once dubbed him the father of the 50-cent series book, noting that he had written "the first of it," the best of it, the worst of it, and "the most of it"—an apt summary of his career ("For It Was . . . ," 86). From the time he began publishing Stratemeyer demonstrated an ability to reach the juvenile market, parlaying his talents into a literary empire as he moved from hack writer to head of his own writing syndicate. When he died in 1930, Edward Stratemeyer left an estate valued at $500,000, a syndicate with 31 different series still in progress, and the legacy of having created some of the most popular characters in children's fiction. He had produced or plotted roughly 900 stories for children. The Syndicate he created—which would continue beyond not only his death but that of his daughter—went on to publish almost 800 more books and still flourishes today.

Series Books

Stratemeyer's role was not in inventing the series genre but in helping to reshape it to reach twentieth-century readers and in creating many of its best-sellers. Books in series—that is, books using continuing characters or a central theme—had been around since at least the 1830s. Early series took two forms, both of which differed from twentieth-century series. What could be called the library-approved series combined heavily didactic or informational material, frequently historical or geographical, with continuing characters and less sensational adventures. These were often published in expensive editions. The second type of series was used for adventure novels, including those by popular authors such as Horatio Alger. Limited to three to six volumes, they followed characters for a set period of time, usually through a particular type of experience, such as military service, an expedition westward, or a planned outing. Compared with the other kind of series, they contained more sensational adventures and more exaggerated triumphs and thus were less realistic.

160

By the end of the series the characters are ready to settle into respectable (and usually financially comfortable) adulthood. A variation of the genre was the thematic series, in which each volume follows a different character as he gains economic and social success.

The Stratemeyer Syndicate's early offerings, such as the Rover Boys and Tom Swift, helped alter these formulas. They combined continuing characters with somewhat exaggerated adventures but structured the stories so that success in one book did not mark the end of the protagonists' adventures. At the end of each story the heroes remain available for new challenges. Later, the use of characters who do not age made it possible to continue a series indefinitely. These tactics had already been used in dime novels, but Stratemeyer and others adapted them to clothbound books.

The shift to clothbound books and to younger protagonists freed series books from some of the negative connotations of dime novels. Other aspects of series books also offered a surface respectability. The cover designs (and later, dust jackets) highlighted all-American boys and girls engaged in athletics, sampling new technologies, or visiting striking settings. Ads and book blurbs continued this theme, employing phrases like "clean," "bright," and "up-to-date" and an occasional reference to the factual information in the stories. Any parent inspecting a series book would find that the heroes do not indulge in vices or even read dime novels. All of this must have assuaged the worries of many adults, for inscriptions in books show that older relatives bought series titles for children and teachers gave them as prizes for good conduct or attendance.

Although Stratemeyer was among the first to use these techniques, it is difficult to establish precisely what part his series played in the rapid development of twentieth-century series. The Rover Boys premiered in 1899, and by 1909 there were at least 115 series available; the real explosion, however, occurred between 1910 and 1930, when over 480 series began. In 1926 and 1927 the American Library Association published the *Winnetka Graded Book List* and a supplement based on a survey of books read by schoolchildren from 34 cities across the country. It was one of the earliest surveys to show—and deplore—the popularity of series books. As the authors noted, "The books of one series—seventeen of them—were unanimously rated trashy by our expert librarians and almost unanimously (98%) liked by the 900 children who read them."[1] The series referred to was the Bobbsey Twins; other Syndicate series were also prominently featured in the supplement.

Similarly, a 1929 study tracking one week's reading by boys in junior high showed that Tom Swift books were second only to the Bible as the books most frequently read. When the same boys were asked to list the novels they had read during the school year, the Tom Swift series topped the list, with the Rover Boys third. A survey of the girls elicited similar results, with the Syndicate's Outdoor Girls as the first choice.[2] Five years later, an article on series books estimated that the top three publishing houses turned out over 5,000,000 series books a year, and that works by Stratemeyer and the Syndicate had already sold approximately 20,000,000 copies, roughly 6,500,000 of which were Tom Swift titles, and another 5,000,000 Rover Boys books. In the Christmas season alone of 1933, Macy's sold 6,000 Nancy Drew and 3,750 Bomba the Jungle Boy books ("For It Was . . . ," 86, 88, 208). George Dunlap's reminiscences, published in 1937, mention five of Grosset & Dunlap's best-selling juvenile series—four of them by the Stratemeyer Syndicate (193). In short, although the Stratemeyer Syndicate's series constituted only a small percentage of the total number of series published, by the 1920s and 1930s its creations ranked among the most popular.

During the 1940s and 1950s the number of series published decreased. Comic books, radio, movies, and, later, television began supplanting them. Many old favorites were discontinued— including the majority of the Stratemeyer Syndicate's series—and fewer new ones developed. Despite the occasional flurry of new series, this trend appears to have continued through the 1960s and early 1970s. Syndicate series experienced a drop in sales, even Nancy Drew and the Hardy Boys (later reversed when the sleuths appeared as a television show in the late 1970s).

In 1978 the Syndicate switched to a paperback format for most of its series, just in time for the paperback revolution. The mid-1980s witnessed the genre's renaissance in paperback. Over 210 girls' and tots' series began in this decade, including several Syndicate series, such as the Nancy Drew Files and Hardy Boys Casefiles.[3] The Syndicate continues to issue titles in the Bobbsey Twins, Nancy Drew, and Hardy Boys series and has just begun the Tom Swift (IV) series, which reached nine volumes after only eleven months of publication. Thus, even without Stratemeyer or his descendants managing the Syndicate, new titles—and even new series—have continued to appear. The Syndicate has managed to adapt to changing styles and, judging by the steady stream of new titles, seems to retain a secure place in the market.

Attitudes toward Series Books

The evolution of series books has been accompanied by changing attitudes from librarians and educators; Stratemeyer is the writer they most frequently single out for attention. Early in the century librarians viewed the preponderance of series books with dismay and were concerned about their effect on children. In 1914 Franklin K. Mathiews, chief librarian for the Boy Scouts of America, began a campaign against substandard reading, attacking the series books through articles in journals, appeals to publishers, and campaigns to enlist parents and others concerned about children's reading. His most famous article, "Blowing out the Boy's Brains," lambastes the series books and describes their deleterious effect on the country's youth: "One of the most valuable assets a boy has is his imagination. In proportion as this is nurtured a boy develops initiative and resourcefulness. . . . Story books . . . of the viler and cheaper sort, by over stimulation, debauch and vitiate. . . . As some boys read such books, their imaginations are literally 'blown out,' and they go into life as terribly crippled as though by some material explosion they had lost a hand or foot." He also criticized the books' assembly-line methods of production, writing that "one man . . . is as resourceful as a Balzac sofar [*sic*] as ideas and plots for stories are concerned. He cannot, though, develop them all, so he employs a number of men who write for him"—almost certainly a reference to Stratemeyer.[4]

In the following decades, journals for librarians and educators also tried to discourage children from reading series books. In 1929 the *Wilson Bulletin* attempted to help librarians weed their collections by publishing a list of "books in series not circulated by standardized libraries."[5] The article cited 64 series authors and pseudonyms; Stratemeyer and Syndicate pseudonyms comprise almost one-fifth of those named.

At this point Stratemeyer was still considered one among many writers responsible for series books, but an article published anonymously in *Fortune* magazine in 1934 helped bring him to prominence—or infamy. "For It Was Indeed He" dealt with the phenomenon of series fiction. The bulk of it concentrated on Stratemeyer's empire and the fortune he had acquired through series books. *Fortune* also described Stratemeyer's method of production—sending outlines of stories to hired writers, who turned them into full-length manuscripts. Critics who had previously faulted authors for being too prolific learned that there were authors who were not even authors, merely plotters of stories. Now Stratemeyer stood revealed as one of the main perpetrators of such works. From then on rarely did an article on series books fail to mention Stratemeyer and his methods of production.

Articles published in library journals over the following years also singled out Stratemeyer for censure. Hope White labeled him an "arch-fiend," gave a flawed biography of him based on information from *Fortune*, and ended by urging librarians to "pledge ourselves anew to battle the fifty-cent thrillers until they are completely routed."[6] A librarian wrote to say she was now using White's article and the author biographies from *The Junior Book of Authors* "to win children away from such yellow literature as the Tom Swift and the Nancy Drew books." She referred to "the dark deeds of Edward Stratemeyer, author of more than 800 cheap series books," and faulted him for "the machine-like regularity with which he and his hack writer assistants produced books about places where they had never been and people who acted like automatons."[7] In 1956 the *South Carolina Library Bulletin* carried Janie Smith's "History of *Bobbsey Twins*," another summary of the *Fortune* information; five years later the *Kansas Library Bulletin* reprinted it (as "*Bobbsey Twins* History Told") to explain "why standard libraries refuse to spend limited book funds for children's serials."[8]

For all their discussion about the undesirability of series books, these articles devoted few words to the content, literary or otherwise, of the books. White dismisses the subject entirely, saying there is "no need to enumerate to [librarians] the undesirable features of the series" (113). Other criticisms frequently take the form of sweeping generalizations. Those comments that do appear fall into four categories: poor or ungrammatical style, questionable moral tone, unrealistic characters, and improbable adventures—plus a fifth catchall category, general mediocrity.

Criticism of the morals and values conveyed through the books occurs primarily in articles from the first three decades of the century. Most confine themselves to vague comments; a 1914 article, for example, states that the series "give a false ideal of life," with no further elaboration.[9] Beginning with Mathiews's piece in 1914, observations about near-omnipotent heroes and unrealistic adventures frequently accompanied, and later supplanted, remarks about the books' moral values. This observation was only another way of saying the heroes' continuing success arouses false expectations in the reader.

Other articles also criticized the extraordinary competence of the protagonists and their implausible adventures, but only in vague terms. In 1924 one librarian referred to the "mock heroics and cheap modern stunts" found in series like the Motor Boys and Radio Boys.[10] Later, Janie Smith would criticize "the superhuman exploits of adolescent heroes" (15).

Although the articles rarely went beyond these references, the series' actual crime, one suspects, was that they did not present proper or acceptable role models for children. It was not that their heroes are not moral, but that they do not teach children to be children. As R. Gordon Kelly has observed, one of the purposes behind children's literature is socialization, teaching children how a child should act and which principles and values to adopt (56–116). Stratemeyer's books are laden with the proper moral values: his protagonists are honest, generous, industrious, and courageous—the same values espoused in traditional stories—but they do not act like children. Traditionally, in the more acceptable children's literature of the period, adults give children necessary advice and impose restraints on them. In series fiction, however, the adolescents make their own crucial decisions. They demonstrate the intelligence, capability, and freedom of adults, in violation of this tradition. Children, not adults, become the moral arbiters and shapers of their fate. They willingly enter the adult world and compete on an even footing—a fantasy, certainly, but one that appeals to almost every child.

By the 1960s attitudes toward series books were beginning to change. Margaret Beckman's "Why Not the Bobbsey Twins?" is notable not for her stance on series—a reiteration of the traditional arguments—but for the reactions she describes. When Beckman objected to her daughter's school library carrying Nancy Drew books, a local newspaper picked up the story, which then attracted the attention of city papers and radio and television commentators. Judging by Beckman's comments, the press sided with supporters of the series books, who felt that children "will read, unencouraged, everything they can find and jump easily from the Hardy Boys to *Treasure Island*."[11] Beckman also suggested that some of the personnel connected with libraries—notably, board members and trustees—had begun to adopt the position that a library should acquire any book that encourages a child to read, an attitude Beckman hoped to counter.

That the tide was turning was also evidenced by an editorial in *Library Journal* in 1970. Ervin Gaines, the director of the Minneapolis

Public Library, addressed the serious drop in the circulation of children's books and suggested it was time for librarians to reevaluate their position. One of his suggestions was that libraries acquire comic books and series, to lure children back. He believed that opposition to series such as Nancy Drew and the Hardy Boys was "a sign of brittle rigidity that is ultimately harmful to the promotion of reading."[12]

By 1974 an article on Nancy Drew noted that the series was "winning acceptance on the library shelves of major cities."[13] In 1982 an article coauthored by a professor of teacher education and a homemaker stated, "The reading of series books should not be discouraged," for "the child's reading of these books is not a waste of time. He or she experiences genuine pleasure in meeting again the familiar acquaintances in each succeeding story and wants to share in the next adventure."[14] And in 1990 an article in an Alabama newspaper noted the continuing popularity of series books. One librarian remarked, "Once a child gets started on a series, they [sic] won't stop until they have read everything in that series. I have to keep ordering more," further evidence of librarians' capitulation.[15]

Although series books are still not universally accepted, and many of the early ones have received belated criticism for their racial and ethnic stereotypes, they are gaining wider acceptance. Objections to style and content occasionally surface, but the books' value as an inducement to reading has earned them some librarians' support. In an age dominated by television, the books' messages and role models no longer seem as controversial.

Conclusion

It is now over a century since Edward Stratemeyer sold his first story, a tale of a young boy, influenced by popular fiction, who runs away to the big city. There he finds not fame but misery; he returns home with a greater awareness of the deceptions in books. In retrospect, it seems ironic that such a tale should have been Stratemeyer's first sale, for he never repeated this theme. Instead, his stories, like his career, accentuated success: the triumph of young protagonists over any and all obstacles.

Stratemeyer founded his empire not on one or two series but on many, which he developed through a process of adaptation and experimentation. Part of Stratemeyer's success lay in his readiness to adapt the form and content of his books to the changing times. He negotiated the shift from nineteenth-century dime novels and success stories to the newer style of twentieth-century series fiction, managing this change so well that his books became the virtual blueprint for the genre. A practical man, he recognized the value of reusing successful material: his stories contain favorite plots, characters, and even names, recycled and reissued as new products. At the same time he experimented with series of every type imaginable, from career stories to historical fiction and travel tales to school adventures. And, always, he wrote of enterprising young protagonists overcoming incredible odds.

His earliest work in dime novels shows his willingness to adapt style and content to the market. Many of the questionable values endorsed in these tales disappeared when Stratemeyer had the freedom to create his own series. Other features from the dime novels remained in his later stories, among them continuing characters, courageous, self-reliant heroes who demand respect, human and mechanical obstacles, competitions, and tangible triumphs.

While Stratemeyer was working predominantly with story-paper fiction, he drew on nineteenth-century models for some of his characterizations and plots. A transitional writer, he recognized the necessity of modifying his material to reach a changing audience, children interested in contemporary settings, characters, and situations. With his series fiction, Stratemeyer found a formula that suited the requirements of the new readership. By using continuing characters who neither age nor attain a permanent success Stratemeyer was able to add to a series indefinitely. Forming a Syndicate and hiring others to write books that he outlined allowed him to increase production and try all types of series. Although his methods earned disapproval from literary quarters, they ensured not only his success but ultimately the continuation of his empire after his death.

Stratemeyer's books reflected the tone of the times. His career stories placed boys in popular occupations, whether they were nineteenth-century surveyors or twentieth-century aviators or filmmakers. While the early career stories were patterned after Alger's "rags to riches" formula, later series recognized the importance of the new technology and readers' desire to learn more about the modern world.

The travel stories, written when Americans were becoming more conscious of the world beyond U.S. borders, provided glimpses of foreign lands and new possessions. Similarly, the historical fiction fed Americans' national pride and their interest in current conflicts. With their shift from hunting trips in the northeastern woods to rides across the south-western deserts, the outdoor tales chronicle changes in the environment and in the form of the western story.

Stratemeyer's boys' school stories marked a further shift in the status of the hero. Natural leaders, they impress others with their abilities in almost all areas and also possess ample material goods. The series follow their many adventures and travels as they repeatedly demonstrate their ability to master challenges in different environments. The stories also recognized new emphases in children's lives, reaching readers who could expect to spend close to 12 years in school and who were involved in athletics and school organizations.

With his girls' and tots' series, Stratemeyer extended his audience, modifying plots and themes accordingly. While these series also display materialistic values, the themes of nurturing and the family become more important. However, technology and current events still play a part in these series.

Finally, after Stratemeyer's death, his daughter, Harriet Stratemeyer Adams, continued his work, shifting the Syndicate's emphasis to mystery series. Although the number of series dropped, those that remained enjoyed strong sales and even engendered artifacts and spinoffs. Even today, under the aegis of Simon & Schuster, Syndicate mysteries continue to appeal to a new generation of readers.

Originally written at a time when children were beginning to spend more time with other children outside of the home—because they had fewer family responsibilities—the series books depict young heroes and heroines leading lives away from their parents' influence yet behaving in a moral manner. They contain—and still promulgate—values that are acceptable, even admirable, not only to their readers but often to read-ers' parents and other book-buying adults.

Above all, Stratemeyer and the Stratemeyer Syndicate's books preached success, the same message found in numerous other series, past and present. Children could be powerful, competent, and victorious through such books. No matter what the situation, a Stratemeyer or Syndicate hero or heroine eventually triumphs. No obstacle is too great, no adult too powerful, no competitor too skilled or too devious to fell the protagonist permanently. A 1925 study of children's reading detailed the satisfaction children received from series books: "They gratify the child's desire to find in his reading the fulfillment of his daydreams and subconscious wishes to excel, to be popular, to lead group or gang, to show heroism in a dangerous situation, or to display astonishing physical prowess."[16]

In a world of changes, uncertainties, and disempowerment, series books provided children with a means of security and control. These elements were further heightened through the use of continuing characters, for here was an even greater security, the guarantee not just of a happy ending but of meeting old friends over and over again. And when the adventure is over and the triumphant hero or heroine is toting treasures home, there is the promise of another round of adventures in a forthcoming book, reassuringly advertised on the last page.

The same deceptions in fiction that Stratemeyer criticized in his first tale—adolescents finding exciting adventures and ready success in the outside world—characterize his later stories, but in a positive fashion. Stratemeyer's legacy to children past, present, and future is hours of reading pleasure, an escape to a world where children and adolescents face all manner of contemporary challenges and emerge triumphant.

Notes

Preface

1. R. Gordon Kelly, *Mother Was a Lady: Self and Society in Selected American Children's Periodicals, 1865–1890* (Westport, Conn.: Greenwood, 1974), xv–xvi, hereafter cited in the text.

2. John G. Cawelti, *Adventure, Mystery, and Romance: Formula Stories as Art and Popular Culture* (Chicago: University of Chicago Press, 1976), 13, hereafter cited in the text.

Chapter 1

1. Edward Stratemeyer, *Oliver Bright's Search; or, The Mystery of a Mine* (Boston: Lee & Shepard, 1899), iv.

2. "Newarker Who Writes for Most Critical of All Readers Has Far Exceeded Standard of Success His Mother Set," *Newark Evening News*, 4 June 1927, hereafter cited in the text as "Newarker."

3. Peter Walther, "Bibliographic Rambles No. 7: Louis Charles and Edward Stratemeyer," *Newsboy* 28 (November–December 1989): 4.

4. Pat Pflieger, "The Stratemeyers of New Jersey; or, The Secrets in the Old Archives" (paper presented at the American Culture Association Convention, Louisville, Kentucky, 21 March 1992).

5. Karen DeWitt, "Nancy Drew's Author—She's No Mystery," *San Antonio Express News*, 7 August 1977, hereafter cited in the text; "Services at Home Tonight for Edward Stratemeyer," *Newark Evening News*, 12 May 1930, hereafter cited in the text as "Services."

6. "Newark Author, Great Favorite with Young Boys," *Newsboy* 26 (November–December 1987): 76; reprinted from *Newark Sunday News,* ca. 1904, hereafter cited in the text as "Newark Author."

7. Peter A. Soderbergh, "The Great Book War: Edward Stratemeyer and the Boy Scouts of America, 1910–1930," *New Jersey History* 91, no. 4 (Winter 1973): 236, hereafter cited in the text; Wallace Palmer, "Some Stratemeyer Miscellany," *Newsboy* 26 (November–December 1987): 90.

8. This correspondence is in the Edward Stratemeyer–Harriet Adams Collection, University of Oregon, Eugene.

9. Peter A. Soderbergh, "Edward Stratemeyer and the Juvenile Ethic, 1894–1930," *International Review of History and Political Science* 11, no. 1 (February 1974): 64.

10. Edward Stratemeyer, *The Automobile Boys of Lakeport; or, A Run for Fun and Fame* (Boston: Lothrop, Lee & Shepard, 1910), vi.

11. Edward Stratemeyer, *Dave Porter at Star Ranch; or, The Cowboy's Secret* (Boston: Lothrop, Lee & Shepard, 1910), iv, hereafter cited in the text as *DPSR*.

12. Edward Stratemeyer, *The Baseball Boys of Lakeport; or, The Winning Run* (Boston: Lothrop, Lee & Shepard, 1908), vi.

13. "Uncle Wiggily's Creator Joined News 50 Years Ago," *Newark Evening News*, 1 October 1946.

14. Roger Garis, *My Father Was Uncle Wiggily* (New York: McGraw-Hill, 1966), 7–8.

15. Harry K. Hudson, *A Bibliography of Hard-Cover Boys' Books*, rev. ed. (Tampa: Data Print, 1977), 60, 160.

16. J. Edward Leithead, "Pulp King—W. Bert Foster," *Relics* 2 (Summer 1968): 11–12, hereafter cited in the text.

17. Leslie McFarlane, *Ghost of the Hardy Boys* (New York: Two Continents, 1976), 10, hereafter cited in the text.

18. Mildred Wirt Benson, "The Ghost of Ladora," *Books at Iowa* 19 (November 1973): 25.

19. "Mildred A. Wirt," *Iowa Authors* (University of Iowa, 1967), 197–208, hereafter cited in the text as "Mildred A. Wirt."

20. Bernard A. Drew, letter to the editor, in *Mystery and Adventure Series Review* 22 (Spring 1990): 29.

21. Photos of the grave are in *Newsboy* 26 (November–December 1987): 88.

22. "Author: Harriet Stratemeyer Adams '14" [source unknown], hereafter cited in the text as "Author"; "Harriet Stratemeyer Adams," *American Women Writers from Colonial Times to the Present: A Critical Reference Guide* 1 (New York: Ungar, 1979), 15, hereafter cited in the text as "Adams"; Sidney Field, "Whatever Happened to . . . ?" *New York Daily News*, 4 April 1968, hereafter cited in the text.

23. See also Judy Foreman, "The Saga of a Mysterious Author," *Newsboy* 19 (November 1980): 18–19; reprinted from *Boston Globe*, 3 July 1980.

24. Judy Klemsrud, "100 Books—and Not a Hippie in Them," *New York Times*, 4 April 1968.

Reconstructing an accurate picture of Adams's girlhood and early years with the Syndicate is difficult—perhaps impossible—for the Syndicate seems to have deliberately avoided publicity until the late 1940s. Even in the infrequent interviews from the late 1940s through the early 1960s, Adams usually publicized the series and withheld personal information. By the time she began discussing the Syndicate's past over half a century stood between the events and her recollections. In addition, just as Stratemeyer had guarded the secret of his many pseudonyms and ghostwriters, so, too, did Adams try to shield young readers from learning that some much-loved authors were collective pseudonyms. For whatever reasons—faulty memory, errors or misunderstandings on the interviewer's part, or deliberate evasions—articles based on interviews with

Adams and other members of the Syndicate are rarely in complete agreement on any aspect of the Syndicate's past.

Additionally, for years Syndicate publicity linked the Nancy Drew and Dana Girls titles to Adams; on occasion, articles stated that Adams had written all the Nancy Drew books. During the 1980 trial it became evident that Adams had plotted and edited the books and, of course, owned rights to the characters, making the books hers, but that she had not written them all. Since many published lists of her works do not distinguish between titles she wrote and those she plotted and/or edited, it is difficult to attribute authorship of specific works accurately.

This account combines information from various published interviews and assumes, perhaps incorrectly, that Adams exaggerated her writing and her early involvement as time progressed; it thus deemphasizes her early Syndicate work.

25. "Harriet Stratemeyer," Wellesley reunion booklet, 1914 [source unknown]; reprinted in David Farah, "Basic Nancy Drew," *Yellowback Library* 14 (March–April 1983): 16.

26. "For It Was Indeed He," *Fortune* (April 1934): 204, hereafter cited in the text as "For It Was . . . ."

27. Anita Susan Grossman, "The Ghost of Nancy Drew," *Ohio Magazine* (December 1987): 42; David Farah, "Collecting Nancy Drew Books," *Paper Collectors' Marketplace* (February 1990): 27.

28. "Walter Karig," in *American Novelists of Today*, ed. Harry R. Warfel (New York: American Book, 1951), 238–39.

29. John T. Cunningham, "Where the Bobbseys Live," *Newark Sunday News*, 23 March 1969; see also Field.

30. Geoffrey S. Lapin, "Jim Lawrence and the Stratemeyer Syndicate," *Yellowback Library* 31 (January–February 1986): 5–8.

31. "Omar S. Barker," in *Contemporary Authors* 2, permanent series (Detroit: Gale Research, 1978), 43–45.

32. Ernie Kelly, "Inside the Stratemeyer Syndicate," 2 parts, *Yellowback Library* 52, 54 (October and December 1988): 1:11, hereafter cited in the text. More detailed information about Syndicate ghostwriters can be found in the article.

33. Mike McGrady, "The East Orange Gold Mine Mystery," *Newsday's Weekly Magazine* (29 June 1968): 3W, 33W.

34. Roger May, "Nancy Drew and Kin Still Surmount Scrapes—and Critics' Slurs," *Wall Street Journal*, 15 January 1975.

35. Edward Wakin, "Solving the Nancy Drew Mystery," *American Way* (September 1979): 16.

36. "Tom, Jr.," *New Yorker* (20 March 1954): 26, hereafter cited in the text as "Tom, Jr."

37. Peggy Herz, *Nancy Drew and the Hardy Boys* (New York: Scholastic, 1977), 8.

38. James V. O'Connor, "All under One Roof: Andy's," *Rotarian* (September 1973): 33.

39.Elizabeth Bumiller, "Squeaky-Clean and Still Eighteen: Nancy Drew, Girl Detective, Marks Half a Century," *Washington Post*, 17 April 1980; Lee Daniels, "Hardy Boys Named in Literary Suit," *New York Times*, 10 June 1980.

40. Elaine D'Aurizio, "Rejuvenating Juvenile Legend," *The Record*, 22 March 1983.

Chapter 2

1. Bibliographic information about most of Stratemeyer's Street & Smith dime novels can be found in John T. Dizer, Jr.'s "Early Stratemeyer Writings," *Dime Novel Round-up* 50 (June 1981): 50–60, and in Deidre Johnson's *Stratemeyer Pseudonyms and Series Books: An Annotated Checklist of Stratemeyer and Stratemeyer Syndicate Publications* (Westport, Conn.: Greenwood, 1982), hereafter cited in the text.

2. E. F. Bleiler, Introduction to George W. Peck, *Peck's Bad Boy and His Pa* (rpt., New York: Dover, 1958), v–vii.

3. Peter Pad {Edward Stratemeyer}, "Mayor Liederkranz of Hoboken; or, The Jolly Captain of the Pretzel Schuten Corps," *New York Five Cent Library* 40 (13 May 1893): 3.

4. Background, publication, and reprint information for the Nick Carters is given in J. Randolph Cox's *Bibliographic Listing: Nick Carter Library* (Fall River, Mass.: Edward T. LeBlanc, 1974). Stratemeyer's authorship is noted in the typed errata sheets issued with this work.

5. More detailed bibliographic information about the Old Cap Collier Library dime novels can be found in Peter C. Walther's "Edward Stratemeyer and the 'Old Cap Collier Library,'" *Newsboy* 26 (November–December 1987): 86–87.

6. Lew James {Edward Stratemeyer}, "Cool Dan, the Sport; or, The Crack Shot of Creede," *Log Cabin Library* 180 (25 August 1892): 3, hereafter cited in the text as "CD."

7. Jim Bowie {Edward Stratemeyer}, "Dead Shot Dave in Spokane; or, A Lone Hand and a High Stake," *New York Five Cent Library* 24 (21 January 1893): 2, hereafter cited in the text as "DSD."

8. Zimmy {Edward Stratemeyer}, "Jack and Jerry, the Bicycle Wonders; or, Lively Times on the Wheel," *New York Five Cent Library* 52 (5 August 1893): 2–3.

9. Jim Daly {Edward Stratemeyer}, "Gentleman Jack; or, From Student to Pugilist," *New York Five Cent Library* 14 (12 November 1892): 5, hereafter cited in the text as "GJ."

10. Zimmy {Edward Stratemeyer}, "Jack and Jerry's Spurt; or, The Bicycle Wonders' Ride for Life," *New York Five Cent Library* 56 (2 September 1893): 6.

11. Martha Wolfenstein, *Children's Humor: A Psychological Analysis* (1954; rpt., Bloomington: Indiana University Press, 1978), 12.

12. Jim Daly [Edward Stratemeyer], "Gentleman Jack's Tour; or, The Ring Champion and His Enemies," *New York Five Cent Library* 36 (15 April 1893): 15.

Chapter 3

1. Gary Scharnhorst, *Horatio Alger* (Boston: Twayne, 1980), 67–68, hereafter cited in the text.

2. Russel Nye, *The Unembarrassed Muse: The Popular Arts in America* (New York: Dial, 1970), 66.

3. Frank Luther Mott, *A History of American Magazines*, 5 vols. (Cambridge, Mass.: Belknap Press of Harvard University Press, 1930–68), 3:178, hereafter cited in the text as Mott, *History*.

4. Stanley A. Pachon, *Bibliographic Listing of "Golden Argosy" and "Boys' World"* (Fall River, Mass.: Edward T. LeBlanc, 1962), 5; James E. Knott, "The Golden Argosy," *Reckless Ralph's Dime Novel Round-up* 12 (September 1944): 2.

5. J. P. Guinon, "The Young Sports Series," *Dime Novel Round-up* 26 (August 1958): 113. Information about *Bright Days* can be found in Chester G. Mayo, *Bibliographic Listing: "Bright Days"* (Fall River, Mass.: Edward T. LeBlanc, 1962).

6. Bibliographic information about publication dates and clothbound reprints of Stratemeyer's story-paper fiction can be found in John T. Dizer, Jr., *Tom Swift and Company* (Jefferson, N.C.: McFarland, 1982), hereafter cited in the text; and Johnson 1982.

7. Ed Ward [Edward Stratemeyer], "Harry's Trial," *Our American Boys* 1 (January 1883): 5, hereafter cited in the text as "HT."

8. Edward Stratemeyer, *True to Himself; or, Roger Strong's Struggle for Place*, (Boston: Lothrop, Lee & Shepard, 1900), 3; originally published as "True to Himself; or, Roger Strong's Struggle for Place," *Argosy* 13 (17 October 1891– 9 January 1892).

9. Ralph Hamilton [Edward Stratemeyer], "Alvin Chase's Search; or, The Mystery of Cedar Cove," *Golden Days* 11–12 (11 October–20 December 1890): 721, hereafter cited in the text as "ACS."

10. Edward Stratemeyer, "Paul Raymond's Rovings; or, In Quest of Name and Fortune," *Golden Days* 16 (27 July–5 October 1895): 585 (emphasis added).

11. Theodore Roosevelt, *An Autobiography* (New York: Scribner's Sons, 1925), 25.

12. Joseph Campbell, *The Hero with a Thousand Faces*, 2d ed. (1968; rpt., Princeton: Princeton University Press, 1973), 69–77, 98–109.

13. Edward Stratemeyer, *Joe the Surveyor; or, The Value of a Lost Claim* (New York: Grosset & Dunlap, 1903), 122; originally published as "Joe the

Surveyor; or, The Value of a Lost Claim," *Good News* 9 (5 May–28July 1894).

14. The publishers ran descriptive ads in the back pages of the series books; each ad appeared in numerous series titles. Edited and altered versions were then sometimes run in new printings of old titles and in new titles. This ubiquity precludes citing individual sources for these ads.

15. Allen Chapman, *A Business Boy's Pluck* (1908; rpt., Chicago: Donohue, n.d.), 14, hereafter cited in the text as *BB*; originally published as *A Business Boy; or, Winning Success*.

16. Frank V. Webster, *The Young Firemen of Lakeville; or, Herbert Dare's Pluck* (1909; rpt., Akron: Saalfield, 1938), 30, hereafter cited in the text as *YFL*.

17. Victor Appleton, *The Movie Boys' First Showhouse; or, Fighting for a Foothold in Fairlands* (1913; rpt., Garden City, N.Y.: Garden City, 1926), 9; originally published as *The Motion Picture Chums' First Venture; or, Opening a Photo Playhouse in Fairlands*. The original plates were used for the retitled edition.

18. Eugene Martin, *Randy Starr Leading the Air Circus; or, The Sky Flyers in a Daring Stunt* (rpt., Akron: Saalfield, 1932), 197.

19. Franklin W. Dixon, *The Lone Eagle of the Border; or, Ted Scott and the Diamond Smugglers* (New York: Grosset & Dunlap, 1929), 19, hereafter cited in the text as *LEB*.

20. Franklin W. Dixon, *Over the Ocean to Paris; or, Ted Scott's Daring Long Distance Flight* (New York: Grosset & Dunlap, 1927), 48, hereafter cited in the text as *OOP*.

21. Franklin W. Dixon, *First Stop Honolulu; or, Ted Scott over the Pacific* (New York: Grosset & Dunlap, 1927), 5, hereafter cited in the text as *FSH*.

22. Roy Rockwood, *Dave Dashaway around the World; or, A Young Yankee Aviator among Many Nations* (New York: Cupples & Leon, 1913), 73.

23. Richard H. Stone, *Sky Riders of the Atlantic; or, Slim Tyler's First Trip in the Clouds* (New York: Cupples & Leon, 1930), 167.

24. Victor Appleton, *Moving Picture Boys; or, The Perils of a Great City Depicted* (New York: Grosset & Dunlap, 1913), 105.

Chapter 4

1. Roy Rockwood [Edward Stratemeyer], "The Rival Ocean Divers; or, A Boy's Daring Search for Sunken Treasure," *Golden Hours* 675–82 (5 January–23 February 1901): 12.

2. Theodore Roosevelt, *The Strenuous Life* (New York: Review of Reviews, 1910), 133, hereafter cited in the text.

3. Frank Luther Mott, *Golden Multitudes: The Story of Best Sellers in the United States* (New York: Macmillan, 1947), 207, hereafter cited in the text.

4. Edward Stratemeyer, *A Young Volunteer in Cuba; or, Fighting for the Single Star* (Boston: Lee & Shepard, 1898), iv, hereafter cited in the text as *YVC*.

5. Hal Harkaway [Edward Stratemeyer], "Holland, the Destroyer; or, America against the World," *Golden Hours* 669–76 (24 November 1900–12 January 1901): 13.

6. Bob Chenu, "Winning World War I," *Dime Novel Round-up* 49 (June 1980): 50–51.

7. Dan Scott, *The Secret of Hermit's Peak* (New York: Grosset & Dunlap, 1960), 14, hereafter cited in the text as *SHP*.

8. Quoted in Robert L. Beisner, *From the Old Diplomacy to the New, 1865–1900* (New York: Crowell, 1975), 76.

9. Captain Ralph Bonehill [Edward Stratemeyer], *For the Liberty of Texas* (Boston: Estes, 1900), 297, hereafter cited in the text as *FLT*.

10. Captain Ralph Bonehill [Edward Stratemeyer], *When Santiago Fell; or, The War Adventures of Two Chums* (New York: Grosset & Dunlap, 1899), 279, hereafter cited in the text as *WSF*.

11. Edward Stratemeyer, *With Washington in the West; or, A Soldier Boy's Battles in the Wilderness* (Boston: Lothrop, Lee & Shepard, 1898), 17, 31, 259, hereafter cited in the text as *WWW*.

12. Captain Ralph Bonehill [Edward Stratemeyer], *With Boone on the Frontier; or, The Pioneer Boys of Old Kentucky* (New York: Grosset & Dunlap, 1903), 103, 165, hereafter cited in the text as *WBF*.

13. Edward Stratemeyer, *Marching on Niagara; or, The Soldier Boys of the Old Frontier* (Boston: Lothrop, Lee & Shepard, 1902), 181, hereafter cited in the text as *MN*.

14. Edward Stratemeyer, *At the Fall of Montreal; or, A Soldier Boy's Final Victory* (Boston: Lothrop, Lee & Shepard, 1903), 42–43.

15. Edward Stratemeyer, *Under the Mikado's Flag; or, Young Soldiers of Fortune* (Boston: Lothrop, Lee & Shepard, 1904), 17, hereafter cited in the text as *UMF*.

16. Edward Stratemeyer, *On to Pekin; or, Old Glory in China* (Boston: Lee & Shepard, 1900), 25, hereafter cited in the text as *OP*.

17. Edward Stratemeyer, *Treasure Seekers of the Andes; or, American Boys in Peru* (Boston: Lothrop, Lee & Shepard, 1907), 112.

18. Captain Ralph Bonehill [Edward Stratemeyer], *Young Hunters in Porto Rico; or, The Search for a Lost Treasure* (Chicago: Donohue, 1900), 114; Captain Ralph Bonehill [Edward Stratemeyer], *A Sailor Boy with Dewey; or, Afloat in the Philippines* (New York: Mershon, 1899), 202, hereafter cited in the text as *SBD*.

19. Captain Ralph Bonehill [Edward Stratemeyer], *Pioneer Boys of the Great Northwest; or, With Lewis and Clark across the Rockies* (New York: Grosset & Dunlap, 1904), 107, hereafter cited in the text as *PBGN*.

20. J. Frederick MacDonald, "'The Foreigner' in Juvenile Series Fiction, 1900–1945," *Journal of Popular Culture* 8 (Winter 1974): 536, hereafter cited in the text.

21. Edward Stratemeyer, *Under Otis in the Philippines; or, A Young Officer in the Tropics* (Boston: Lee & Shepard, 1899), 155.

22. Captain Ralph Bonehill [Edward Stratemeyer], *Off for Hawaii; or, The Mystery of a Great Volcano* (New York: Grosset & Dunlap, 1899), 91.

23. Donald A. Colberg, "Moral and Social Values in American Adventure

Novels for Boys, 1865–1900" (dissertation, University of Minnesota, 1973), 276, hereafter cited in the text.

24. Paul C. Deane, "A Century of Xenophobia in Fiction Series for Children," *Youth Services in Libraries* 3 (Winter 1990): 119; MacDonald, 535.

25. Edward Stratemeyer, *The Campaign of the Jungle; or, Under Lawton through Luzon* (Boston: Lee & Shepard, 1900), 97.

26. These themes are discussed throughout Henry Nash Smith's *Virgin Land: The American West as Symbol and Myth* (1950; rpt., Cambridge, Mass.: Harvard University Press, 1970), esp. book 2 (51–120).

27. Captain Ralph Bonehill [Edward Stratemeyer], *Four Boy Hunters; or, The Outing of the Gun Club* (New York: Cupples & Leon, 1906), 175–76, hereafter cited in the text as *FBH*.

Chapter 5

1. Corey Ford, "The Father of Those Famous Rover Boys," *New Age Illustrated* (April 1928): 102.

2. See also Arthur Prager, "Edward Stratemeyer and His Book Machine," *Saturday Review* (10 July 1971): 16–17.

3. Carol Billman, *The Secret of the Stratemeyer Syndicate: Nancy Drew, the Hardy Boys, and the Million Dollar Fiction Factory* (New York: Ungar, 1986), 9, hereafter cited in the text.

4. Arthur M. Winfield [Edward Stratemeyer], *The Rover Boys at School; or, The Cadets of Putnam Hall* (1899; rpt., Racine, Wisc.: Whitman, n.d.), hereafter cited in the text as *RBAS*. The quote is from the unpaginated introduction to a Grosset & Dunlap reprint of the 1899 Mershon edition; all page numbers cited hereafter refer to the Whitman edition.

5. Benjamin A. Rader, *American Sports: From the Age of Folk Games to the Age of Spectators* (Englewood Cliffs, N.J.: Prentice-Hall, 1983), 204.

6. Gregory S. Sojka, "Going 'From Rags to Riches' with Baseball Joe: Or, A Pitcher's Progress," *Journal of American Culture* 2 (Spring 1979): 115.

7. Clarence Young, *The Racer Boys at Boarding School; or, Striving for the Championship* (New York: Cupples & Leon, 1912), 34, hereafter cited in the text as *RBBS*.

8. Arthur M. Winfield [Edward Stratemeyer], *The Rover Boys at College; or, The Right Road and the Wrong* (1910; rpt., Racine, Wisc.: Whitman, n.d.), 91.

9. Spencer Davenport, *The Rushton Boys in the Saddle; or, The Ghost of the Plains* (Racine, Wisc.: Whitman, ca. 1916), 119, hereafter cited in the text as *RBS*.

10. Edward Stratemeyer, *Dave Porter at Oak Hall; or, The Schooldays of an American Boy* (Boston: Lothrop, Lee & Shepard, 1905), iii–iv (emphasis added), hereafter cited in the text as *DPOH*.

11. Roy Eliot Stokes, *Andy at Yale; or, The Great Quadrangle Mystery* (Cleveland: Goldsmith, 1914), 21; Allen Chapman, *Fred Fenton, the Pitcher; or,*

The Rivals of Riverport School (New York: Cupples & Leon, 1913), 4; *DPOH*, 5; *RBS*, 9; Clarence Young, *Jack Ranger's Schooldays; or, The Rivals of Washington Hall* (New York: Cupples & Leon, 1907), 13; *RBAS*, 9.

12. Allen Chapman, *Tom Fairfield's Schooldays; or, The Chums of Elmwood Hall* (New York: Cupples & Leon, 1913), 12.

13. Arthur M. Winfield [Edward Stratemeyer], *The Rover Boys in New York; or, Saving Their Father's Honor* (New York: Grosset & Dunlap, 1913), 71.

14. Arthur M. Winfield [Edward Stratemeyer], *The Rover Boys on Land and Sea; or, The Crusoes of Seven Islands* (New York: Grosset & Dunlap, 1903), 123.

15. Edward Stratemeyer, *Dave Porter's Return to School; or, Winning the Medal of Honor* (Boston: Lothrop, Lee & Shepard, 1907), 187.

Chapter 6

1. Leithead, 94; "Mildred A. Wirt," 197–200.

2. Alice B. Emerson, *Ruth Fielding and Her Crowning Victory; or, Winning Honors Abroad* (New York: Cupples & Leon, 1934), 210; quoted in Billman, 77.

3. Society of Phantom Friends, *The Girls' Series Encyclopedia* (n.p.: Society of Phantom Friends, 1988), 137–39.

4. Gertrude W. Morrison, *The Girls of Central High; or, Rivals for All Honors* (New York: Grosset & Dunlap, 1914), 5, hereafter cited in the text as *GCH*.

5. Jane S. Smith, "Plucky Little Ladies and Stout-Hearted Chums: Serial Novels for Girls, 1900–1920," *Prospects* 3 (1977): 156, hereafter cited in the text.

6. Alice B. Emerson, *Ruth Fielding of the Red Mill; or, Jasper Parloe's Secret* (New York: Cupples & Leon, 1913), 51, hereafter cited in the text as *RFRM*.

7. Helen Beecher Long, *Janice Day at Poketown* (New York: Sully, 1919), 77, hereafter cited in the text as *JDP*.

8. Alice B. Emerson, *Betty Gordon at Bramble Farm; or, The Mystery of a Nobody* (New York: Cupples & Leon, 1920), 60, hereafter cited in the text as *BGBF*; reprinted from the original plates in *Popular Stories for Girls* (New York: Cupples & Leon, ca. 1934).

9. Margaret Penrose, *Dorothy Dale at Glenwood School* (New York: Cupples & Leon, 1908), 169, hereafter cited in the text as *DDGS*.

10. Margaret Penrose, *Dorothy Dale and Her Chums* (New York: Cupples & Leon, 1909), 214.

11. Alice B. Emerson, *Betty Gordon at Boarding School; or, The Treasure of Indian Chasm* (New York: Cupples & Leon, 1921), 90, hereafter cited in the text as *BGBS*.

12. May Hollis Barton, *Three Girl Chums at Laurel Hall; or, The Mystery of the School by the Lake* (New York: Cupples & Leon, 1926), 60; Grace Brooks Hill, *The Corner House Girls: How They Moved to Milton, What They Found, and What They Did* (New York: Barse & Hopkins, 1915), 23; *BGBS*, 38.

13. Alice B. Emerson, *Betty Gordon and Her School Chums; or, Bringing the Rebels to Terms* (New York: Cupples & Leon, 1924), 33.

14. Amy Bell Marlowe, *The Girl from Sunset Ranch; or, Alone in a Great City* (New York: Grosset & Dunlap, 1914), 50.

Chapter 7

1. George Terry Dunlap, *The Fleeting Years: A Memoir* (New York: privately printed, 1937), 193, hereafter cited in the text.

2. Bobbie Ann Mason, *The Girl Sleuth: A Feminist Guide* (Old Westbury, N.Y.: Feminist Press, 1975), 30, hereafter cited in the text.

3. Ramy Allison White, *Sunny Boy in the Country* (New York: Barse & Hopkins, 1920), 12, hereafter cited in the text as *SBC*.

4. Alice Dale Hardy, *The Flyaways and Cinderella* (New York: Grosset & Dunlap, 1925), 5, hereafter cited in the text as *FC*.

5. Laura Lee Hope, *The Bobbsey Twins at the County Fair* (New York: Grosset & Dunlap, 1922), 64.

6. Laura Lee Hope, *Six Little Bunkers at Cousin Tom's* (New York: Grosset & Dunlap, 1918), 49.

7. Laura Lee Hope, *Bunny Brown and His Sister Sue* (New York: Grosset & Dunlap, 1916), 51, hereafter cited in the text as *BBHSS*.

8. Laura Lee Hope, *Bunny Brown and His Sister Sue on Jack Frost Island* (New York: Grosset & Dunlap, 1927), 2; *BBHSS*, 9.

9. Laura Lee Hope, *The Bobbsey Twins at School* (New York: Grosset & Dunlap, 1913), 104–5, hereafter cited in the text as *BTS*.

10. Helen Louise Thorndyke, *Honey Bunch: Just a Little Girl* (New York: Grosset & Dunlap, 1923), 146, hereafter cited in the text as *HBJLG*.

11. Mabel C. Hawley, *Four Little Blossoms and Their Winter Fun* (New York: Sully, 1920), 7.

12. Ramy Allison White, *Sunny Boy in School and Out* (New York: Barse & Hopkins, 1921), 30, hereafter cited in the text as *SBSO*.

13. Laura Lee Hope, *The Six Little Bunkers at Aunt Jo's* (New York: Grosset & Dunlap, 1918), 23.

14. Laura Lee Hope, *The Bobbsey Twins on a Ranch* (New York: Grosset & Dunlap, 1935), 62.

15. Helen Louise Thorndyke, *Honey Bunch: Her First Visit to the Zoo* (New York: Grosset & Dunlap, 1932), 176.

16. Deidre Johnson, "Child Labor in the Stratemeyer Syndicate Series Books: A Preliminary Study," *Dime Novel Round-up* 52 (April 1983): 17–30.

Chapter 8

1. Franklin W. Dixon, *The Missing Chums* (New York: Grosset & Dunlap, 1928), 15; Franklin W. Dixon, *The Tower Treasure* (New York: Grosset & Dunlap, 1927), 2, hereafter cited in the text as *TT*.

2. Arthur Prager, *Rascals at Large; or, The Clue in the Old Nostalgia* (Garden City, N.Y.: Doubleday, 1971), 118, hereafter cited in the text.

3. Ed Zuckerman, "The Great Hardy Boys Whodunit," *Rolling Stone* (9 September 1976): 40.

4. Carolyn Keene, *The Secret of the Old Clock* (New York: Grosset & Dunlap, 1930), 1, hereafter cited in the text as *SOC*.

5. Carolyn Keene, *The Hidden Staircase* (New York: Grosset & Dunlap, 1930), 2–3, hereafter cited in the text as *HS*.

6. Patricia Craig and Mary Cadogan, "A Sweet Girl Sleuth: The Teenage Detective in America," in *The Lady Investigates: Women Detectives and Spies in Fiction* (New York: St. Martin's, 1981), 151–52, herafter cited in text.

7. Deborah Felder, "Nancy Drew: Then and Now," *Publishers' Weekly* (30 May 1986): 31.

8. Carolyn Keene, *The Whispering Statue* (New York: Grosset & Dunlap, 1937), 27.

9. Anne Scott MacLeod, "Nancy Drew and Her Rivals: No Contest," *Horn Book* 63 (May–June 1987): 315, hereafter cited in the text.

10. Carolyn Keene, *The Phantom of Pine Hill* (New York: Grosset & Dunlap, 1965), 74.

11. Carolyn Keene, *Secrets Can Kill* (New York: Simon & Schuster/Pocket Books, 1986), 19, hereafter cited in the text as SCK.

12. Clinton W. Locke, *Who Closed the Door; or, Perry Pierce and the Old Storehouse* (1931; rpt., Cleveland: Goldsmith, n.d.), 6, hereafter cited in the text as WCD.

13. Jerry West, *The Happy Hollisters* (Garden City, N.Y.: Doubleday, 1953), 31.

14. Jerry West, *The Happy Hollisters at Mystery Mountain* (Garden City, N.Y.: Garden City Books, 1954), 33–34.

Chapter 9

1. Carleton Washburne and Mabel Vogel, *Winnetka Graded Book List* (Chicago: American Library Association, 1926), 44.

2. Joe Jennings, "Leisure Reading of Junior High School Boys and Girls," *Peabody Journal of Education* 6 (May 1929): 340, 344–45.

3. *Girls' Series Books 1840–1991* (Minneapolis: University of Minnesota, Children's Literature Research Collections, 1991), 337–44.

4. Franklin K. Mathiews, "Blowing out the Boy's Brains," *Outlook* 108 (November 1914): 652–53

5. Mary E. S. Root, "Not to Be Circulated," *Wilson Bulletin* 3 (January 1929): 446.

6. Hope White, "For It Was Indeed He," *Illinois Libraries* 16 (October 1934): 113–16.

7. Lucille Shanklin, "Tom Swift's Last Stand," *Wilson Bulletin* 9 (June 1935): 588.

8. [Janie Smith], "*Bobbsey Twins* History Told," *Kansas Library Bulletin* (December 1961): 15, hereafter cited in the text; reprinted from *South Carolina Library Bulletin* (May 1956).

9. Adeline B. Zachert, "What Our Children Read and Why," *Library Journal* 32 (January 1914): 23.

10. Elizabeth Wisdom, "The Development of Good Taste in Little Children's Reading," *Library Journal* 49 (October 1924): 876.

11. Margaret Beckman, "Why Not the Bobbsey Twins?" *Library Journal* 89 (November 1964): 4613; reprinted from *Ontario Library Review* (August 1964).

12. Ervin J. Gaines, "Viewpoint: Closed Circuit Children's Books," *Library Journal* 95 (April 1970): 1455.

13. Barbara S. Wertheimer and Carol Sands, "Nancy Drew Revisited," *Language Arts* 52 (November–December 1975): 1131.

14. Dorine Geeslin and Anita Dishman Sanders, "Children's Book Choices in the Eighties," *Delta Kappa Gamma Bulletin* 48 (Winter 1982): 57.

15. Quoted in Gil O'Gara, "From the Editor," *Yellowback Library* 76 (October 1990): 3.

16. Lewis M. Terman and Margaret Lima, *Children's Reading: A Guide for Parents and Teachers* (New York: Appleton, 1926), 78.

Selected Bibliography

PRIMARY WORKS

Selected Series by Edward Stratemeyer

Publishers listed are major publishers. Grosset & Dunlap series beginning prior to 1907 were usually first published by the Mershon Company (1890s–1905), then by Stitt (1905) and Chatterton-Peck (1906–7). Lee & Shepard publications were issued by Lothrop, Lee & Shepard from 1904 or 1905.

Alger, Horatio, Jr. Rise in Life. 11 vols. New York: Grosset & Dunlap, 1901–12.
Bonehill, Captain Ralph. Boy Hunters. 4 vols. New York: Cupples & Leon, 1906–10.
———. Flag of Freedom. 6 vols. New York: Mershon, 1899–1902.
———. Frontier. 3 vols. New York: Mershon, 1903–6.
———. Mexican War. 3 vols. Boston: Dana Estes, 1900–1902.
———. Outdoor. 2 vols. New York: Barnes, 1904–5.
———. Young Hunters. 2 vols. New York: Allison, ca. 1900.
———. Young Sportsman. 5 vols. New York: Allison, 1897–ca. 1902.
Stratemeyer, Edward. American Boys' Biographical Series. 2 vols. Boston: Lee & Shepard, 1901–4.
———. Bound to Succeed. 3 vols. New York: Merriam, 1894–99.
———. Bound to Win. 12 vols. New York: Allison, 1897. See Stratemeyer, Bound to Win series.
———. Colonial. 6 vols. Boston: Lee & Shepard, 1901–6.
———. Dave Porter. 15 vols. Boston: Lothrop, Lee & Shepard, 1905–19.
———. Lakeport. 6 vols. Boston: Lothrop, Lee & Shepard, 1908–12.
———. Old Glory. 6 vols. Boston: Lee & Shepard, 1898–1901.
———. Pan-American. 6 vols. Boston: Lothrop, Lee & Shepard, 1902–11.
———. Ship and Shore. 3 vols. Boston: Lee & Shepard, 1894–1900.
———. Soldiers of Fortune. 4 vols. Boston: Lothrop, Lee & Shepard, 1900–1906.
———. Working Upward. 6 vols. New York: Allison, ca. 1893–1903. Volumes 1–4 also published as Bound to Win.
Winfield, Arthur M. Putnam Hall. 6 vols. New York: Grosset & Dunlap, 1901–11.
———. Rover Boys. 30 vols. New York: Grosset & Dunlap, 1899–1926.

Selected Stratemeyer Syndicate Series

Allen, Captain Quincy. Outdoor Chums. 8 vols. New York: Grosset & Dunlap, 1911–16.

Appleton, Victor. Don Sturdy. 15 vols. New York: Grosset & Dunlap, 1925–35.

———. Motion Picture Chums. 7 vols. New York: Grosset & Dunlap, 1913–16.

———. Moving Picture Boys. 15 vols. New York: Grosset & Dunlap, 1913–22.

———. Tom Swift. 40 vols. New York: Grosset & Dunlap, 1910–41.

———. Tom Swift (III). 12 vols. New York: Simon & Schuster/Wanderer Books, 1981–84.

———. Tom Swift (IV). 9 vols. New York: Simon & Schuster/Pocket Books, 1991– .

Appleton, Victor, II. Tom Swift, Jr. 33 vols. New York: Grosset & Dunlap, 1954–71.

Barnes, Elmer Tracey. Motion Picture Comrades. 5 vols. New York: New York Book Co., 1917.

Barnum, Richard. Kneetime Animal Stories. 17 vols. New York: Barse & Hopkins, 1915–22.

Barnum, Vance. Joe Strong. 7 vols. New York: George Sully, 1916.

Bartlett, Philip A. Roy Stover. 4 vols. New York: Barse, 1929–34.

Barton, May Hollis. Barton Books for Girls. 15 vols. New York: Cupples & Leon, 1926–31.

Beach, Charles Amory. Air Service Boys. 6 vols. New York: George Sully, 1918–20.

Carr, Annie Roe. Nan Sherwood. 7 vols. New York: George Sully, 1916–37.

Carson, Captain James. Saddle Boys. 5 vols. New York: Cupples & Leon, 1913–15.

Chadwick, Lester. Baseball Joe. 14 vols. New York: Cupples & Leon, 1912–28.

———. College Sports. 6 vols. New York: Cupples & Leon, 1910–13.

Chapman, Allen. Boys of Pluck. 5 vols. New York: Cupples & Leon, 1906–11. Volumes 1–3 originally published as Boys of Business, 4 vols. (New York: Cupples & Leon, 1906–8).

———. Darewell Chums. 5 vols. New York: Cupples & Leon, 1908–11.

———. Fred Fenton Athletic Series. 5 vols. New York: Cupples & Leon, 1913–15.

———. Radio Boys. 13 vols. New York: Grosset & Dunlap, 1922–30.

———. Railroad (Ralph of the Railroad). 10 vols. New York: Grosset & Dunlap, 1906–28.

———. Tom Fairfield. 5 vols. New York: Cupples & Leon, 1913–15.

Cooper, John R. Mel Martin Baseball Stories. 6 vols. New York: Cupples & Leon, 1947–53.

Davenport, Spencer. Rushton Boys. 3 vols. New York: Hearst's International Library, 1916.

Dawson, Elmer A. Buck and Larry Baseball Stories. 5 vols. New York: Grosset & Dunlap, 1930–32.

———. Garry Grayson Football Stories. 10 vols. New York: Grosset & Dunlap, 1926–32.

Dixon, Franklin W. Hardy Boys. 117 vols. New York: Grosset & Dunlap; Simon & Schuster, 1927– .

———. Hardy Boys Casefiles. 70 vols. New York: Simon & Schuster/Pocket Books, 1987– .

———. Ted Scott Flying Series. 20 vols. New York: Grosset & Dunlap, 1927–43.

Duncan, Julia K. Doris Force. 4 vols. Chicago: Henry Altemus, 1931–32.

Emerson, Alice B. Betty Gordon. 15 vols. New York: Cupples & Leon, 1920–32.

———. Ruth Fielding. 30 vols. New York: Cupples & Leon, 1913–34.

Endicott, Ruth Belmore. Carolyn. 2 vols. New York: Dodd, Mead, 1918–19.

Ferris, James Cody. X Bar X Boys. 21 vols. New York: Grosset & Dunlap, 1926–42.

Forbes, Graham B. Boys of Columbia High. 8 vols. New York: Grosset & Dunlap, 1912–20.

———. Frank Allen. 17 vols. Garden City, N.Y.: Garden City Publishing Co., 1926–27.

Gordon, Frederick. Fairview Boys. 6 vols. New York: Graham & Matlack, ca. 1914–1917. First three volumes originally published as Up and Doing series (1912).

Hardy, Alice Dale. Flyaways. 3 vols. New York: Grosset & Dunlap, 1925.

———. Riddle Club. 6 vols. New York: Grosset & Dunlap, 1924–29.

Hawley, Mabel C. Four Little Blossoms. 7 vols. New York: George Sully, 1920–30.

Henderley, Brooks. Y.M.C.A. Boys. 3 vols. New York: Cupples & Leon, 1916–17.

Hill, Grace Brooks. Corner House Girls. 13 vols. New York: Barse & Hopkins, 1915–26.

Hope, Laura Lee. Blythe Girls. 12 vols. New York: Grosset & Dunlap, 1925–32.

———. Bobbsey Twins. 115 vols. New York: Grosset & Dunlap, 1904–92.

———. Bunny Brown and His Sister Sue. 20 vols. New York: Grosset & Dunlap, 1916–31.

———. Make-Believe Stories. 12 vols. New York: Grosset & Dunlap, 1920–23.

———. Moving Picture Girls. 7 vols. New York: Grosset & Dunlap, 1914–16.

———. Outdoor Girls. 23 vols. New York: Grosset & Dunlap, 1913–33.

———. Six Little Bunkers. 14 vols. New York: Grosset & Dunlap, 1918–30.

Hunt, Francis. Mary and Jerry Mystery Stories. 5 vols. New York: Grosset & Dunlap, 1935–37.

Judd, Frances K. Kay Tracey Mystery Stories. 18 vols. New York: Cupples & Leon, 1934–42.

Keene, Carolyn. Dana Girls. 34 vols. New York: Grosset & Dunlap, 1934–79.

———. Nancy Drew Files. 78 vols. New York: Simon & Schuster/Pocket Books, 1986– .

———. Nancy Drew Mystery Stories. 110 vols. New York: Grosset & Dunlap; Simon & Schuster, 1930– .

———. Nancy Drew Picture Books. 2 vols. New York: Grosset & Dunlap, 1977.

———. River Heights. 11 vols. New York: Simon & Schuster/Pocket Books, 1991– .

Lancer, Jack. Christopher Cool/TEEN Agent. 6 vols. New York: Grosset & Dunlap, 1967–69.

Locke, Clinton W. Perry Pierce Mystery Stories. 4 vols. Chicago: Henry Altemus, 1931–34.

Long, Helen Beecher. Do Something (Janice Day). 5 vols. New York: Sully & Kleinteich, 1914–19.

Marlowe, Amy Bell. Amy Bell Marlowe's Books for Girls. 7 vols. New York: Grosset & Dunlap, 1914–16.

———. Oriole. 3 vols. New York: Grosset & Dunlap, 1920–27.

Martin, Eugene. Randy Starr (Sky Flyers). 4 vols. Chicago: Henry Altemus, 1931–ca. 1933.

Moore, Fenworth. Jerry Ford Wonder Stories. 4 vols. New York: Cupples & Leon, 1931–32.

Morrison, Gertrude W. Girls of Central High. 7 vols. New York: Grosset & Dunlap, 1914–19.

Penrose, Margaret. Dorothy Dale. 13 vols. New York: Cupples & Leon, 1908–24.

———. Motor Girls. 10 vols. New York: Cupples & Leon, 1910–17.

———. Radio Girls. 4 vols. New York: Cupples & Leon, 1922–24.

Ridley, Nat, Jr. Nat Ridley Rapid Fire Detective Stories. 17 vols. Garden City, N.Y.: Garden City Publishing Co., 1926–27.

Rockwood, Roy. Bomba the Jungle Boy. 20 vols. New York: Cupples & Leon, 1926–38.

———. Dave Dashaway. 5 vols. New York: Cupples & Leon, 1913–15.

———. Dave Fearless. 17 vols. Garden City, N.Y.: Garden City Publishing Co., 1926–27. Volumes 1–3 also published as Dave Fearless series by George Sully & Co. (1918).

———. Great Marvel. 9 vols. New York: Cupples & Leon, 1906–35.

———. Speedwell Boys. 5 vols. New York: Cupples & Leon, 1913–15.

Roe, Harry Mason. Lanky Lawson. 4 vols. New York: Barse, 1929–30.

Scott, Dan. Bret King Mystery Stories. 9 vols. New York: Grosset & Dunlap, 1960–64.

Sheldon, Ann. Linda Craig. 23 vols. New York: Grosset & Dunlap; Simon & Schuster/Pocket Books, 1962–90.

Speed, Eric. Wynn and Lonny. 6 vols. New York: Grosset & Dunlap, 1975–78.

Stokes, Roy Eliot. University. 2 vols. New York: Sully & Kleinteich, 1914.

Stone, Alan. Tolliver Adventure Stories. 3 vols. New York: World, 1967.

Stone, Raymond. Donald Dare. 2 vols. New York: Graham, 1914.

———. Tommy Tiptop. 6 vols. New York: Graham & Matlack, 1912–17.

Stone, Richard H. Slim Tyler Air Stories. 6 vols. New York: Cupples & Leon, 1930–32.

Thorndyke, Helen Louise. Honey Bunch. 34 vols. New York: Grosset & Dunlap, 1923–55.

———. Honey Bunch and Norman. 12 vols. New York: Grosset & Dunlap, 1957–63.

Todd, Burbank L. Hiram (Back to the Soil). 2 vols. New York: Sully & Kleinteich, 1914–15.

Warner, Frank A. Bobby Blake. 12 vols. New York: Barse, 1915–26.

———. Bob Chase Big Game. 4 vols. New York: Barse, 1929–30.

Webster, Frank V. Webster Series. 25 vols. New York: Cupples & Leon, 1909–15.

West, Jerry. Happy Hollisters. 33 vols. Garden City, N.Y.: Doubleday, 1953–70.

Wheeler, Janet D. Billie Bradley. 9 vols. New York: George Sully, 1920–32.

White, Ramy Allison. Sunny Boy. 14 vols. New York: Barse & Hopkins, 1920–31.

Young, Clarence. Jack Ranger. 6 vols. New York: Cupples & Leon, 1907–11.

———. Motor Boys. 22 vols. New York: Cupples & Leon, 1906–24.

———. Racer Boys. 6 vols. New York: Cupples & Leon, 1912–14.

SECONDARY WORKS

Books

Billman, Carol. *The Secret of the Stratemeyer Syndicate: Nancy Drew, the Hardy Boys, and the Million Dollar Fiction Factory*. New York: Ungar, 1986.

Dizer, John T. *Tom Swift and Company*. Jefferson, N.C.: McFarland, 1982.

Garis, Roger. *My Father Was Uncle Wiggily*. New York: McGraw-Hill, 1966.

Johnson, Deidre. *Stratemeyer Pseudonyms and Series Books: An Annotated Checklist of Stratemeyer and Stratemeyer Syndicate Publications*. Westport, Conn.: Greenwood, 1982.

Mason, Bobbie Ann. *The Girl Sleuth: A Feminist Guide*. Old Westbury, N.Y.: Feminist Press, 1975.

McFarlane, Leslie. *Ghost of the Hardy Boys*. New York: Two Continents, 1976.

Prager, Arthur. *Rascals at Large; or, The Clue in the Old Nostalgia*. Garden City, N.Y.: Doubleday, 1971.

Articles

DeWitt, Karen. "Nancy Drew's Author—She's No Mystery." *San Antonio Express News*, 7 August 1977.

"For It Was Indeed He." *Fortune* (April 1934): 86–89. Reprinted in *Newsboy* (November–December 1987).

"Funeral Tonight for E. Stratemeyer." *New York Times*, 12 May 1930.

Johnson, Deidre. "Early and Miscellaneous Stratemeyer Writings." *Dime Novel Round-up* 57 (August 1988): 60–62.

Kelly, Ernie. "Inside the Stratemeyer Syndicate." 2 parts. *Yellowback Library* 52, 54 (October and December 1988): 5–11, 5–12.

Lapin, Geoffrey. "The Ghost of Nancy Drew." *Books at Iowa*, No. 50 (April 1989) 8–27

"Newark Author, Great Favorite with Young Boys." *Newsboy* 26 (November–December 1987): 75–77. Reprinted from *Newark Sunday News*, ca. 1904.

"Newarker Who Writes for Most Critical of All Readers Has Far Exceeded Standard of Success His Mother Set." *Newark Evening News*, 4 June 1927.

Walther, Peter. "Edward Stratemeyer and the 'Old Cap Collier Library.'" *Newsboy* 26 (November–December 1987): 86–87.

Wirt Benson, Mildred. "The Ghost of Ladora." *Books at Iowa* 19 (November 1973): 24–29.

Index

The Author

Deidre Johnson received her B.A. in English literature from Knox College, her M.A. in children's literature from Eastern Michigan University, and her Ph.D. in American studies from the University of Minnesota–Twin Cities. She is the author of *Stratemeyer Pseudonyms and Series Books* (1982) and various articles on series books, as well as an avid collector of series and literature about them. Currently, she teaches courses in children's literature at West Chester University of Pennsylvania.

The Editor

Ruth K. MacDonald is a former professor of English and head of the Department of English and Philosophy at Purdue University. She received her B.A. and M.A. in English from the University of Connecticut, her Ph.D. in English from Rutgers University, and her M.B.A. from the University of Texas at El Paso. To Twayne's United States and English Authors series she has contributed the volumes on Louisa May Alcott, Beatrix Potter, and Dr. Seuss. She is also the author of *Literature for Children in England and America, 1646-1774* (1982).